THE TERRITORY

OF

Jimmy Divine

FREEPORT

MARSH
HARBOUR

SPANISH WELLS

BIMINI
ISLANDS

NASSAU

ANDROS
ISLAND

RUM CAY

GEORGE TOWN

LONG
ISLAND

THE
BAHAMAS

GREAT
INAGUA

Praise for

Weed Man

"This reads like a bestseller. It's about time we hear from a genuine pot smuggler of Jimmy Divine's caliber who opens our eyes to the high times and high jinks on the high seas."

— Tommy Chong,
comedian and actor
of Cheech & Chong fame

"McCaslin was a 20-something White House correspondent covering my dad, Ronald Reagan, when I first read his unique musings. Maybe I'm not surprised, given the cast of characters and shenanigans he calls attention to every day in his *Inside the Beltway* column, that he's now somehow made his way to a distant tropical island and uncovered the colorful if not hilarious escapades of drug trafficker Jimmy Divine."

— Michael Reagan,
presidential son and nationally-
syndicated radio host

"Facts are easy. Anyone can find facts for a story. What McCaslin always finds is heart."

— Brad Meltzer,
author of New York Times best-selling
mystery/suspense novels *The Tenth
Justice, Dead Even, The First Counsel,
The Millionaires, The Zero Game,
The Book of Fate, The Book of Lies*

"This story is so compelling . . . John McCaslin has put it all together in a way that simply made me want to just keep on reading. Wow."

— Wolf Blitzer,
anchor, host of CNN's
The Situation Room

"For years everybody in Washington has turned to John McCaslin's *Inside The Beltway* column for the inside skinny on what is going on in our nation's capital. Now, in *Weed Man: The Remarkable Journey of Jimmy Divine*, McCaslin brings his exceptional reportorial talent to bear in a fascinating expose of the drug trade."

— G. Gordon Liddy,
Watergate figure and nationally-
syndicated radio host

"I'm delighted to see that John McCaslin has climbed out of his political trench in Washington long enough to set sail on this astonishing journey through the precarious Caribbean reefs, and beyond. Somehow, in typical McCaslin fashion, he manages to bring his readers back to the nation's capital in a chapter that will certainly have official tongues wagging in Washington."

— Katie Couric,
anchor and managing editor
of the *CBS Evening News* and former
co-host of *NBC's Today*

"Proof positive that the extras in James Bond movies are far more interesting than the films, the story of Harbour Island's Jimmy Divine is so colorful it is hard to believe . . . or put down. Told in a breezy, witty style, McCaslin's book captures moments in relatively recent Caribbean history when it was again possible to make a fortune by the ability to steer a boat stealthily through dangerous seas."

— Mark Bowden,
author of *Black Hawk Down*,
Guests of the Ayatollah and *Killing Pablo*

Weed Man

Also by John McCaslin

*Inside the Beltway: Offbeat Stories, Scoops, and Shenanigans
from Around the Nation's Capital*

WEED MAN

The Remarkable Journey of Jimmy Divine

John McCaslin

THOMAS NELSON
Since 1798

NASHVILLE DALLAS MEXICO CITY RIO DE JANEIRO BEIJING

Published in Nashville, Tennessee, by Thomas Nelson. Thomas Nelson is a registered trademark of Thomas Nelson, Inc.

Thomas Nelson, Inc., titles may be purchased in bulk for educational, business, fund-raising, or sales promotional use. For information, please e-mail SpecialMarkets@ThomasNelson.com.

Library of Congress Cataloging-in-Publication Data

McCaslin, John.
    Weed man : the remarkable journey of Jimmy Divine / John McCaslin.
      p. cm.
    Includes bibliographical references.
    ISBN 978-1-59555-153-5 (hbk.)
      1. Moree, Jimmy, 1952- 2. Drug couriers—Caribbean Area—Biography. 3. Drug traffic—Caribbean Area. 4. Drug traffic—United States. 5. Marijuana industry—Caribbean Area. I. Title.
HV5805.M67M33 2008
363.45092—dc22
    [B]   2008054290

Printed in the United States of America

09 10 11 12 13 QW 5 4 3 2

FOR LANE AND FINNEAS AND THEIR CREW
ON HARBOUR ISLAND

AUTHOR'S NOTE

THIS BOOK IS BASED ON A TRUE STORY TOLD FOR THE first time by Jimmy Moree, who lives on a tiny Bahamian island accessible only by boat. Several of the story's characters are identified by their actual names or by nicknames. Identities of others have been changed to protect the guilty.

— JOHN MCCASLIN
Washington, D.C.
October 2008

INTRODUCTION

THE SUN-BAKED BOTTLE OF KALIK SPEWS SUDS AS Robert Arthur's golf cart, the primary mode of transportation on tiny Harbour Island—spoken "Briland" by the locals—bounces along a rough road called Coconut Grove, past the sand dance floor of Gusty's Bar, and onto a crater-filled path leading to the Narrows, a secluded stretch of paradise where some of the world's wealthiest people try to avoid the rest of us.

"You'll enjoy meeting the couple," Robert says as I suck the foam from the beer neck. "Jimmy's Bahamian—a white Bahamian—and Hannah is Canadian. There aren't two nicer people on the island."

That was all the tri-tiered baker/Realtor/minister bothered to say beforehand about the Morees (pronounced Mor-ease), although I knew Robert ran with good company. Before he began glazing donuts, peddling properties, and preaching God's Word every Sunday, Tuesday, and Thursday in his Kingdom Hall (attached to Arthur's Bakery) of Jehovah's Witnesses, the handsome black Bahamian had worked in broadcast journalism, as I did early in my career. During the 1970s he was splicing tape in the same studio where a budding broadcaster named Lawrence Zieger, better known today as Larry King, hosted a local talk show over Miami television station WTVJ. Like Larry, Robert would rise to become a star in his own right, "blessed with one of those one-in-a-million success stories in TV and film," as he describes it. Now he's come back home to this charming speck of coral floating off the northeast coast of Eleuthera his ancestors helped settle centuries ago.

Indeed, despite being raked by an untold number of hurricanes, Harbour Island's colonial-era homes still stand today, lathered in tropical shades of pink, green, and blue long before Lilly Lee Pulitzer painted her house a watermelon sorbet. One 1935 visitor to the island, Nora Benjamin, described a storybook setting for *Nassau Literary Magazine*: "We found ourselves facing a perfect model of a town, a candy box of a town. There was a coffee-colored house with raspberry shutters; a lemon house with chocolate shutters; a strawberry mousse mansion on the hill all decorated with white sugar icing. Spotless paved streets and walks ran between gardens flaming with bougainvillea and hibiscus."

Today, the narrow lanes bordered by salt-bleached fences and pargeted walls still bear allegiance to the British crown:

King, Queen, Princess, and Pitt, to name a few of the streets. In other words, little has changed on the three-mile-long island since the last of the redcoats surrendered the thirteen colonies, and the loyalist governor of Virginia fled to this very cay, where he ceremoniously crowned himself "Lord Dunmore."

Ironically, of all the West Indies in the California-sized archipelago to choose from, Lord Dunmore evacuated to one inhabited by a religious flock that first landed in 1647 to escape persecution in England. He immediately ordered their subsequent generations expelled, and only then was he able to christen the British Empire's newest capital—what else?— Dunmore Town.

In fact, after he baked his final dozen donuts one day, Robert put on his real estate hat and arranged for my family to buy a two-hundred-year-old colonial—pink with blue-green shutters—directly next door to the original site of Lord Dunmore's cottage on Crown Street.

"What's the name of Jimmy's wife again?"

"Hannah. She keeps a beautiful home, as you will see," says Robert, maneuvering his backfiring ride along a bumpier stretch that leads to Harbour Island's world-famous pink-sand beach, where a shapely Elle Macpherson has struck some of her finest poses.

"Oh, and Jimmy doesn't drink," adds Robert, watching as I pry my sticky fingers from the beer bottle. *Lovely*, I think to myself, wishing suddenly that I hadn't accepted the baker's invitation to "meet some locals," which I assumed required climbing out of my bathing trunks and into the one pair of decent pants I generally pack in case the president of the United States bombs Iran and cuts my vacation short.

A virtual canopy of flowering trees and coconut palms shades our way to the couple's lovely house, built tall on concealed pilings and tucked behind thick dunes of sand. Robert parks his cart near the sweeping set of front steps, where awaiting our arrival is the barefoot Hannah, who, I learn later, was born in Toronto, went to art school in Nova Scotia, owned a horse farm with her first husband in Ontario, and sold real estate in New Orleans, before meeting Jimmy during her vacation and subsequently marrying him. My reputation precedes me, as the strawberry-blonde hostess is anxious to hear the latest political news from Washington: Is George W. Bush's "surge" really working? Who is this Barack Obama fellow? Has Bill Clinton calmed down any?

Like Hannah, Jimmy is a gracious host. Relaxed in shorts, Lacoste polo, and cement-splashed Crocs, which he sheds at the front door (so much for my urban threads), he sports a healthy head of jet-black hair with matching goatee, and is amazingly fit for somebody his age, which I guessed to be mid-fifties. He credits the carpentry trade, which he first learned as a teenager, for being in such good shape, although I come to find out he was once the top-ranked kickboxer in all of the Bahamas. He briefly explains the history behind his small construction and renovation business—preferably one house at a time, given that he's semiretired. Just that morning, in fact, he and his crew of carpenters set out to save a termite-consumed colonial at the corner of King and Princess Streets, although he hinted the prognosis was not good.

As Robert and Hannah weigh the latest Harbour Island gossip—what Bahamians call *sip-sip*—Jimmy serves everybody mixed drinks or wine, pouring himself one of those trendy lemon-lime sodas imported from Europe with the red star on the side. Soon, he chimes in more and more, until such time he's the captivating master of ceremonies.

For the next two hours I can't believe what I'm hearing. I sit on a kitchen bar stool as Jimmy spins one amazing yarn after another, in a lilting Bahamian accent unlike any I've ever heard cross the lips of a white man. He recalls growing up on Long Island, just due west of San Salvador, where Christopher Columbus dropped anchor and first set foot in the New World. I hadn't known it, but Long Island was the Italian explorer's third discovery, the second being pint-sized Rum Cay.

Jimmy explains how his mother, Perline, took to her bed after his delivery—"I weighed almost fourteen pounds," he reasons—and as a result he was bundled up in his baby blanket and sent by mail boat to the Bahamian capital of Nassau, where he would live with his father's sister, Olive, a big-boned, outwardly religious woman who, besides her own strict guiding principles, relied on the black preachers from the Church of God and the white nuns from the Catholic school to teach Jimmy right from wrong.

He relives the summers he spent on Long Island with his father, Jacob, helping farm, fish, and ferry spices between the various islands, including Cuba. I hear of his unrehearsed Hollywood acting roles: a childhood part in the original *Flipper*, as well as a speedboat racer alongside James Bond. He tells of his first marriage, which coincided with his first business venture—as a scuba-diving instructor off the coast of Abaco, the Bahamian island due north of here. It was on that secluded cay one otherwise ordinary morning that the health-conscious Jimmy went for his usual jog on the beach—one that changed his life forever.

After all, how many people stumble upon several million dollars when they're out exercising? Soon, millions more dollars would fall into his lap. And with each million Jimmy has an incredible story to tell, the next one more amazing than the last, all recalled in his sweet-flowing "Conchy Joe" (slang for minority white Bahamians) accent I never grow tired of hearing. One minute my jaw is agape—like when he describes the view from his pew at the royal wedding of Prince Charles and Lady Diana—and the next I'm laughing myself to tears when he's a child again, trying to poison his crusty old neighbor with a deadly barracuda.

I wipe away real tears when he recounts the times he would return to Long Island and pay back the poor families of farmers and fishermen who helped care for his ailing mother when he couldn't. He'd give each family two envelopes—one for the wife and one for the husband—containing more money than they would ever see from a bumper year of potatoes and lobsters.

By the time he pours my third or fourth Mount Gay rum—one great thing about Harbour Island is a person forgets how to count—I can't help but realize Jimmy never bothered to mention what it was he stumbled upon on the beach that otherwise ordinary morning that changed his life so drastically. So I ask him.

He suddenly becomes quiet and looks to Hannah, who turns and looks to Robert, who turns to look my way. On cue I look back at Jimmy.

"Should I tell him?" he asks.

ONE

RUSTED WHEELS CLUNG TO WORN TRACKS AS THE rickety train climbed the *sabana*, or high plateau of the Andes mountains. Slouched so as to be less noticed in the passenger seat nearest the locomotive, the Reverend Jerome Constantakis felt inside his scarlet-red tunic for his passport, which identified him as a Catholic priest from the Bahamas. Proof of citizenship and motley vestments wouldn't be required once he reached his final destination in the Sierra Nevada de Santa Marta, the world's highest coastal mountain range he'd soon be ascending on the back of a donkey—the day's final mode of transportation that began in the backseat of a Miami taxi. He zipped his travel documents into a small suitcase kept at his

1

feet—where he could feel it—realizing in doing so that he forgot his toothbrush again.

Father Jerome, as he called himself—for fear of butchering the last name—had never grown comfortable administering blessings to the appreciative Colombians who squatted in the mountainous villages between Bogotá and the northern coast. Seldom did these peasants come face-to-face with visiting clergymen of his caliber—dressed to the hilt and sporting an ecclesiastical stone ring so gigantic it should have belonged to the pontiff.

"Full regalia," he now describes the wardrobe with its dangling tassels and trinkets. "Sometimes I wore purple, sometimes I wore red. I didn't wear just the black outfit with white collar. I didn't have the pope's hat, but I had the cardinal's hat."

Mothers and grandmothers alike, babies forever glued to their arms, swarmed around the handsome priest with the jet-black hair and matching goatee. *"Padre, bendiga a mi bebé, por favor,"* they pleaded, asking for blessings for their children.

Father Jerome managed a smile with each request, grateful when the women extended the infants so he wasn't at a loss for their requests. He then placed the palms of his suntanned hands atop each silky scalp and recited his trademark Latin blessing—the few holy words he could recall from his years as an altar boy in 1960s' Nassau. At which point the unsuspecting Colombians, who spoke Castilian Spanish peppered with Colombian vernacular or one of 180 other indigenous languages overheard in the third-world country, knelt down before the holy imposter to kiss his magnificent ring.

Without fail, Father Jerome followed each Latin blessing with a separate prayer that he whispered to himself in a language he could understand. "God, forgive me," he repeated, over and over again.

More often than not his mind turned to the real Father Jerome, his principal at Sacred Heart Catholic School in Nassau and a guiding force in his life. How would that servant of the Lord, a Pennsylvanian from blue-collar Bethlehem, have reacted if he'd known that one of his more promising non-Catholic altar boys and pupils had literally hijacked his name and most sacred vow?

The guilt would have been unbearable had the phony priest not recalled the strap. Once the unruly boys had grown taller than the nuns, Father Jerome would be summoned to administer more memorable punishments. The children called it "strap time"—when they would bend over their desks for lashings, the specific number hinging on the severity of the crime.

So what if I'm not an ordained channel to God? Father Jerome reasoned with himself. *Isn't my presence alone a good thing? Aren't my prayers and blessings among these masses of spiritually deprived people better than having none at all?*

He recalled one of his former Sacred Heart classmates, whose surname was Constantakis. The boy had been enrolled in the Catholic school for maybe a year before his Greek parents shipped him off to boarding school. It took one of his classmates so long to memorize his name that he hadn't forgotten it to this day. Still, it was difficult for him to pronounce. And then the school's stern principal popped back into his mind, haunting him again.

"Pour the wine," the principal would encourage his timid altar server, who would start to pour and then stop, the chalice half-full. Maybe it was because he'd grown up knowing that too much alcohol—whether orange-colored altar wine or the clear hooch his father drank—was not such a good thing. "More wine, more wine; it's okay, Jimmy."

No, it wasn't the Colombian police or military that Father Jerome dreaded bumping into during his risky journeys into these unfamiliar mountains. He wasn't afraid of the rebel groups that kidnapped foreigners for a living, holding them for ransom. What petrified him more than anything else was crossing paths with a Catholic priest or a nun and having to lie about being in the poor South American country in hopes of opening an orphanage. It was a tough sell to begin with, but the fact that he didn't speak a lick of Spanish made such ungodly deception all the more difficult.

He glanced down at the shiny cover of his Bible, realizing how unread it looked. He slumped further into his stiff seat, its fabric worn to wood many journeys ago. Fatigued, his stomach growling, he stared through the train's filthy windows into the muddied-green countryside until the rocking and rhythm of the wheels lulled him to sleep.

=
=

"*Padre, padre, me marido se está muriendo! Venga, venga por favor!*"

The shrill cry was coming from the rear of the car. Startled awake, Father Jerome sat upright, turning to see an old woman wearing a colorful *pollera* skirt, her dark gray hair wrapped neatly in a bun, waving her hands wildly into the air as she rushed to the front of the train.

The priest looked to his fellow passengers for a clue, unable to comprehend the woman's pleas: "Father, Father, my husband is dying," she was repeating in Spanish. "Come, please come!"

The train's riders stared wide-eyed at the larger-than-life priest—wearing everything but a halo on his head—no doubt expecting to witness their first miracle. Father Jerome knew enough to grab his Bible—and, on second thought, his suitcase—place his zucchetto (skullcap) on his head, and follow the hysterical woman back down the aisle to the rear of the train.

"Her husband had suffered a heart attack," he explains now. "I went to him, but unfortunately he was already gone. So I recited some of my Latin words and traced a cross on his forehead—just like the priests do on Ash Wednesday. I figured that was a good touch.

"'Ahd Doh'mee-noom Day'oom noh'stroom [*ad Dominum Deum nostrum*]'—I had no idea what I was saying. But the old woman seemed relieved, given the circumstances. Giving him the last rites—whatever the case was—it made her feel good, and that made me feel good. And the people who had gathered around for my send-off were all thanking me, handing me various tokens of their appreciation—whatever possessions they carried with them on the train, some breathing, some not. I kept saying, 'No, thank you, no, thank you.'"

Last rites administered, a weary Father Jerome carefully made his way back up the swaying aisle of the train, keeping his suitcase clutched to his chest. Now more than ever he relished the seclusion of his forward space, where he could reflect on his sins. And then, as if on sacred cue, the sun's rays broke through the storm clouds that shrouded the nearby mountains and streaked yellow through the car's muddied windows. "Light from God," proclaimed one elderly passenger, rising up from his seat to bow in homage.

Father Jerome passed row after row of these adoring peasants, some shouting accolades, others grabbing at his colorful mozzetta (bishop's cape), cassock, and silk sash. It reminded him of the annual May Day processions in Nassau, except in this unholy aisle it wasn't the Blessed Mother the throngs were worshiping.

Ashamed of himself, he found his seat and stared one last time at his Bible—still no worse for the wear. "I've really done it this time," he mumbled. "I'm going straight to hell for this performance."

He felt like ripping off his cross and leaping from the slow-moving train. He tried to concentrate on his two-day itinerary, which culminated as guest of honor with one of the more influential drug cartels in Colombia—the Cardinals.

It took longer than usual, but the priest began to relax and came close to nodding off, when he felt a light tapping on his shoulder. He turned to first notice the crusted tear streaks, twisting like dried mountain streams down the widow's wrinkled cheeks. Her eyes were bloodshot, but determined.

"Padre," she offered, her voice a mere whisper in comparison to the screech of her time of need. "*Gracias por su bendición. Por favor, acepte este pollo en agradecimiento.*"

And with that she placed a simple wooden and wire-mesh box on Father Jerome's lap, turned, and shuffled away. The cackling chicken inside it looked as confused as the priest.

TWO

THE MOREE BROTHERS—RENO, FLOYD, AND JAMES (whenever the latter was back visiting)—didn't have to pore over the pages of Robert Louis Stevenson's *Treasure Island* to dream about buccaneers and buried gold. Pirates and pillaging were in their blood. The boys' father, Jacob, delighted in recalling the maritime adventures of the family's ancestors—genuine French-rooted *boucaniers* licensed by the British crown as privateers to attack any and all galleons and coastal cities from the Caribbean to the Americas that flew the Spanish flag.

Surely Jacob spared his sons the most gruesome details of the family's diaries, given the sport of buccaneering in the seventeenth and eighteenth centuries wasn't bound by any manual of niceties. Buccaneers attacked without warning and seldom took prisoners—it was that simple. Except for a diversion or two, the family's days of swashbuckling ended in the 1780s, Jacob assured his barefoot boys, which is when the Morees first settled on this sliver of an island that Christopher Columbus had christened Fernandina some three centuries before. Their bloodline, their father told them, fished and farmed on the same five-hundred-acre tract—a pirate's payment by the crown—they farmed and fished from today.

"Tell us more about the wreckers!" one of the boys begged.

"There was one spell during the nineteenth century that the Moree clan helped darken the lighthouse a couple of times and set a fire in the middle of the island—they were called wreckers," Jacob explained. "They did it to survive, you see, or else you boys might never have been born. And when the ships, loaded to the decks with goods and treasures, sailed past our island, the captains would confuse the fire in the field for the lighthouse, and they'd run their boats up on the reef. The wreckers would then go out to the sinking ships and collect whatever supplies they needed. Does that make sense?"

If a Caribbean cowboy ever existed, it was Jacob. Tall and thin, he wore all black, from his Stetson hat to his pointy-toe boots. A cantankerous fellow, he welcomed fistfights with each snort of hooch—a corn-based moonshine made by a neighbor farmer the islanders called Mr. John. When he wasn't fishing for grouper, snappers, yellow tails, and grunts— plentiful lobsters were used to catch the grunts—or growing potatoes, pumpkins, and corn; or tending to his chickens, goats, and sheep, Jacob was riding his black and gray horse, named

Smokey. Jacob used to irritate his wife by galloping his stud into her kitchen—separated from the one-bedroom pink rubble (stone mixed with mud) house—and tying him up to the table while the family ate.

A renowned womanizer, Jacob was always telling his boys that their mother, Perline Daville, was the most gorgeous woman he'd ever laid eyes on. Of Portuguese descent, she stood just over five feet, weighed fewer than 110 pounds, and had a hardened beauty to her. The Long Islanders were most impressed with her flowing black hair, which hung below her hips. She was, Jacob realized, the prize catch on the island. To court her, he would jump on his horse and gallop halfway up the eighty-mile-long shard of land, past five-hundred-acre tracts owned by the Millers ("Mr. John" and "Ma Miller"), Dillards, Knowleses (pronounced "Nalls"), Farrellses, and Wellses. A single date with Perline would last the entire day, but given the distance involved, Jacob would spend most of it with Smokey. The three dated like this for two years, until Jacob asked Perline to give him and his horse a rest. She accepted the pair's proposal and left the five-hundred-acre Daville tract her family farmed and fished to settle on the five-hundred-acre tract the Moree family farmed and fished.

———

The earliest settlers employed by the British crown had been doled out like-sized parcels of land, what came to be called "generational property"—passed down from one generation to the next, so long as there was a son in the family to inherit the property. Deeds stating as much were issued by the Bahamas

House of Assembly when it first convened in 1729 to draw up a constitution, which recognized the English king and queen as its rulers, with an appointed governor to oversee the tropical archipelago of seven hundred islands and cays—fourteen of them prosperous enough to sustain populations.

Stretching north to south on the map, Long Island resembles a chewed toothpick, albeit there was less wood and more rock, and not much of that. Stand anywhere on the island and all you see is ocean. In fact, the waterlogged geology confused the original inhabitants of the island, which in turn served to confuse their children, their children, their children, and so on, despite the fact the subsequent generations, unlike their forebearers, had state-of-the-art maps at their disposal. Even the Moree brothers were confused.

"The entire time growing up, the east side of the island was known as the north side," Jimmy recalls. "I never knew why, and I learned not to question it. Early one morning Jacob—I almost always called him Jacob because that's what he wanted to be called; he refused to believe that he was older than the rest of us . . . Anyway, this one morning Jacob and I were eating breakfast before we went out to check the pots. And up comes the sun, dead in the east—where it's supposed to come up, you know? And I said, 'Jacob, I realize I'm not that bright, but why is the sun rising in the north?' And he said, 'Son, let me explain something to you. It's not up to us to step in and change something that has stood for centuries. That has always been the north side of the island, and it will stay the north side.'"

———
———
———

Perline had delivered her third and last son, James—who henceforth answered to Jimmy—on the morning of November 15, 1952. When it came to a baby's size, the two older Moree siblings had been larger than most newborns, but a mother's intuition told Perline that Jimmy would be no ordinary arrival. And he wasn't—topping Jacob's fish scale at almost fourteen pounds, a Long Island record as far back as the neighbors could remember.

Anemic to start with, Perline never fully recovered from the difficult delivery. From that day forward she barely stepped foot out of her pink house and kitchen, except to use the bathroom or attend church, which was as close as the outhouse. Jacob and the older boys carried in all the fish and vegetables, and Perline always managed to set a hot meal on the table. But she and Jacob knew—indeed the entire island knew—that the huge addition to the Moree family would be too much for Perline to handle. On that inevitable day, tears welled in her eyes and, drawing all the emotional strength she could muster from her frail body, she kissed her six-month-old on the nose and told him to always remember his mother (as it was, she lived another twenty-two years). She then handed the baby to Jacob, who wrapped a blanket around his youngest son and told the boy's speechless brothers to see to their mother's needs while he was away on the boat, and to call on the neighbors if needed. He then placed his black cowboy hat on his head, grabbed the small bag that Perline had packed with what few possessions belong to somebody Jimmy's age, and set off for the water's edge, where the father and son boarded the mail boat bound for Exuma Sound and the Bahamian capital of Nassau.

Ironically, it was the most bonding Jacob had ever done with one of his babies. He didn't normally step into the picture until his children were old enough to run the fields and learn how to set the fish traps. For the first time, guilt gripped him as the boat churned its way north, past a few large islands and hundreds of smaller ones, christened with curious names like Man-O-War Cay, Rat Cay, Bitter Guana, Rudder Cut, Sail Rocks, Booby Island, and, once beyond Salt Cay, the big island of New Providence and its bustling harbor of Nassau.

There, to her brother's relief, standing impatiently on the pier in her extra-large muumuu dress, was six-foot-two-inch, 240-pound Olive Pearce—Jimmy's new "mother"—who, having already raised her own brood, welcomed her small nephew with half-open arms.

THREE

JIMMY KNEW EARLY ON HE HAD NO EAR FOR MUSIC. On the nights the Pearces sat down to sing, whenever Jimmy attempted to open his mouth, he was teased to no end by Godfrey and Patricia, his older cousins who, by Olive's estimation, sang like angels.

"You know you're adopted," they enjoyed reminding him.

Usually orchestrating the songfests was Olive's husband, Kirkwood, whose musical talents impressed Brother Bell and Brother Franks, the pair of Bahamian preachers at the nearby Church of God ("the black man's country club," Olive whispered when the brothers weren't around). The two preachers proclaimed "Alleluia!" whenever Kirkwood filled the air with the chords of his guitar and accordion, whether it was the classic "Amazing Grace" beside the altar during Sunday services or the Bahamian spiritual "Sheep Know When Thy Shepherd Calling" on the front porch of Miss Olive's aqua-colored house on rough-and-tumble Kemp Road.

"There was lots of singing; all the neighbors used to come by," Jimmy recalls. "They put in a streetlight right above our house there, so that became the place to congregate. There were only three streetlights on the whole road. Mr. Willie Good, he would come down, and Mr. French and Mr. White. There were no chairs on the porch, so they'd sit on the porch wall or else pull up buckets, and we'd sing into the night. And when the singing was over, the sip-sip would begin. And after everybody got their fill, Kirkwood would start playing again."

It was quite the honor in the impoverished Kemp Road neighborhood, several blocks away from more affluent Bay Street, to have the Church of God preachers stop by your house when nobody was dying.

"These two guys were as black as the ace of spades, and characters in themselves," Jimmy says. "They were notorious for having sweethearts, and they would act like they were preaching to the congregation about such awful things when they were really preaching at each other. They weren't educated men—the majority of the people in those days got as far as the eighth grade before they'd have to find work. But they were men of the cloth, so you respected them. It was apparent they knew few of the Scriptures—they would preach the same story every Sunday. Sometimes it was livelier than other times, sometimes it was funny, but it always dealt with dying and going to hell if you didn't repent beforehand. And they'd preach in their Bahamian accents, which gave it all the more flavor.

"Brother Bell, he was tall and thin and in great shape—had muscles everywhere, which he got from being the grave digger. Brother Franks, he looked like Don King—gray hair going everywhere. He spoke with a raspy voice, so Brother Bell was always considered more of the preacher because he spoke plain and direct. And we'd have to speak back, and when I say *we*, I mean we were maybe one of six or seven white families in a congregation of a couple hundred people. But we still had to shout and scream, carry on, jump up and down, the whole works.

"I'll never forget one Sunday after the Scriptures were read—usually by somebody who had made it to high school, which is why they often called on me to read—and Brother Bell would recite the customary, 'Now, let the church say amen!' And we'd answer, 'Amen, Brother Bell!'

"'Now, before I start my sermon tonight, I want to let you know that somebody stole my bicycle. But by the grace of God, by the time this service is out, I will know who stole my bicycle. And no, I did not leave it nowhere, so don't nobody ask me. Somebody stole it.'

"It was hilarious," Jimmy recalls, "but nobody dared laugh. And then, sure enough, Brother Franks interrupted the sermon. 'Come to think of it, are you sure you lost your bicycle, Brother Bell?' And Brother Bell said, 'I said someone stole it. Now let's get back to the service.' And at that point he started preaching about the Ten Commandments, looking out across the congregation: 'Do you know one of the commandments?' he'd point to somebody and say. 'Do you know a commandment?' he asked another. And then Brother Bell pointed straight at me and said, 'Do you know a commandment, young man?' And out of my mouth comes, 'Thou shalt not commit adultery.'

"And amazingly, Brother Bell got real quiet; you could actually see him thinking to himself. And after enough time passed, he announced to the congregation, 'Don't worry, I remember where I left my bicycle.' As if everybody in the congregation didn't know what had crossed his mind. He'd left his bicycle by his sweetheart's house, had left in a hurry and forgot about it, and everybody in church knew it."

The preaching continued in such fashion every Sunday, every holy day, every Easter, every Christmas, and every time the preachers buried somebody in the cemetery—but not before Brother Bell finished digging the grave, which often delayed entry into the pearly gates, granted the soul repented. But anytime Brother Bell would be frantically digging, Kirkwood would always be there to fill the voids with his playlist of spirituals.

Jimmy grew to understand Kirkwood more than his stepfather ever came to understand the boy who had suddenly arrived on his doorstep. But the same blood that ran through Olive ran through Jimmy, and Kirkwood, who drove a taxi part-time, did his best to be at least a part-time stepfather. In retrospect, the best thing he ever did for Jimmy was teach him how to fend for himself, especially when confronting the many bruisers in his tough Nassau neighborhood.

"Back in the day, when someone called you Conchy Joe for some reason, we didn't like it. They were fighting words. So from the time I was about eight, Kirkwood took me down to this little place just below Kemp Road called Nassau Stadium, and Charlie Major had a boxing gym in there. Kirkwood said, 'Son, when you're dumb, you've got to be tough. And since you're fighting every day to begin with, you've got to learn to do it properly.' Charlie Major was one of the nicest men you'd ever meet in your life. And in the back of his wrestling area he had this boxing gym, and all the local boxers used to train there. I would walk home from school—you had to walk everywhere in those days—and I would go to the gym for an hour or hour and a half. And it was tremendous for me because I was the little white kid that would not stop. I would box every day, doing my push-ups and my sit-ups, everything you could do, right alongside the big boys. Then when the boxing matches came around, I'd always work their corners—Boston, Blackie, all the Bahamian boxers."

Soon, the first-of-its-kind martial arts studio opened on the island of New Providence, and for Kirkwood and Jimmy it was a no-brainer. The boy began studying the various forms of karate at a very young age, and soon got into sparring—or *kumite*—which means "meeting of the hands." Once he mastered blocking and counterattacks with his hands, Jimmy turned to kickboxing, which he not only enjoyed but excelled in to the point that everybody up and down Kemp Road, black or white, young or old, would allow Jimmy ample space to pass. Little did Kirkwood ever dream that Bahamians one day in the not-too-distant future would be paying money to see Jimmy fight.

Otherwise, the stepfather and stepson mostly kept their distance, including on special occasions like Christmas, when Olive, for whatever odd reason, would present Jimmy with the same gift-wrapped present every year: a toy gun—the same toy gun, in the same plastic holster. And every Christmas Jimmy would play with the gun for a few days, and then it would mysteriously disappear only to reappear the next Christmas in wonderful new wrapping. It was apparently all that Olive and Kirkwood could afford.

"Everybody on Kemp Road was poor," Jimmy says, "although you never stopped to think about it. You had no yardstick to compare who was rich and who was poor, because everybody was poor. I'll never forget my uncle Preston, my father's brother—he was a character too. We were having an outdoor barbecue one Friday night, and he said, 'You know, times really change. I remember when we used to poop in the yard and eat in the house. Now we poop in the house and eat in the yard.' I mean, when I was growing up in Nassau, you had to shower with a bucket you pulled up from the well—just pour it over you. The water was cold unless you had time to light the fire between the three rocks and boil it in our number five tub."

When he wasn't driving his taxi—which was usually six months out of the year, since most hotels in Nassau were open only during the most pleasant months—Kirkwood made up for the downtime by harvesting whatever vegetables he could grow in his garden. This would see to a continuous serving of corn and tomatoes and greens on the family's dinner table. And Jimmy, who like most islanders was an excellent swimmer, would often be sent by Olive to dive for some lobsters. In those days the ocean was swarming with the marine crustaceans—he'd bring home thirty or forty at a time. She'd then boil them in the fifty-five-gallon drum that Kirkwood cut in half and put in the backyard. The people on Kemp Road ate lobster like it was hot dogs or bologna. It was the poor man's food, provided by Jimmy while Kirkwood quietly tended his garden.

"I understood Kirkwood's position," Jimmy says. "He'd raised his children, had gotten through all the hard times, and then this big hungry baby floats up on the mail boat. It took me a long time to get my head around it, but I could understand the resentment. The family story was told that when I came off the boat, I was the lightest-colored one on the block—I was lighter than Kirkwood's own children because he was from the island of Eleuthera. Unfortunately in the Bahamas it was an issue back in those days: no white Bahamians wanted to raise any dark children. Kirkwood was sensitive about that. So he and I always had a problem from the time I first showed up. But he had no say in the matter because Olive controlled the roost. She was in charge. 'She was large, and she was in charge;' that's what we used to say."

One time when Olive's oldest child, Godfrey, was in his early thirties, he, his wife, and their two children were visiting the house on Kemp Road for one of Olive's weekly barbecues. Every Friday, Olive insisted on cooking a hot meal for her now-expanding family of children and grandchildren—to nourish their souls, so to speak. It was important to Olive that her grandchildren get to know their grandmother, particularly since they weren't fortunate enough to grow up beneath her roof.

Having lived most of his life in the two-bedroom house, Godfrey knew better than anybody that his mother did not allow one drop of alcohol on her property. Whether it was poured in the house or in the outhouse, she made no distinction. Smoking anything besides fish was also completely out of the question.

"Neither existed as far as she was concerned," Jimmy explains.

But now that he was a grown adult with children of his own, Godfrey somehow came to the conclusion, at least on this particular Friday night, that if he wasn't man enough to enjoy a nip under Olive's roof, he surely was clever enough to conceal a cooler beneath a blanket on the backseat of his car and step outside every now and then for a sip—which always tasted better when accompanied by a cigarette, of course.

"This one Friday, I was flipping the burgers," Jimmy recalls, "and everybody's just sitting around as usual, shooting the bull. When out of the corner of my eye, I see my brother Godfrey take out a pack of cigarettes and flip one up into his mouth. I remember saying to myself, 'This boy has gone and lost his mind.' I don't know what he was on, but sure enough, Olive suddenly filled the entire doorway—this gigantic woman, right? And she just stood there for a moment, as if she was taking it all in. It took her thirty seconds or more to realize what her son was doing, because she didn't think anybody possessed that much stupidity to smoke a cigarette on her property. And as I stood there and watched, she calmly walked over to the side of Godfrey, drew back her hand, and slapped that boy hard—and when I say *hard*, she slapped him silly. His cigarette went one way and his face went the other. And I never ever saw Bobo—I called him Bobo affectionately, and he called me Pumpkin—I never saw Bobo smoke anything again. He told me later that every time he saw a pack of cigarettes, his head ached. No sir, you did not mess with Olive, no matter who you were."

Jimmy remembers one family in the neighborhood and "their child had some type of problem and had to go through a twelve-step rehab program. And I remember Olive saying, 'That child doesn't need twelve steps; all that child needs is one swift kick in the you-know-where. That's a waste of steps.'" She had no tolerance for ignorance.

Besides being large and stubborn, Olive was a God-fearing woman. After her two oldest children had flown the nest, she made sure Jimmy received her undivided attention. Meaning she was bound and determined to keep Jacob's son—her son now, as far as she was concerned—on the straight and narrow. "She was my real mother," Jimmy says. "I called her mom, and she called me son."

And whereas she all but owned her favorite pew at the Church of God, from a distance Olive always admired the Catholic Sisters of Sacred Heart School. She would watch, impressed, as the sisters, clad in their sparkling white habits, marched their neatly pressed charges around the streets of Nassau, as if they were training little black soldiers. She'd made up her mind long before Jimmy shed his diapers that—baptized Catholic or not—he would spend his days as near the nuns' convent as possible. The way she figured it, between the pope's strict teachings and the sermons of Brother Bell and Brother Franks, Jimmy's childhood would be divinely blessed. And whatever spiritual guidance the men and women of the cloth could not instill in the boy, she would be there to pick up the slack.

"Olive read somewhere in the Bible that if you spare the

rod you spoil the child. I think that's the only Scripture she ever memorized in her life," Jimmy points out. "She used to beat me once a week for the things I did that she didn't know about. The tamarind tree was the switch of choice, because it's really, really thin—and it stings. And the sad part about it is she used to send me to fetch the switch. You can't pick a thin switch either, because if it breaks while she's beating you, then you're in a world of trouble. Then she has to go to the tree to get what you didn't get in the first place. Just think of the mental anguish you go through when you have to choose the right switch. First, you have to find the right one. Then you have to strip the leaves off. And as you're coming back to the house, you're swinging it like she's going to swing it. And it's making this sound—*ssswishhh-ssswishhh-ssswishhh*—and you realize that every one of those *swishes* is going to be headed in your direction, and they're going to be painful. It was a tough walk to take. And we actually had the tamarind tree right in our yard, and I visited it often, because let me tell you, when you're young, you're dumb. That was another one of Olive's sayings."

One day Jimmy was hanging out with his best friend, David French, a strikingly handsome boy born to a mulatto mother and white father. David had a severe stuttering problem, and Olive sought to console him by commenting how blessed he was to be born with wavy red hair and skin the color of mango. One hot afternoon, after Jimmy and David sweated through a game of rounders in the Church of God cemetery—"First base was Miss Pinda, second base was Mr. Rolle, and I can't remember who third base was, but we used their gravestones as our bases"—they hurried down to the Savoy Theatre on Bay Street for the three o'clock show of *Hercules Unchained*, starring Steve Reeves, who, apart from acting, was famous for winning several bodybuilding titles, including Mr. America 1947 and both Mr. World and Mr. Universe 1950. Despite what the critics considered a lackluster performance, Jimmy was captivated by the scene where Hercules uproots a tree with his bare hands and throws it into the path of a pursuing chariot. He was so intrigued that he and David stayed for the five o'clock show and watched Hercules do it all over again.

"I sat right in the front, and I watched Hercules very closely," Jimmy recalls. "I saw exactly how he grabbed this tree. He put one arm this way, one arm this way, and then he squatted down and pulled the tree right up out of the ground. Man, you couldn't beat me and David rushing home after that—flying up Kemp Road on our bicycles."

Y-y-y-yer g-g-g-going to p-p-p-pull that tree out of y-y-y-yer y-y-y-yard, aren't you?

Yep, I'm going to pull it out of the ground right now, David. Just watch.

A-a-a-are you s-s-s-sure y-y-y-you can lift it?

Don't worry about it. I can lift it. I saw the way Hercules did it. I can do it. I know I can.

"Let me tell you, I went into the backyard, and David is stuttering his best to coach me along and cheer me on, and I'm hanging on to this tamarind tree, trying to yank the roots out of the ground. Of course, all I'm doing is scraping my arms real bad. But I kept at it. And sure enough, Olive appears in the door, just like the Ghost Rider."

Boy, what are you doing?

I'm pulling this tree out of the yard.

What tree?

This tamarind tree.

Why?

I saw Hercules do it in the movie just a little while ago.

Boy, come this way. But first break off a switch and bring it with you for being stupid.

FOUR

ONE THING ABOUT OLIVE IS NO SOONER DID SCHOOL let out for the summer and she was stashing Jimmy among the boxes that were loaded onto the mail boat leaving for Long Island. He would spend the summer months beside Perline— but only after he and Jacob finished hoeing the fields, picking the *keneps*, feeding the horse, and setting the fish pots.

"When you were small, it was just like you were big: you worked like a man," Jimmy says. "You go into the fields, you go out in the boat—digging potatoes and catching fish. From the minute you got up in the morning you worked. And when it got too hot in the fields, you'd go out on the boat. And after you came home at sundown, you'd split firewood to boil the

25

water to cook the food. And after you finished eating, you often went 'torching.' We'd take a bottle, fill it with kerosene, light the wick at the end, and walk along the beach in ankle-deep water. Lobsters come into the shallow water at night to feed, and you'd strike them and put them in the basket. You'd get as many lobsters as you wanted. They were plentiful."

Next to his three boys and his horse, Jacob was most proud of his twenty-four-foot, one-mast sailing sloop, which he christened the *Windward* after the nearby Windward Passage. He fished "hand line"—a line attached to a piece of wood—and he planted coconut-straw pots that measured four feet square that he baited with leftover crawfish heads he hadn't sucked. Twice a day he pulled pots, more often than not, loaded to the gills with grouper and other delectable fish—unless the sharks got to them first.

"Jacob fished every day but Sundays; that was his day of rest. Fortunately for us, the Church of God was right in our yard. It was a very small church, holding I'd say fifty people," Jimmy says. "But it was nice having it right next door to you, since a lot of the neighbors had to come a long way—they either walked, rode horseback, or came via horse and buggy. It sounds primitive, but you have to realize that Long Island didn't get electricity until 1992. We had generators before that, but we relied on kerosene lamps and lanterns, and open-flame cooking."

Frail and anemic, Perline avoided most anything public except church, which given its close proximity, she'd attend regularly. And after the preachers said amen, and she exchanged a few words with the other parishioners, she would walk the few steps back home to the family's two-room pink house with its outdoor kitchen, which for her held comforting aromas of baked bread and fried fish. The boys slept in the main room—"There was just one bedroom, where Jacob and Perline slept, and then there was the rest of the house," Jimmy says—and they would normally be in bed by dark because Jacob would have them back up before first light.

The sea usually bathed everybody but Perline. The boys watched with interest one day as Jacob configured a wide faucet to a fifty-five-gallon drum, which he then set atop some two-by-fours. At that point he turned on the closest thing to a shower anybody on Long Island ever stood under. "As far as we were concerned, he'd invented the wheel," his youngest son remembers.

Jimmy's favorite part of the summer was bittersweet, because it would usher in the end of his stay on Long Island. He would accompany Jacob on his spice runs, which started with picking up large baskets of harvested salt from the famous salt flats (Morton Salt is produced there today) of Great Inagua, one of the more southerly islands in the Bahamas, also popular for its large colony of fiery pink flamingos. Once the salt was loaded, they would transport it to Cuba, their entire voyage under sail. Once it grew dark, and they had eaten their dinner of dried fish, the father and son would sit together in the well of the boat and talk about everything under the moon. And when they were tired, they would sleep on the linens Perline stuffed with straw and sewed shut.

When the warm sun smiled down on the little sloop again, Jimmy would watch in awe as his father expertly navigated his boat across an endless palette of blue and green—first southeast through the Crooked Island Passage, then into the Windward

Passage, constantly bound for watery landmarks that only he could identify.

"I once saw him take a piece of cloth, roll it up, and throw it overboard," Jimmy remembers.

Jacob, what's that?

A current ball.

What does it do?

It gives you the direction of the tide, which helps tell you where you've been and where you're going. Along with everything else, you've got to work the tide.

"You have to remember this man did not have a GPS [Global Positioning System] or any other instrument. He only had what was in his head. He was amazing to watch, because he always knew where he had to go. Jacob eventually taught me how to read the water too. And it came in handy throughout my life, all because of what I had experienced at that young age."

Havana was a fabulous, vibrant place, unlike any city Jimmy had ever been to in his life, which at present count was one, if you rank Nassau as a city. Every street the Bahamian boy peered down was a kaleidoscope of color and chrome—an endless Detroit parade of tail fins mounted to Fords, Chryslers, and Cadillacs, all with throbbing V-8 engines.

"The cars were everywhere, and for a youngster like me, it was like being in a candy store. And talk about city lights and the music on every street corner! Havana got me hooked on cities to this day."

On one journey to the Western Hemisphere's communist capital, the father and son tied the *Windward* to the seawall next to *el Malecón*, Havana's bustling and busiest boulevard that bared the Cuban soul in more ways than one.

"My father would always bring girls back to the boat," Jimmy admits. "Oh yeah, he was a womanizer. But they weren't prostitutes. He could just go to a bar and pick up most of the ladies. And I'd be right up on the bow of the boat, told to watch over it. That was my job, watch the boat, you see? Jacob made me feel important because I was in charge. He and the ladies would drink rum and carry on, and I never told nobody a thing. Even now I don't say anything when I see guys doing foolish things."

On the other hand, Jimmy never had to remind his father to pick up a special gift to take home to Perline. "And don't forget," Jacob would always remind his youngest son while sailing home from Cuba, "your mother is the most beautiful woman in the islands." That seemed to make everything that ever happened all right, at least as far as Jacob was concerned.

Despite the relatively short amount of time they spent together, Jacob taught Jimmy everything he possibly could about life, both on land and at sea. Of his three sons, he considered Jimmy the most special: "You were born with gold letters in your head," he would later tell his son.

"I didn't know what he meant, so I asked him," Jimmy says.

"When you were younger, I used to put you on the bow of the boat, and I would tell you to set a course, and more times than not, you'd run the boat aground. I would curse and carry on, but soon you learned to read the water—read the letters—on your own: you knew what was underneath, knew the tide, worked the currents, and linked the channels. And before long all I could do was sit back and watch—just let you go. You might have thought I was too tough on you and not paying attention, but I only wanted to make you a better person."

———
———

Stacked up against Jacob's and Olive's obedience training, atonement paid to the nuns at Sacred Heart was a breeze, as far as Jimmy was concerned: usually nothing more than tiny circular bruises on his chest from the one nun who "talked with her finger, punching you with it as she spoke. We used to joke that she could do push-ups with that finger," Jimmy laughs.

Always his biggest fear was that Olive would hear some *sip-sip* from the Catholic sisters about those times Jimmy would be acting up in school. Like Jacob, hardly a day went by that he wasn't in a fistfight, which could be serious for the taker, given Jimmy's knowledge of martial arts. He would sit on pins and needles waiting for Olive's big feet to come marching into his room, demanding answers. But the Sisters of Charity came to know Jimmy and his family situation, and they tried to spare their non-Catholic pupil and altar boy—who earned some of the best grades in his class—further punishment.

"One time I really messed up in school, and I was sent to Father Jerome and Sister Marie. My mother was sent for, and when she walked in, I thought it was over. Sister Marie laid out everything on the table, and then Olive looked her dead in the eye and said: 'You know, sometimes you have to overlook Jimmy because he's only half-right.' She was serious as a heart attack, because in her mind and in the mind of the government, I was 'mixed'—my mother was Portuguese, and the

Bahamian government classified that as mixed. Not being pure white, in other words.

"Either way, I was one of those bright kids," Jimmy says, getting back to his course of studies. "The nuns used to give you a number, and I always came in third or fourth in my class every year. So this next year I decided that I was really going to study hard, and I actually came in first in the class. I was so proud, as you can imagine. And in time there was a school assembly, and they called everybody up to get their report cards in sequence—the student who came in first place, second place, and so on. So Olive came down to the school, and Sister Marie called my name. And my mother was right there to see me walk up and get my report card. Now remember, there were only five white children in the whole school. So I walked back to my mother, my face beaming, and she looked me straight in the eye and said, 'Son, before you start bragging, look at your competition.'"

Olive's outspokenness, while sounding racist, reflected the culture of the Bahamas during the 1950s and '60s. In truth, she certainly had more black Bahamians as friends and acquaintances than she did whites, granted there were fewer of the latter to sit on Olive's porch in the evening. That said, she was extremely proud of her stepson's performance in the Catholic school. She cared for him and loved him as if he had come from her own flesh and blood, which she argued he did, since she and Jacob had the same mother. She always made sure Jimmy completed whatever homework he'd brought home—which was very little, if any—supervised all of his chores, filled him with well-rounded meals, and sent him to bed in the loft at the appointed time each night.

Mostly she concerned herself with Jimmy's spiritual development. She had successfully seen to it that his daily path crossed at least one house of worship—either the Catholic Church or the Church of God—although further down the road she was keeping an eye on the Baptists and Methodists too.

"We were Pentecostal, so church was a social event," Jimmy says. "Every time the church doors opened, we would stroll in. Monday night was the young people's fellowship, Tuesday was regular church, Wednesday was Bible study, Thursday was regular fellowship, and Friday was church sports. Saturday was your only free day, because on Sunday you went to church three times: in the morning for Sunday school, midday for church, and then you had to go to church that night. Everything surrounded church."

Which for all the blessings heaped on the Pearce family did pose one particular problem for Olive. Roughly 80 percent of the Bahamian population was of African descent, while 11 percent was "coloured" or "mixed." That left fewer than 10 percent of Bahamians who were white, and figure fewer than 5 percent of those were white women, and say 2 percent were white girls. If Jimmy was lucky, maybe 1 percent of the population consisted of white girls his own age.

"You had to go far and wide to find a white person," he describes it. "I think there were five of us in the whole school, and three were girls. There was Virginia Roberts. There was Jackie. And there was Sheryl Fletcher. But then again, Sheryl didn't last long—she got transferred out."

His larynx growing larger and thicker by the day, the eighth grader settled for Naomi Bowleg. "She was from Andros, and she was absolutely gorgeous," Jimmy reminisces. "The blacks in Andros have Seminole—Indian blood—in them, so they have very fine features. But she was black, that was obvious, and she and I were together for a long time."

Too long, as far as Olive was concerned, her motion seconded by Kirkwood.

"She finally said to me one day—actually it was another one of her sayings—she said, 'Let me explain something to you, son. If she can't use your comb, don't bring her home.' I thought about that long and hard, and there was no way Naomi could have used my comb, so that right there signaled the end of the relationship."

Whereas Jimmy constantly feared Olive's wrath, as he grew older he realized his stepmother was forever looking out for his best interests. And in time she would be coming to his defense—particularly when the entire family's reputation was on the line.

"We had a gentleman up the hill—his name was Mr. Willie Good. And Mr. Willie Good had a *kenep* tree in his yard, right next to his septic tank, which always made the fruit sweet. In fact, these *keneps* were so sweet and tasty that he would sell them and make some money. So he didn't allow any of the children to get any. He and his wife would actually alternate going to church so that one of them could always be home to guard the *kenep* tree.

"Anyway, my uncle Berlin was the captain of a fishing boat, and he would always bring fish home to our family. And on this particular day, barracuda was the fish of the day. I mean, when you got barracuda, it was like having the best sushi in the world. We just loved barracuda, but you had to be very careful because of its poison [the toxin *ciguatera*]. The bigger the barracuda, the better chance it has of being bad. Back then, what you used to do with barracuda was give a little piece to a stray cat. I mean, it's not as bad as Michael Vick with his dogs, but that's how we tested it. You'd boil a little chunk and give it to the cat, and then you'd have to watch closely to see if the cat ate it or not, because sometimes it would trick you. And if the cat ate it, sometimes it would die, or else it would get very sick, and then you knew the barracuda wasn't okay to eat.

"Anyway, Uncle Berlin drops this barracuda off, and Olive cuts off a little piece and has it tested. Sure enough, it was poison. So she said, 'Jimmy, go throw the fish in the trash barrel.' And while I walked to the barrel, my mind, for whatever reason, ran on Mr. Willie Good and his special *keneps*. And I thought, *Oh, Mr. Willie Good, have I got something for you today.* So I walked up to him."

Good morning, sir.

What's happening, young boy?

I got some barracuda here. Uncle Berlin dropped it in. Mommy said she already had one, so I brought it for you.

Did she test it?

Oh yes, she tested it.

"Well, he took it, and let me tell you, we missed Mr. Willie Good for about a week. I was actually beginning to worry, when all of a sudden he was leaning up against the wall outside the house. And I could hear Olive saying, 'Who's that calling?' She went out front and I heard her say, 'My Lord, what has happened to you?' I went to the door to look for myself, and Mr. Willie Good could barely stand up."

It's about that barracuda you sent me the other day.

What barracuda?

34

Jimmy brought it to me.

What did you take to Willie?

I took him that barracuda.

Olive all but grabbed Jimmy by the ears and dragged him back inside the house.

You trying to kill that man?

Yeah, he's too mean.

Olive went back out on the porch.

Yeah, Willie, I gave him the fish, but I didn't tell him to give it to you. I was sending it up the street.

Well, did you test it?

Yeah, yeah, I tested it.

Did you look at the cat you gave it to?

Yeah, yeah, I looked at it.

"Let me tell you," Jimmy says, "I thought I would get the whippin' of my life. But Olive just kept quiet and didn't admit to anything. Everybody in the house just kept real quiet."

FIVE

IF JIMMY MOREE AND HIS GANG FROM KEMP ROAD owned their own playground, it was Hog Island, better known by millions of vacationers today as Paradise Island. Apart from a few wealthy homeowners, including the silent-film clown Charlie Chaplin, the island's primary inhabitants were iguana and parrots.

Tourists who ventured to Hog Island arrived from Nassau by small passenger ferry and then were lifted in horse-drawn carriages to the lone beach pavilion, which featured a refreshment bar and pool table. There they would spend the day relaxing, sunning, and swimming—and, if they were so inclined, smoking marijuana supplied by Jimmy and his crew of Conchy Joes.

"We were barely teenagers, you know? And I didn't smoke—never smoked cigarettes, never smoked pot, and still haven't to this day," Jimmy stresses. "But some of my friends did. Anyway, one day they were smoking their weed on the beach and somebody smelled it and said they wanted to buy some. It didn't take us long to realize that this could turn into a profitable business. Better yet, we could grow this business cheaply from seeds."

To launch their green enterprise, the budding entrepreneurs picked uninhabited Rose Island, a few cays up the coast. For starters, each of the boys obtained a dozen plastic buckets and filled them up with the richest soil a coral island can give up. Next, with their index fingers they pressed the marijuana seeds one at a time about a half inch deep into the dirt. Then they placed the pails in the sunniest spot of the island that wasn't visible to a passing boat. Finally, being typical boys, they painted personalized insignias on the buckets, no different than pirates did with their treasure chests. Jimmy's friend P. A., for instance, drew a skull and crossbones on the side of his twelve buckets, while the forever smart-aleck Max had everybody laughing by branding his pots MP—a swipe at the Bahamian members of parliament who followed the canons of the Westminster system. On his buckets, Jimmy traced a circle that he filled with three *x*'s. "Everybody had their own little symbols for their pots because, you know, you had to look after them," Jimmy explains.

With balmy temperatures and virtually uninterrupted sunlight, save the occasional beneficial sprinkle provided by Mother Nature, Rose Island turned out to be the ideal environment for growing marijuana au naturel. In fact, it took only five days for the seeds to sprout and the plants to begin growing.

Soon, instead of measuring themselves against a knobby tree on Kemp Road—boasting who'd grown the tallest—the barefoot boys were on Rose Island, bragging about whose cannabis plants reached highest—every leaf and stalk individually nursed and cared for.

It wasn't long before tourists were reaping the benefits of the boys' harvests. And it wasn't too much longer before Nassau's CID (Criminal Investigation Department) officers also caught wind of the distinctive aroma that encircled the Hog Island pavilion, particularly after school let out. When word leaked out that a certain group of boys from Kemp Road had been spending a lot of time plying the waters between Nassau and Rose Island, the Bahamian police gassed up a patrol boat and started to sniff around.

"So they picked up all of our buckets and took them down to the Central Police Station. Then they rounded up all of us and took us in—a bunch of the white boys, the Conchy Joes from Kemp Road—and they started asking if we owned the pot. Everybody denied it, obviously. And then they noticed the MP on some of the buckets, and they knew right away to go to Max. 'Do you know anything about these marijuana plants?' And Max, who was known for his smart tongue, said, 'Yes sir.' And the CID officers' eyes got as big as saucers, as if to say, 'Fantastic! This boy is stupid enough to admit to it.' The officers thought they finally had an arrest on their hands, you know? And one officer said, 'What do you know about it, young man?' And Max replied, 'Whoever owns it, if he don't water it, it's gonna die.'"

The CID investigation came up as dry as the plants. None of the boys was ever charged with a crime, although a few of them were handed sentences by their parents. It was about that time that a talent scout from Hollywood showed up at Sacred Heart School in dire need of a white child or two to appear as extras in the movie *Flipper*, starring Chuck Connors, with Luke Halpin as the white island boy named Sandy. Given there were only a handful of white kids to choose from, Jimmy got the part without ever trying out.

"There was one time in the movie when the kid said he had a dolphin that could do tricks, and another kid didn't believe him. So the kid with the dolphin said, 'You bring some of your friends around, and I'll show you the very best of the tricks.' So they had me standing with these mixed kids on this little dock, and Flipper was doing his tricks. And one of the producers would yell out, 'Applause!' after each trick. If you watch the movie, you can see that I'm a little late with the clapping— looking all around me to see what everybody else was doing because I didn't know what the word *applause* meant. I never heard that word before. The fool should have just said, 'Clap!' If he'd said, 'Clap,' I would've done what he said."

Being a Hollywood extra didn't impress Jimmy in the least, even though Flipper—actually a dolphin named Mitzie—would soon swim into the hearts of millions of moviegoers. Instead, Jimmy was consumed with his kickboxing, and nobody could dampen his enthusiasm for the sport. As he grew stronger and more talented, he would appear at various venues around Nassau, including a club called the King of Nights, where Bahamians would have to buy a ticket to see Jimmy go foot to foot with other top boxers. Before long, Jimmy scored his first sponsor, and soon other promoters lined up behind the boy wonder. Obviously his friends on Kemp Road were impressed, and Olive and Kirkwood were thrilled when Jimmy started competing in kickboxing tournaments outside of the islands. Not only did he win competitions in the United States; he was invited to a tournament in Thailand, where he outkicked everybody he faced in the ring. Suddenly there was hardly space in the Kemp Road house for all the trophies he carried home. Similarly, there was hardly a person left in Nassau—short of Olive and a concerned parent or two—who dared tangle with the mighty and powerful—and cocky—Jimmy Moree.

Grounded in the principles of the Catholic faith, able to recall the morals of the colorful stories told by Brother Bell and Brother Franks, the obvious next step for Jimmy in his religious upbringing was to enroll at Bahamas Baptist School for his post–eighth-grade studies.

"It was great, because these guys were liberal," he remembers. "We had American teachers and we had Bahamian teachers, and all of them liked to discuss things. It wasn't like in the Catholic school system, where you memorized the catechism but seldom discussed it. Here, everything was discussed, and then you wrote about it. By then I hated homework with a passion, and if you didn't do it, the Baptists would put you in detention, which was understandable. And if you didn't show up for detention, they would double it. I remember Mr. Bryant, my history teacher. He was from Indiana, near Notre Dame. He said, 'James, where's your homework?' I told him I didn't do it, and he said that I'd have to go to detention. I said, 'Mr. Bryant, I would love to, but this semester is completely booked already.' It was always cool with the Baptists. I think when I graduated I had twenty years of detention waiting to be served."

In more ways than one, Jimmy had grown too big for his britches, especially when it came to dating. While he had several girlfriends throughout his high school years, Francesca was the love of his life—or at least for one frustrating phase of it.

"She was mixed. She was gorgeous. But her father didn't like me. He didn't like me being around," Jimmy says. "They were eating their lunch one day, and I was hanging around, and her father looked at me and said, 'You know, Jimmy, I notice you coming around the house a lot. What are your intentions towards my daughter?' Now, to be honest, my aim was to sleep with her before graduation. That was my intention. And something wasn't right in my head, because I decided to come clean. The facts were that I did not, at that young age, intend to marry his daughter. I was just like every other kid and wanted to go to bed with her. So I told him as much."

The very next day, Jimmy was riding his bicycle home from school when a car carrying four people pulled up alongside him and cut him off. Three men jumped out, grabbed him by the shirt, and threw him into the car. They drove to an area behind Nassau called Sea Breeze, where few homes were built. While three of the men held the teenager down, the fourth proceeded to beat him with a garden hose.

"And let me tell you, because there were four of them, they put a whippin' on me," Jimmy says. "And it changed me. You talk about falling out of love fast. When I would see Francesca, I would turn completely around and go the other way."

As Jimmy grew older and more independent, Olive found

that she had more personal time on her hands to pursue interests outside the home. Incredibly, she launched a small construction business, initially crowning Kirkwood chief carpenter until she could hire somebody for the position. With the help of bank lenders, she was soon purchasing enough land to build an average of three houses per year, which would bring the family more money than it had ever earned before. Enough profit that Olive expanded her commercial enterprise to include a rental-car business, what with all the tourists starting to appear in Nassau. And what better place to park the rental cars, she figured, than on the pier—right where the cruise ships docked.

"The people come down the gangway, and we are right there," Jimmy explains of his stepmother's plan. "It was a good idea at least. Olive tried and tried, but she couldn't get permission from the Bahamian government to park her fleet of cars on the dock because it was just not allowed—government policy, she was told. So instead we put our company around the corner and then went out and hustled the tourists with our little brochures. We even had motorcycles to rent. But the problem was you had to walk a good stretch from the dock to the rental location."

If Olive was ever angrier in her life, Jimmy never witnessed it, which tells you something. A wealthy foreign businessman, who on previous occasion vacationed in Nassau, had apparently padded enough ministerial palms to park his own fleet of twenty-five rental cars on the touristy pier.

"Olive used to say that the Bible tells you to turn the other cheek when somebody slaps you. And she was prepared to turn the other cheek. But one thing about Olive, she was always prepared to turn her cheek back," Jimmy says. "So we were having dinner one night, and out of the blue she remarked, 'If I was a man and somebody did that to me, I'll tell you what I would do. I would roll every vehicle off the end of the dock.' Well, I was young. I was a rebel (had some bad boys in my camp), so I felt that Olive had given me the green light. And that's what we did. We rolled every car off the pier, all British-made cars— Humbers and Hillmans and what have you. We put them all in neutral and pushed them over the side into the drink."

SIX

JIMMY HAD EXCELLED AT BAHAMAS BAPTIST SCHOOL, despite his long list of unsatisfied demerits, so much so that he graduated before his seventeenth birthday. Somehow he had not only impressed the Baptists, but the Methodists as well, whose church elders presented the white Bahamian with a full-paid scholarship to attend London Polytechnic. Jimmy wasn't keen about continuing with his education—particularly across the pond—however, an ecstatic Olive gladly accepted the valuable gesture on Jimmy's behalf.

And here now he stood, days later, unable to muster the nerve to ring his stepmother from London with his surprise news. So he checked his suitcase, boarded his flight, and called Olive upon his arrival at Nassau International Airport.

What happened?

I didn't like it. It rained, it was cold, and it rained some more. Every day it rained.

No problem.

"And that was it," Jimmy says. "She was just as cool as cool could be. We ate dinner, had the normal small talk, and the next morning at seven o'clock she was knocking on my bedroom door."

Are you ready to go?

Go where?

I'm taking you down to Bacy Lee.

The old gentleman lived down the hill from Olive's house, and he had a basement efficiency apartment that few people on Kemp Road would ever consider paying money they didn't have in the first place to live in.

Good morning, Miss Olive, what can I do for you today?

You know that basement room?

Yeah, it's still there, Miss Olive.

Well, Jimmy's moving in.

This Jimmy?

Here's his first and last months' rent. Son, you're on your own.

Jimmy just stood there speechless, still wiping the trans-Atlantic cobwebs from his eyes. When he had gone to bed the night before, everything seemed fine. Now he had awakened to a nightmare.

He had fully appraised England before he ever stepped foot in it. Now his perception and subsequent first impression of the country—and its people—was coming back to haunt him.

"When I grew up, I thought I was British; there was no such thing as a Bahamian. We didn't get our independence until '73," Jimmy recalls. "So I went down to the British embassy in Nassau to get my visa, because I would be in the UK for longer than six months. I couldn't comprehend needing one, figuring I was already British, but I went through the motions and had a meeting with an English gentleman who sat me down to talk."

Young man, let me explain something to you. You will never be British. If you look closely at your passport, it says "British subject." Rest assured you will always be a British subject and nothing more.

The arrogant envoy had no idea that Jimmy wasn't your typical white Bahamian, so to speak. Surely the diplomat assumed that anybody in Jimmy's shoes would kowtow if not curtsy to be awarded such a scholarship—the opportunity for an islander to attend school in England, no less.

"I've never been subject to nobody, especially your country," Jimmy told the snotty diplomat, who was shocked beyond words. Retreating from the room, his tail tucked between his legs, the envoy quickly prepared the required paperwork and then sent his confused secretary back into the room to hand Jimmy his admission papers.

Otherwise, the other big mistake the Methodists made was issuing Jimmy a round-trip ticket to London.

"I was sixteen years old, and as you can see, I was dropped into a situation where I had to learn a whole new system," he says. "I had to move to another country. I had to live with people I didn't know. I had to catch the bus. I had to learn my way around a big city. And I got up in the rain, I went to class in the rain, and I came home in the rain. One day I was on the bus, and this fool looked at me and remarked, 'What a lovely day.' I wanted to kickbox the guy silly—what was lovely about this day? I looked out the window, and it was dark and miserable. I decided right then and there that none of it made sense. I'd been in England two weeks and I was going home. If this was the mother country I'd heard about my entire life, then I'm glad I came from the child."

Now, instead of waking up in London's West End, Jimmy was staring at a lizard slithering across the peeling ceiling of Bacy Lee's stifling basement from a none-too-comfortable cot that Olive didn't bother to turn down after she threw him out of her house to fend for himself. It also dawned on him that inaugural morning in his musty cement cave that his protracted course of divine education, taught in strategic sequence year after year by the Church of God, the Catholics, the Baptists, and, for a few short weeks, the Methodists, had come to an abrupt end.

The least Olive could do now was provide him a job in the family construction business. After all, he had to pay his rent somehow.

"No, no, no," she would say, shaking her cigar-sized index finger at Jimmy from behind her metal desk. "I don't want you to work for me. Go get your own job. That way you can learn what the real world is all about."

Fortunately, there was another construction company in Nassau that was in need of a manual laborer who could handle a shovel. And shovel he did, from dawn to dusk. The port city, commercially speaking, was booming, and new buildings were going up everywhere. Once upon a time he used to have to swim to Hog Island. Now there was a bridge built to reach the luxury hotels and marinas that sprang up on what was now renamed Paradise Island. If digging deep holes in the sand was what Olive meant by learning about the real world, then Jimmy figured three months of shoveling was long enough. Fortunately, his stepmother also agreed that her stepson had served penance enough, and soon she placed him behind the wheel of one of her supply trucks. And when he finished hauling materials to the building sites, she saw to it that Mr. Johnson, her best carpenter, taught him everything he needed to know about saws, levels, squares, protractors, foundations, siding, roofing, and the blueprints to put them all together.

Jimmy kept busy with his kickboxing, and soon an opportunity came for him to travel to New York City, where one of his fellow competitors was enrolling in an advanced regimen of martial-arts training. Jimmy was more than anxious to tag along—to see the lights of the city that he'd heard never slept. To do so he would have to approach Olive and request a leave of absence. To his surprise, knowing the benefits and satisfaction Jimmy got from his martial-arts training, Olive was more than supportive of him taking the trip up the Atlantic coast.

Go. This could be good for you, especially if you continue with your kickboxing.

Wouldn't you know, Jimmy had no sooner arrived in the Big Apple than he and his friend were riding the subway through the Bronx when a severe gang fight broke out unlike any brawl his band of Conchy Jocs had ever found themselves in along Kemp Road.

"I'd always seen controlled fights—in the school yard, in the boxing gym, but I'd never seen a stabbing. This fight involved a knife, and it was really bad. I was pretty upset and got myself to the nearest pay phone because I was suddenly ready to come home. I called my mother collect, and the operator repeated each name clearly, so it's not like there was any confusion."

Jimmy is calling for Olive. Will you accept the charges, ma'am?

Operator, would you mind telling my son that I love him, but to write instead? Thank you.

SEVEN

JIMMY FELL IN LOVE JUST SHY OF HIS TWENTIETH birthday. But remembering Olive's advice, he first ran his comb through Charon's hair. Charon's parents, both white, had lived on separate Bahamian Out Islands, two hours apart by boat, until they found each other and married.

"She was pure Conchy Joe," Jimmy says of the couple's daughter. "She was one of the few white women my age in Nassau. She was attractive, certainly, but she was bright and she was sharp—a lot smarter than I would ever be."

They'd met at a weekend dance, began dating, grew serious, and with Olive's blessings and Kirkwood's encouragement,

Jimmy popped the question. In time, he escorted his bride down the aisle of the Evangelistic Temple (if there had been a Jewish synagogue in Nassau, Olive would have found a reason for Jimmy to worship there too).

Besides Charon being Caucasian, another positive aspect of Jimmy getting married, Olive figured, was it would keep his nose clean—and in one piece.

"We were starting to get ourselves in a lot of trouble. All the guys I was running with were on their way to jail," Jimmy recalls. "There was a lot of tension at the time—no violence, but a lot of tension. Independence was in the air, especially after the transition from an all-white government to an all-black government."

The first black majority in the Bahamas was elected in 1967, but it wasn't until July 10, 1973, shortly after Jimmy and Charon exchanged their vows, that Bahamians discarded their British shackles, lowered the Union Jack that had flown for centuries over Nassau, raised a sun-sand-and-sea-themed Bahamian flag, and broke out in song—singing for the very first time a new national anthem, "March on, Bahamaland."

About this time, Jimmy and his good friend Oswald Hall, the most handsome of the Kemp Road gang, whose father at one time was the lighthouse keeper on Hog Island—"He used to ask us to go over there in the morning and turn the light off for him, because you had to do it manually," Jimmy says— were approached by the owners of a new resort. They wanted Jimmy and Oswald to run their scuba-diving shop on touristy Treasure Cay, a spit of land shaped like a high-heeled shoe that extends toe first out of eastern Abaco, the most northerly island in the Bahamas chain.

It was difficult enough for Jimmy to say good-bye to Olive, cutting a decades-long apron string that had pulled him through thick and thin. A more urgent matter dealt with the fact that Jimmy and Oswald, if they were going to certify divers, needed to become certified divers themselves—unless holding your breath for sixty seconds while scooping up handfuls of pinching lobsters counted. So the very first thing the pair did before hanging out the "Treasure Cay Diving" shingle was sign up for a diving course.

"I will never forget this one older lady who came down to Treasure Cay from New York who wanted to go diving so that she could look at the fish," Jimmy recalls. "There was just one problem. She couldn't swim."

Ma'am, I'll try anything, but I've never heard of a woman going diving who can't even swim.

I don't intend to swim.

Okay, if you say so. But I'm going to put you in the shallow end of the pool first and get you familiarized with the equipment, show you how to breathe properly. After that, I'll take you out to the reef, attach you to a lifeline, and then I'll help tip you overboard. And don't worry—I'll always be next to you.

The silver-haired New Yorker sank like a rock—fifteen feet straight down to the ocean floor, with Jimmy swimming furiously after her to make sure she hadn't stopped breathing. After she had landed and gotten her bearings, he couldn't believe his eyes. The woman who couldn't swim transformed her oversized flippers into street shoes and literally started walking along the sandy bottom adjacent to the coral reef—careful with each step not to disturb the rainbow of tropical fish and their fragile hiding places.

"She was so relaxed, just stepping along the bottom of the sea as if she was looking into an aquarium, it was amazing to watch," he says. "There were barracuda and all these beautiful sea creatures right in front of her mask, and she was just having a wonderful time, using up all the air in her tank. Then it came time for me to bring her up."

Ma'am, is there any fear you have in life? You really weren't afraid to drop overboard when you can't even swim?

The way I look at it, son, is I came all the way from New York on a plane, and I can't fly.

It reminded Jimmy of the excuse his father's mother, Mom Millie, once came up with for refusing to fly in a plane from Long Island to Nassau.

You know, Mom, this makes no sense. It's going to take you fourteen hours on the mail boat.

I'm not going to fly, Jimmy. When I come to see you, it's going to be by boat.

But you're religious, Mom. When your time's up, it's up.

Jimmy, it might not be my time. It might be the pilot's time.

───

The Treasure Cay resort that owned the dive shop provided Jimmy and Oswald each with a dive boat and staff villa, seeing to it that the newlyweds moved into the more spacious of the two accommodations. For Jimmy and Charon, it was a perfect business opportunity—too good to be true, as it turned out. Oswald was another story.

Oswald had had a reputation in Nassau for being a playboy

from the moment he'd reached puberty—each of his conquests, black and white, made simply by being blessed with an olive complexion, chiseled features, and tall frame. Now that he was zipping boatloads of bikini-clad Americans into dive suits, he found himself constantly wanting to play. And Jimmy was left to pick up the slack.

"It was a seven-day-a-week job to begin with. I'm married, I'm settled, and he's like a breeding horse," Jimmy says. "All the girls would come down to the Bahamas wanting to party, and Oswald was always happy to oblige. We'd have a dive set up to take fifteen people out, and where's Oswald? He's off on some deserted island with a girl, or partying in a hotel room somewhere. He wasn't serious about the business, so I decided I was going to split and look for another job."

Contemplating his future while jogging along a distant and secluded stretch of beach, the health-conscious diving instructor rounded a point and had fun trying to jump over a large bale of what appeared to be hay.

"I ran a bit farther along the beach and there was another bale, wrapped in burlap like the other one, with three stripes on it," Jimmy recalls. "And that's when I said to myself, *What's hay doing in the Bahamas?* So I stopped jogging and noticed that other bales were floating in with the surf. And then it hit me: *This isn't hay. This is weed!* So I dragged several of the bales up behind the dune and stacked them there, but there were so many more floating in. What was the point, right? I mean, I would be there all day. So I ran back to my place and drove to the police station in Coopers Town, where a friend of mine I called Sarge was on duty."

———
———

Always looking dapper in his Royal Bahamas Police Force (RBPF) uniform—black pants and tan shirt, the insignia beneath his red-crown emblem bearing the words *Courage, Integrity, Loyalty*—Sarge was the biggest, blackest, friendliest Bahamian Jimmy ever met. He had broad, muscular shoulders and arms the shape and size of Popeye's, their pulsating veins glistening with an oily sweat that flowed continuously from the taut cuffs of his short-sleeved shirt. Being two of the few locals that weren't always out fishing, Jimmy and Sarge had become fast friends. If they weren't slamming dominoes in their spare time on the booking counter outside the jail cell, they were shooting billiards at one of the few local watering holes.

One particularly hot day, Jimmy and Sarge had been playing pool and listening to a renowned storyteller and lobster fisherman named Joe Siefus describe a record catch of crustaceans that he swore weighed so much it almost sank his boat. At which point the fisherman seated on the barstool next to Siefus looked up from his beer bottle and said, "Oh Joe, that can't be true." And the lobster diver replied, "If that's not the truth, then Jesus strike me down."

"At the very instant, right in front of our eyes, Joe dropped dead," Jimmy says. "I mean, this guy was only in his forties. I looked at Sarge, and his eyes were as big as white saucers. He was spooked, let me tell you. He slowly made his way over to inspect the body, which is now lying on the floor, expecting Joe at any second to jump up laughing. Then Sarge turned and looked at me."

Jimmy, Joe Siefus is dead.

Well, I guess it wasn't the truth.

Everybody in the bar, shocked as they were, laughed.

Despite his bare feet, Jimmy walked as fast as he could into the police station. Sarge instinctively reached for the box of dominoes kept behind the counter, but Jimmy told him to save them for a sunny day.

What's up, Jimbo?

I just found some marijuana that floated up onto the beach.

Yeah? How much?

A dozen bales at least, and more is coming in. What do you want to do with it?

Where are these bales?

I've got some of them stacked up near the dunes, just around the point where I go jogging every day. Nothin' there but sand and water.

Do you know anybody who might want to buy it?

At first Jimmy assumed the police sergeant was just pulling his leg. Then again, besides putting on his uniform every morning, there wasn't a lot for a policeman to do on a sparsely populated, 120-mile-long island with its necklace of uninhabited cays.

Buy it?

Yeah, man. People pay big bucks for those bales.

They do?

Come on, let's go take a look. I'll follow you.

Jimmy had barely inserted the key into his car's ignition, and

Sarge was already letting go of the clutch of his official RBPF Jeep and speeding off in the direction of the secluded beach that Jimmy normally enjoyed all to himself. The very first thing the giant policeman noticed was the telltale three stripes, hardly different from the ones he wore on his uniform. He smiled a wide grin, turning his pearly whites on Jimmy and informing his white friend that he'd stumbled upon some of the highest-grade marijuana money could buy. Better yet, more bales had been washing ashore, for as far as the eye could see. The pair of Bahamians spent the better part of an hour hauling each and every one from the tidal line to an ever-expanding stockpile.

Surely such a tremendous quantity of marijuana raised more than one red flag as far as the police sergeant was concerned. There was always a thread of possibility that a U.S.-orchestrated drug-interdiction operation was underway out of Nassau that he wasn't privy to. If that were so, how would he answer to his superiors if they were aware a mother ship had dumped its valuable load just offshore of Treasure Cay, yet not a stem or seed was ever found?

Experience told him that in this case the maritime dope smugglers, for whatever reason, probably panicked and threw the precious cargo overboard. Maybe the off-load boats, more often than not piloted by local islanders anxious to earn some extra cash, failed to rendezvous with the mother ship, and the impatient captain cut his losses rather than navigate through precarious waters back to Colombia with a hold crammed with cannabis that nobody claimed. The mother ship, at the same time, might have purposely dumped the load off the secluded stretch of Abaco Beach, telling the buyers—who more likely than not already paid for the marijuana—where they could find it. Who knew why forty bales of superb Colombian grass suddenly washed ashore on a stretch of sand with nothing between it and Africa? All the police sergeant knew was the contraband was now in his hands. And before anybody showed up to claim it, he was going to squeeze as many bales as he could fit into the front and back seats of his Jeep. Three or more times he told Jimmy that he was "arresting" the marijuana. To ensure no one asked any questions, he threw a blanket over his apprehension. Sarge then sped off to Coopers Town, while it was agreed that Jimmy would borrow Oswald's pickup truck to haul off the thirty-four remaining bales. This took three trips.

"I was green, green as the grass," Jimmy says. "I'd never purchased weed before because I never smoked it. I didn't know much about its value, other than what Sarge had told me. But I wasn't worried either, because he stressed that he was arresting it, which sounded official enough to me. We took all the bales and stacked them in the jail—every bud we put behind bars, where it was safe. And then Sarge locked it up, just like he would a prisoner. And then he asked me again if I knew anybody who might want to buy it."

The mail boat that ferried Jimmy so many times from Nassau to his birth home on Long Island would pass the entire length of the hundred-mile-long chain of Exuma cays before reaching the Great Exuma capital of Georgetown. A handful of the seaport's residents, like the Morees, were descendants of seventeenth-century pirates, who'd made good use of Georgetown's deep-water harbor. It also happens that the

Tropic of Cancer, which separates the tepid tropics from the rest of the Northern Hemisphere, runs smack through the middle of the town. Thus, for anybody owning a boat and a map, it has always been a simple destination to reach—and that goes for Jimmy and his Kemp Road crew, who arrived every March for the Georgetown Sailing Regatta. From the time he was a teenager, Jimmy never missed one of the carnival-like flotillas, a Bahamian pastime held on most of the major islands. He and his friends would set off from Nassau aboard a Nova Scotia trawler named the *Flying Swan*, piloted by its debonair and well-to-do owner—a 270-pound Conchy Joe the boys called the Chief.

Born in Nassau to wealthy English parents, the Chief was sent to London to attend private schools. But he never mixed with the formal British classroom environment, and found himself gravitating toward culinary arts, soon securing apprentice positions under several of the country's top chefs. A decade later he would rise from potato peeler to executive chef of London's Dorchester Hotel. And from there his cooking skills carried him across the English Channel to Paris and the prized George V hotel, where he prepared delectable feasts for heads of state and personalities alike. But as time passed, the chef grew weary of the long hours spent in relative obscurity, and he longed to reconnect with his Bahamian roots. When finally he couldn't take it anymore, he packed up his kitchen knives and mixing spoons and, upon arriving in Nassau, launched a catering business that in time would provide its customers with more than food and beverage.

"You only had to be in the Chief's company for five minutes and you knew exactly what he was doing on the side," Jimmy says. "He was six years older than me, and his parents lived in the Eastern Road area of Nassau, a white community where the 'superior' people lived. Living on Kemp Road, I just knew him from a distance. But when we went down to the regatta in the Exumas, the Chief would talk about people in the 'business'—who's doing what, what have you.

"So for the first time in my life I had a reason to hop on a plane, fly to Nassau, and go see him. And the first thing I see is this big Rolex on his wrist, a big ring on his finger, a big chain around his neck—I mean, he had jewelry coming out of his pores, you know? And I thought to myself that this guy made some big money doing something somewhere."

How's life, Chief?

Long time, Jimmy. What's up?

I'm hoping you might know something about moving some weed through the Bahamas.

Yeah, I might know something about that.

Well, let me get straight to it. I just came across some weed that floated into Treasure Cay.

As in floated up in the water?

Yep.

How much are we talking about?

Forty bales. Sarge, my police friend, told me it's really good stuff— it has three stripes on it.

What?

It's got these three stripes—

No, no. You said a policeman told you it was good stuff?

Yeah, he's cool though, a very good friend of mine. You can trust him.

Where is this weed now?

In jail.

It's where?
It's in jail. Locked up in Coopers Town.
You've got to be kidding me!

———

Jimmy drove Oswald's truck into a shaded stretch near the water's edge in Coopers Town, turned off the engine, and waited for the familiar bridge of the *Flying Swan* to cross the horizon. He still couldn't believe what he'd stumbled upon, and more than once he wished he'd left the bales right where he found them for some other beachcomber to discover. The way he figured it, the sooner the Chief arrived and departed, the sooner he could wash his hands of his unintentional predicament.

Signaling the Chief with his arms, Jimmy pointed the trawler to a slip farthest away from the commercial crawfish boats, their deckhands busy unloading bountiful bushels of the lobsterlike creatures that every year earn Bahamian fishermen more money than all other seafood combined. Tossing the lines to Jimmy was the *Flying Swan's* lone mate, Happy, who remained with the trawler while the Chief and Jimmy wasted no time driving Oswald's truck the very short distance to the police station. When he saw the pair of white Bahamians pull up and park, the red-eyed Sarge counted his lucky stars that he'd taken no prisoners that week or else they, too, would be stoned silly from inhaling the marijuana's pungent fumes.

Jimmy introduced the two large men—police officer and drug smuggler—but both realized the fewer words exchanged, the better.

"We loaded the weed onto the truck in broad daylight, then drove it right down to the marina, put it aboard the *Flying Swan*, and then went back for a second load. It went like clockwork," Jimmy says.

In less than thirty minutes' time, forty ninety-pound bales of moist marijuana—confirmed by the Chief as high-grade Colombian—was released from the Coopers Town jail and secured in the hold of the trawler. And five minutes later Jimmy and Sarge were standing on the dock, waving good-bye to the Chief and Happy until the pair of smugglers and the *Flying Swan* disappeared from sight. To say they breathed a sigh of relief at that point was an understatement, particularly for the police sergeant.

I wonder how much it's really worth.

I don't know, Jimmy, and I don't care. Come on. Let's go slam some dominoes.

EIGHT

NOT UNTIL THE LAKE-EFFECT SNOWS BLEW DOWN FROM
Lake Erie would the tourist planes be landing again at Marsh
Harbour, a single strip runway south of Treasure Cay. With
no scuba lessons on Jimmy's schedule, and his bride working
as a secretary at the resort, he and Sarge had more than enough
time on their hands to shoot some pool and *sip-sip.*

It's been ten days, Jimmy.

*You know, the way I look at it is it cost us nothing more than a
plane ticket. And I got to visit Olive, so it was money well spent. We
took a minimum risk, I guess. I mean, who was going to arrest us,
you? Come to think of it, now that the evidence is gone, you couldn't
arrest us if you wanted to, you know?*

Shouldn't you try to reach your Chief buddy, make sure every-thing's on the up-and-up?

I'm not calling him. We'll hear from him, trust me.

Jimmy's phone rang two weeks later. He was surprised to hear that his friend was in Green Turtle Cay, which, given the countless cays dotting the archipelago, couldn't have been more convenient to Jimmy—sitting offshore an equal distance between Treasure Cay and Coopers Town. In no time, the scuba instructor was behind the center console of the resort's diving boat heading north at full bore. He figured the Chief wouldn't have come back to Abaco without a good reason, but not in his wildest dreams did he expect to be handed a duffel bag, and an extremely heavy one at that, the second he jumped from his boat onto the dock. But that wasn't the only reason the Chief had come north.

What's in here?

It's your money. You want it, don't you?

Jimmy's hand shook as he grabbed the canvas handles. He was never so scared to accept anything in his life. "My heart was so far up my throat that if I were to cough, I would have left it on the pier," he recalls. "Then I opened the bag and all I saw was dead American presidents. I couldn't believe they were all mine."

What're your plans, Jimmy?

For the money?

For your future. You staying up here?

I doubt it. Oswald, you know how he is. He's gotten to be a pain.

That's too bad, but maybe I can help you out.

How?

I'm going to Colombia next week, and I could use an extra hand.

Colombia?

South America. We're gonna pick up a boatload of grass and bring it back to the States.

Oh yeah? How does it work?

Well, for this particular trip, it would be me, you, and another guy—his name is Jimmy too. Two Jimmys on my boat—that would be a first. Anyway, all we do is scoot right up to the coast, drop anchor, and the Colombians come out and do the rest. We don't lift a finger. Then we head north again, off-load, and I give you more of what you're holding. It's that simple.

Nothing to it, huh?

That's how it works, piece of cake.

How much risk is there?

I'm covered. You don't need to worry.

Seriously?

Seriously.

Can I think about it and get back to you?

Sure, but don't think too long. The boat leaves this Thursday at 3 p.m. from Yacht Haven. When I get back to Nassau, I'll expect a call, tomorrow night at the latest. If I don't hear from you, I'll get somebody else. Think good and hard about it. You can go back home, Jimmy, be near Olive.

The Bahamian glanced down at the khaki-colored bag sitting at his bare feet, then stared across the radiant turquoise waters toward Treasure Cay, where in one week's time planeloads of Ohio honeymooners and retirees from Quebec, most of whom had never slipped into fins, would be relying on him for a day's instruction and entertainment.

What's the name of the boat?

The South Wind.

===

This time, Sarge didn't reach for the dominoes when he saw Jimmy hurrying down Coopers Town's version of a steamy sidewalk—hard-packed sand—clutching a large bag under his arm.

That's some bag you got there, Jimmy.

Lock the door, Sarge. We've got some counting to do.

The policeman raised his big bones from behind the metal desk (termites far outnumber humans in the Bahamas) to lock the door and close the blinds, which wouldn't be out of the ordinary this time of day with the sun beating down.

"We began counting like a couple of old people," Jimmy says. "'One thousand for you, one thousand for me.' When that took too long, it was, 'Two thousand for me, two thousand for you.' We were so dumb—instead of just counting all the money and splitting it in half, right?"

Regardless of how it was counted, the colossal constable couldn't believe his big eyes. In no time each man's share was thirty-four thousand dollars, and they'd hardly put a dent in the bag.

"We ended up with three hundred and eighty-six thousand dollars," Jimmy says. "Obviously I'd never seen that much money in my life. I'd gotten a loan for five thousand dollars once, but that went straight into my bank account; you know how that goes. Anyway, Sarge took his half and I took mine. And Charon didn't know a thing the entire time, right? So here I come through the door with almost two hundred grand and drop it on the table in front of her."

Who did you rob?

I didn't rob nobody. I was jogging on the beach a few weeks ago, and I came across this weed. I didn't want to tell you about it because I didn't know whether it was a big deal. When I went down to Nassau to see Olive, I called the Chief. You remember him, right? And he came up with his boat and picked it up, and then this morning he came back with all this cash.

Jimmy!

I know, it's unbelievable. We need to talk, Charon. There's an opportunity for us to make even more. The Chief wants me to go to Colombia with him in a few days. It would be a quick trip.

Are you kidding me? You're going to get involved in drugs just like that?

I've been seriously thinking about it.

What, for a few hours?

Ever since Oswald dropped the ball.

Yes, but don't tell me you've been considering getting involved in drugs. That would be the last thing I'd ever imagine you doing. What about your job? What are you going to tell them?

I'm done diving. And now you can quit too. We can go back to Nassau and live.

This is happening so fast I don't know what to say.

Me either.

So this is all your money to keep?

Our money.

I can't believe it. Well, for starters we can pay off our loan; that's one good thing.

Pay off the loan? We can buy a house, live big, you know? Believe me, this is the opportunity of a lifetime, Charon.

But we don't need any more money than this. Why risk it now?

Because I feel I owe the Chief. Plus, he assures me it's all safe. I can make us a ton more money.

The couple debated the pros and cons of drug smuggling, what little they knew of it, for the remainder of the night into the early morning.

Let's make a deal, then, Jimmy. After you make a million dollars, you stop. No more.

That sounds like a good deal.

Then we agree?

We have a deal.

How many trips does it take to earn a million dollars, Jimmy?

You're asking me?

The now suddenly affluent couple packed everything they owned—shorts, shirts, sundresses, and the four-piece stoneware place setting that Olive gave them on their wedding day—and kissed Abaco and a bewildered Oswald good-bye. Jimmy's only regret was not sticking around to see the pot plants sprout from the dirt-filled grooves of Oswald's truck bed, where no doubt a few seeds were already germinating.

After surprising his forever-suspicious stepmother with word of their permanent return to Nassau, Jimmy and Charon walked down to Bay Street with their duffel bag. And with one bank slip, he deposited into his checking account as much cash as he dared without raising red flags. From there, a grown-up but still-stuttering David French gave the Morees a lift to the island's lone luxury car dealer, and one hour later Jimmy and Charon drove off the sunny lot in a shiny Cadillac Coupe Deville—royal blue with light blue interior. His jaw agape, all David could do was stand there and wave. He didn't even try to speak.

"I was dumb, right? The first thing I do is go out and buy a Cadillac," Jimmy says. "One day I'm seen walking down the street with the Chief, and three weeks later I'm driving around in a Cadillac when everybody else drives a Ford Pinto, if they're lucky."

———

Charon took her first spin behind the wheel of the expensive new ride a few minutes before three o'clock on the first Thursday of their return to New Providence. All eyes were on the Cadillac—or else on the couple riding in it—when she pulled into Nassau Yacht Haven, the island's oldest marina, where everybody but the caught crawfish knew Jimmy by name. Then again, he kind of liked the attention, which he missed from his days of kickboxing. Charon turned to her marginally nervous husband and told him to be extra careful, kissed him on the cheek, and said she would see him back home in a few days. No sooner did he shut the heavy door of the Cadillac and he started scanning the slips for the *South Wind*, which took all of two seconds. "It was big as gold, sitting right there at the head of the dock, hiding out in the open," he recalls.

———

The modus operandi the Chief lived and operated by, which Jimmy would hear over and over again from that day forward, was both simple and so far so good: "You've got to have a reason for being there."

In other words, a reason for the *South Wind* to sit so prominently in the choice slip of Yacht Haven; a reason for the large steel-hulled freighter to ply the waters of the Caribbean on a regular basis; a reason for the ship to have an extra-large hold.

"Nobody ever called the Chief dumb," Jimmy notes. "He owned the contract to ship Coca-Cola from the bottling plant in Nassau down to the Turks and Caicos. That was his cover. And fortunately for the Chief, they drank enough Coke down there to keep him navigating back and forth."

Sophisticated and well mannered, thanks in large part to his formal upbringing and the time spent living and working in the European capitals, the Chief was larger-than-life, popular with everybody he met. And he was a hugger. Standing six foot six, he enjoyed encasing people in a bear hug and squeezing the air out of them. When he heard Jimmy walking up the gangplank of the *South Wind*, he skipped every other giant step, rushing down from the bridge to greet him.

"He gave me the usual greeting, saying, 'Come on board.' He obviously was happy I was there, and he quickly introduced me to the other Jimmy. Then the Chief basically told us what we needed to do at that moment to get under way. Soon we're all ready to go. The diesels are fired up, and he tells the other Jimmy to untie the lines. So Jimmy goes down onto the dock and gets everything untied, and the next thing you know he's yelling, 'Bye!'

"I couldn't believe it. Right there on the dock, this guy changes his mind, while I'm standing there pulling up the rope and the boat is pushing off from the dock. This scared me, you know? So I rushed up to the wheelhouse to tell the Chief what happened."

What an idiot. Well, we're not going back now.

Are you sure?

I'm sure—it's just me and you, Jimbo.

How can we do it?

Four hours on and four hours off, that's how.

Meaning?

Well, I will take the wheel for the first four hours, and you will take the wheel for the next four hours. And when I'm not at the wheel, I'm going to be napping right here to the left. And when you're not at the wheel, you're going to be napping over there. And we'll keep up this routine until we've delivered the Coke to the Turks and pull into Aruba.

Aruba?

That's where we pick up van Gogh.

While lonely in London, the Chief had immersed himself in classic literature and poetry, memorizing the familiar lines of renowned authors. He would often recite his favorite passages, whether alone in his basement flat or in the company of his fellow European chefs. He'd carried his favorite pastime with him across the Atlantic, and now Jimmy got an earful.

"He would recite poems all the time. That was his thing," Jimmy says. "It kind of made for an educational trip."

＝
＝

If the Chief was mammoth, van Gogh was towering—he stood well over six feet tall—quintessentially Dutch in appearance, given the Kingdom of the Netherlands, for unknown reasons, has among the tallest populations on the planet. Because so many surnames on Aruba, an autonomous island of the Netherlands, began with "van"—and because the Chief could not for the life of him remember the full name of his weed "loader"—the fair-skinned Dutchman was dubbed "van Gogh," after the Chief's favorite nineteenth-century Dutch post-impressionist painter.

Nickname and nationality aside, van Gogh was Colombian through and through, and his responsibility for the illegal drug runs like this one captained by the Chief began in Aruba and ended along northern Colombia's lengthy Caribbean coastline. It was past dark when the South Wind glided into Oranjestad, the capital of Aruba, and it was before dawn when the three men—two Bahamians and the loader—were gone.

"Van Gogh's job was to oversee the loading," Jimmy explains. It's a short crossing from Aruba to Colombia, rounding Punta Gallinas and dropping anchor in a secluded cove not terribly far from Santa Marta.

"And I'm watching van Gogh make a few hand signals towards the shoreline, and all of a sudden these wooden canoes come out from under the trees—and when I say canoes, I mean long canoes. They were everywhere, paddled by these little guys the Chief called 'F-owes.' He explained they were a jungle tribe that lived in the tall grass, so tall that they would look around and say, 'Where the heck are we?' F—owes, you see?

"So they loaded all of the weed onto the *South Wind*—forty thousand pounds by the time van Gogh finished his count. And then they all disappeared, and it was just me and the Chief again. And that's when it hit me that there was no turning back now. I was in it."

NINE

FOR A BRIEF MOMENT JIMMY WAS A BOY AGAIN, BEING taught a lesson in reading while he and Jacob sailed home—if he could ever call it home—with a boatload of grunts and grouper.

You've got to read the water, son, to know what lurks beneath.

Lurks?

Hides—the lighter the shade of water, the more shallow it is. Likely a sandy bottom. See that chalky-green water off your starboard side? It depends on the draft of a boat, but we can't go there—we'd hit bottom. The bluer or darker the water, the deeper the water.

Like where we are right now?

Right. But you've got to watch out, because if the water's too dark, there's probably a reef underneath. That'll sink a boat—have us swimming back to Long Island.

Treacherous reefs were the least of Jimmy's concerns now. The waters he was piloting the *South Wind* through were lucid blue, the deepest in a Caribbean Sea that stretches south from the Mexican coast to Panama, east across the northern reaches of South America, north again along the many Lesser Antilles, and west along the southern shores of the Dominican Republic, Haiti, and Cuba.

Unlike the voyage south from the Turks and Caicos, when the freighter wasn't sitting so low in the water, Jimmy was now keeping a nervous eye out for any suspicious vessels, although the dozing Chief had bet him a hundred dollars he wouldn't spot anything bigger than driftwood floating in the three hundred miles of open water between Colombia and Jamaica. Within sight of the latter coastline, the eighty-foot *South Wind* would veer northeast into the Windward Passage that separates Haiti and Cuba, skirt Great Inagua—where Jacob and Jimmy used to load their bushels of salt—then head due north the final four hundred miles into Nassau. The Chief was right. If there had been another ship out here, the two passed in the night.

"And we just pulled right into Nassau, into crowded Yacht Haven, filled to the gills," Jimmy says. "The Chief had no worries, although for whatever reason, he did ask me to pick up some scuba gear before I came back to the freighter."

Fill the tanks and bring them back in three days. That's when we leave for the States.

Well, you know, Chief—

Jimmy, we finish this trip together; that was our deal. You promised you would go to the States.

If Jimmy had cold feet when the *South Wind* departed Yacht Haven with its lawful load of Coca-Cola, his toes were now frozen.

"I didn't have a clue what to expect," he explains. "I'm wondering if I'm ever gonna see my family again. Can you imagine Olive's reaction if something were to happen to me? Talk about adrenaline running through your veins. So I go home to Charon, and I decide it would be better if I didn't tell her the boat was sitting down at the dock right then, filled with forty thousand pounds of weed. I told her the Chief needed to get the boat worked on in the States, and he needed my help to get it there. Fortunately, she fell for it, and three days later I was back at the marina. And I had the scuba gear."

And when the big freighter cast off from the pier, the Chief made sure Jimmy Moree had jumped back on board.

Standing on the bow of the boat, the Bahamian smiled at the irony after the *South Wind* glided out of Nassau's bustling harbor and passed just offshore of Rose Island, where barely a decade earlier his dozen buckets of pot plants, innocently marked with *X*'s in circles, seemed to him like an entire plantation. He had steadfastly refused to sample the fruits of his labor when pressured by his Kemp Road friends, even when they teased him that their harvests were far superior to his. To this day, smoking a joint no more interested Jimmy than drinking a beer. Then again, he had never forgotten what became of Godfrey when he indulged in both vices in Olive's company.

As a seagull flies, West Palm Beach is 220 miles northwest of

Nassau. While the Chief set his compass for this last and most risky leg of the felonious journey, Jimmy secured the deck and stowed the scuba equipment.

"I didn't have a clue why the Chief wanted the scuba gear, but I didn't question him. When he said something, I just did it. I was still learning the ropes, and the easiest way to sink a ship is to have two captains. So he called the shots, and I followed them."

Jimmy had kickboxed his way into and out of Miami, but he'd never been to West Palm, which was known more for its decaying downtown and violent crime than it was for its affluent neighborhoods and three hundred varieties of palm trees. Getting mugged, however, was the least of Jimmy's concerns when the fully loaded *South Wind* pushed its large wake onto the rock jetties of the Lake Worth Inlet, which connects the Atlantic Ocean to the Intracoastal Waterway and Port of Palm Beach, one of the busier anchorages in Florida.

Curious where the captain would be docking the *South Wind*, Jimmy took a seat on the forward deck and let his feet dangle between the starboard railing, albeit ready at a moment's notice to start tossing ropes over the side. Clad in his usual cutoffs, T-shirt, and sunglasses, it occurred to him that he'd better remove the blue bandanna that covered practically his entire face. Without fail, whenever he was out on the open water, the health-minded Bahamian would wear the colored, almost sinister-looking handkerchief to protect his nose and lips from the sun's burning rays. Jimmy scanned both shorelines of the inland waterway, this stretch of which, the Chief had told him, was a freshwater lake until dredged open during the nineteenth century. Off the port side sat the eighty-six-acre man-made Peanut Island—a tropical park, of sorts, that on this late afternoon was filled with boaters and sunbathers. Jimmy spotted numerous docks and marinas fronting beachfront homes and condominiums, and paid close attention to the commercial and industrial boatyards, some so rundown and rusty they resembled abandoned scrap yards. The Chief had mentioned something about a boatyard being the final destination, but Jimmy didn't inquire further. Needless to say, he couldn't believe his eyes when the *South Wind* captain cut the engines and dropped anchor practically in the middle of the waterway—in view of a U.S. Coast Guard station, no less.

Now what I want you to do is attach the scuba gear to this chain and hang it from the bow of the boat. And if anybody—and I mean anybody—should approach this boat from any angle, get overboard, get to the gear, and get underwater. Swim in any direction; just get out of Dodge. Any questions?

Yeah, where are you going?

I'll tell you in a minute. Also, make sure that each evening before it gets dark—

Each evening? How long are you going to be gone?

—to flip on all the running lights—white, red, and green. Make sure they're all working. There's spare bulbs on the shelf behind the wheel if you need them. You don't want to give the Coast Guard any excuse to come snoopin' around. Otherwise, don't worry about me. I've got everything figured out.

I'm not worried about you; I'm worried about me. Where are you going?

I'm taking the dinghy to shore, but I'll be back in a couple of days. Just hang tight and be sure to eat all the food, or else it will go to waste. I've got some great jelly cake in the cooler that my caterers gave me. I'd tell you to roll a joint, but fortunately you don't smoke. Read all the books you want; just don't lose my place in Lord of the Flies. *They're under the cot. Actually, I'm taking* Lord of the Flies *with me to read.*

"And so the Chief just left me sitting there. And I mean I could have thrown anything from the deck and hit any one of those Coast Guard guys in the head, that's how close I was. And one day goes by, and then two days go by, and you can imagine me, of all people—I'm like a caged animal. And all kinds of boats and ships are passing by, and the Coast Guard is going in and coming out all the time. But not once did any-body approach the *South Wind*; everybody's just leaving the boat alone. Finally, on the third day, I about had a heart attack. I spot this small boat approaching, and it looks like it's got the commandant of the Coast Guard and his two lieutenants on board. And when I say they arrived, they arrived in full regalia, looking sharp. They had on dress whites, admirals' hats, all the scrambled eggs—these guys were decked out, head to toe. I couldn't believe what I was looking at. And they pulled right up alongside the *South Wind*."

Captain, permission to board?

Gladly, Chief. I never thought you were coming back.

The bare-footed Bahamian, who did all he could not to laugh, lowered the ladder, his first official duty in more than forty-eight hours, apart from eating jelly cake and reading English literature. And the three immaculately dressed offi-cers boarded the freighter.

Good job, Jimmy. We're ready to go.

Go where?

Down to a little boatyard. It's not far from here at all. My friends here will take us in.

The owner of the marine railway, which fronted North Dixie Highway in Lake Worth, was introduced as Nutty Freddy. He carried a small clipboard, and he stood knowingly as the *South Wind*, in all her green glory, was hauled dripping up the rails. Once the freighter was secured, Jimmy watched as he approached the Chief.

So what are we doing?

Well, you can start by plugging any leaks. And then scrape and paint the bottom. I think I'm going to sell her.

"The Chief had an amazing presence. Whenever he spoke he was like the E. F. Hutton TV commercial, except he would do all the talking and little listening. He told Freddy exactly what he wanted done, but it was all for show, you see? Sure, the boat would get painted, but everybody in the boatyard knew we weren't there for that reason. And when they finished discussing the work to be done on the boat, I asked the Chief, 'When are we going to get out of here? I've lived with this load long enough.' And he said, 'Everything's fine, Jimmy. Relax.' But I didn't like the feeling of not being in the know, and I sure didn't know any of these people in the boatyard. All I knew was that my life for the past several weeks had been in the Chief's hands, and I wasn't accustomed to that."

Jimmy felt a little better when he and the Chief and his two lieutenants hopped into a van driven by a little Japanese woman who steered them toward Fort Lauderdale.

"And I'm thinking it's finally over, right? I've done my job, the weed is here, and I'm going home."

We'll unload tomorrow night.

You need me for that?

I need you to count, and that's all—you won't have to touch a seed. What went on the boat has to come off the boat and be put in the right trucks. It's very important for everybody involved. So you just be in charge of the count. In fact, you can be in charge of the count from here on out if you want.

Let's get through this load first.

Long before Jimmy crossed the Straits of Florida on his inaugural drug run into the United States, the Chief had set up a compound of three canal-side houses sitting side by side off busy Las Olas Boulevard in Fort Lauderdale. The house in the middle was used solely as a stash house for storing marijuana, while the homes on either side were for the Chief and his crew to live—and party—in.

And to make sure no eyebrows got raised, the very first thing the Chief did after he moved into the compound was invite over a member of the Fort Lauderdale Police Department, introducing the appreciative officer to his civic-minded neighbor from two doors down, explaining that the pair of concerned citizens were interested in launching and supervising a neighborhood crime-watch program.

Jimmy's first-ever count went smoothly. A caravan of box trucks and vans were driven through the boatyard's chain-link gates, and in no time each was filled with the fragrant Colombian herb. When the last bale was off-loaded, not a seed or stem remained on the high-and-dry *South Wind*. And only then did Jimmy feel the weight of the world drop off his shoulders. He was so invigorated, in fact, he left to find a gym and somebody to kickbox.

He would work out every day for the next two weeks, waiting patiently for the final phase of the operation to wrap up. Not until later would he understand the many facets of the drug trade: from cultivation to distribution, and everything and everybody in between. There never would be an end, in other words, short of Jimmy walking away. Drug-smuggling operations of this magnitude, which sometimes took months to plan and complete, required constant communication and coordination with the drug kingpins in Colombia (or else their representatives in Miami), the loaders in Santa Marta, the off-loaders in the Bahamas, the marina operators in South Florida, and the dope distributors in Orlando and Tallahassee. Unbeknownst to Jimmy, two additional weed runs orchestrated by the Chief were currently underway, and another order was placed during the forty-eight-plus hours Jimmy sat alone on the *South Wind*. In fact, a smaller load of fifteen thousand pounds was at that very moment crossing the Florida Straits, earmarked for Fort Lauderdale and a marina where the Chief owned several slips. No, there never would be an end, unless Charon could somehow hook Jimmy and reel him home.

———

Abaco was difficult enough on a new marriage. Jimmy's spending so much time now in south Florida certainly wasn't what

Brother Franks and Brother Bell had had in mind when they preached that a man "clings to his wife, and the two of them become one body."

If nothing else, he got the "for richer" part of his vows right.

On hump day of his third week in Fort Lauderdale, there was a knock on the door of Jimmy's air-conditioned bedroom overlooking the canal. It was like déjà vu—the Chief standing in the doorway, clutching a duffel bag almost identical to the one he'd handed Jimmy on Green Turtle Cay.

Here's your share—four hundred thousand dollars. You can count it.

Wow! I don't need to count it, Chief, I trust you.

Even after the Chief closed the door, Jimmy didn't open the bag and stare at the presidents. He didn't have to. It wasn't about the money, if it ever was. He'd become more relaxed, more confident of late. He'd been enjoying his independence, the time spent with the Chief and his crew of ocean cowboys, as the tight-knit bunch called themselves. When they weren't out in the boats, they would regularly dine at some of South Florida's finest restaurants, swapping stories and laughing into the wee hours of the morning. The crew even tagged the Bahamian newcomer with a nickname—Jimmy Divine. It was a no-brainer, given the stories he told them about Olive all but nailing him to every denominational crucifix in Nassau, not to mention the fact that he'd never taken a single sip of beer or puff of pot in his life.

No, it wasn't the money. For starters, Jimmy was in a gang again, one that didn't have to act tough to be shown respect. In fact, the cowboys were some of the most decent guys—and gals—he'd ever met. Second, there was the freedom, unlike any he'd ever experienced in his life living with Olive and then Charon. Third was the thrill of sailing the seas, earning his livelihood from the water, like his ancestors had done.

"I can't describe the feeling, or when it first hit me," Jimmy says. "Maybe it was sitting there watching the Coast Guard go in and out, knowing that I was sitting on tens of millions of dollars' worth of weed that the Chief stuck right under their noses. It does something to you, whatever it is."

Jimmy could finally call Charon to tell her that he was coming home. And when he got there, he knew the first thing his wife would say was that he was close to making his million dollars and then he could stop this foolishness and stay home. What Jimmy didn't know was how to tell her that was the least of his intentions.

TEN

He had to hightail it to Nassau one way or another, so why not in style—aboard a go-fast boat? One design that caught his eye had been nicknamed the Reagan, after Ronald Reagan's stepson, Michael, who was busy setting world records in powerboat racing. A few years earlier, the adopted son of the fortieth president had won the world outboard championship by racing a canary yellow Raysoncraft across Lake Havasu in Arizona.

"So I go down to a little boatyard on the Miami River and I bought myself this Reagan," Jimmy says. "I had four hundred thousand dollars, and I spent eighty thousand on a boat.

Can you imagine? As Olive said, you've really got to be dumb. But she was beautiful, named *Sweet Salina*, and she was bright yellow—as yellow as you can find. I mean, I really wanted to keep a low profile, right?"

Jimmy, needless to say, couldn't wait to show off his newest ride, but he needed a mate. He called a cousin in Nassau, who he agreed to fly to Miami if he would accompany him back to the Bahamas. It was a government holiday in the islands, and Jimmy purposely timed his ceremonious arrival to coincide with the traditional family picnics that surrounded such special occasions—when picnic blankets were actually spread by Bahamians on the beach, of all unlikely places. Because the ocean is constantly in the background of everyday life in the islands, Bahamians don't flock to the sand the way landlocked Americans and Europeans do, the one exception being to celebrate national and religious holidays, including Easter and Christmas, but then only after a full day of church services let out. And for those special occasions when islanders hit the beach, you won't find them lugging along a poor man's diet—lobster and fish—in picnic baskets. Bahamians eat meat on holidays, preferably chicken.

"So here I am with three hundred thousand dollars and change shoved under the bow of my boat, and I come screaming up the crowded beach propelled by twin Merc two hundreds drawing power from four-hundred-gallon tanks. I mean, I was doing the whole boat show. And the boat was singing, let me tell you."

Charon had found the couple a home in Blair Estates, an affluent Nassau neighborhood a short walk but world away from Kemp Road. Most Bahamians would give up their life savings to live there, but Jimmy wasn't so impressed. All of which came as no surprise to Charon, of course. In fact, her husband had been in Florida for such a long stretch that she went out and found herself a job she didn't need—working as a secretary for a Nassau attorney.

You're about there, Jimmy. You've got your house, you've got your car—and now you've got your boat. And we have plenty of money left over. I have my job, and you can go back to work for Olive.

Yeah, but it was never about the money.

What's that supposed to mean?

I prefer working with the Chief. Bicycle Joe, Blondie—they're all really great guys to work with. Every day is like an adventure.

Do you hear yourself? There's a difference between adventure and stupidity. I'm scared for you, and don't think for one minute that people in the street aren't talking. "Have you seen Jimmy's new Cadillac?" "Have you seen Jimmy's new house?" After your little stunt along the beach today, they're going to be saying, "Have you seen Jimmy's new boat?" They're not stupid, you know. Can't somebody else do this counting, or whatever it is the Chief needs you to do?

"There was tension, and she had that look in her eye," Jimmy recalls. "And that was when she first realized she was losing me—or I was losing her. Things were starting to go south, and for reasons she had no control over. Charon had a good upbringing, and she didn't like the stigma that came with being married to a drug dealer."

It was the first time the deplorable job title had come up when the couple discussed what it was, exactly, that Jimmy was now doing for a living. But as far as he was concerned, being one of the "weed people" was a far more respectable—and certainly more lucrative—position to be in than zipping tourists into wetsuits and spitting into their masks so they would have a clear view of the rainbow fish.

A week passed before the Chief checked in with Jimmy, and the two agreed to meet in Fort Lauderdale, a quick forty-five-minute flight from Nassau. When Jimmy went to kiss Charon good-bye, she turned her cheek. When he couldn't tell her when he'd be coming home, she turned and walked out the door.

Can you go south?

How far?

Colombia.

On the freighter?

No, you'll be flying down.

Flying?

A few of the crew are on their way down in the trawler, and what you're going to do is select the weed and then see how it gets put on the boat.

How do I do that?

I'll explain everything beforehand, don't worry. But this is an opportunity for you to meet the cartel, be introduced to the various players, see how the operation works. I've told them all about you, and they're looking forward to meeting you. You'll get feted and fed like a king and be back home in two days. How does that sound?

Following the Chief's instructions, Jimmy booked a round-trip flight from Miami to the old Caribbean port city of Barranquilla—Colombia's *La Puerta de Oro*, or Golden Gate. He arrived at the first airport ever built in South America, and it was his first time stepping foot onto the continent. The travel bug was biting him, and he was enjoying every minute of it. He couldn't get over how close and convenient the country was to South Florida, a geographical blessing the Colombian drug kingpins had realized long before Jimmy got into dealing grass. Better yet, the Bahamian's passport was barely examined when leaving Miami and upon his arrival in Colombia—*A piece of cake*, he thought. Getting back into the United States, he didn't stop to think, might be another story.

He was greeted by three Colombians, two of them bodyguards for an extremely thin man dressed in a snow-white cotton suit. In fact, his entire outfit, silk scarf to loafers, was white. He introduced himself as Flaco, which actually means skinny. Jimmy had heard all about Flaco, the notorious drug lord of the Cardinals. "He was so skinny you could almost see through him," he recalls.

The Bahamian and his carry-on bag were deposited in the back of a black four-wheel-drive Jeep Commando, and the four men set off in the direction of the towering Sierra Nevada de Santa Marta, a breathtaking granite massif with one snow-covered peak reaching 18,947 feet. It was the tallest mountain the Bahamian had ever seen, and the rest of the landscape was similarly eye-opening, although he couldn't help but glance occasionally at the semiautomatic weapon resting between the legs of the Colombian seated next to him. They traveled for almost two full hours into a region called Guajira, through villages and farms, across a series of basins and ranges, until they were surrounded by fertile green foothills that from a distance resembled neatly manicured golf courses. Accustomed his entire life to offshore breezes, Jimmy struggled to catch his breath in the high humidity, which seemed to lessen somewhat the higher the Jeep climbed into the lush countryside.

Flaco, it turns out, was well versed in English, and surprisingly up-to-date on current events around the world. He would constantly turn around from the front seat to inquire about the latest news from the United States—not that a Bahamian national would know much to tell him. He was particularly curious how a petty crime like Watergate, where nobody's throat was slit or body riddled with bullets, could threaten to bring down an entire presidency.

You want to see corruption, then stay in my country for a while. You will die a bloody death before you can even think of resigning like Richard Nixon.

If it was jitters Jimmy was feeling, he didn't want anybody to notice. He gulped the thick air, which dripped as warm sweat from his body. *No wonder the grass grows so green up here*, he thought. Colombia is blessed with prevailing winds that blow the moist sea air over the various mountain ranges, which form clouds and the country's frequent rain showers. The local farmers, as a result, are awarded some of the Western Hemisphere's finest crops, including the most potent marijuana. All of which is how Colombia became the planet's largest purveyor of pot. Cannabis was the country's most profitable business too, providing far more pesos to its farmers, people, and government than, say, coffee. Juan Valdez, for that matter, was the creation of an advertising agency.

Whether Jimmy realized it or not, the illegal drug trade was also now the largest retail business in south Florida. But to supply the retailers, he had to pull himself together emotionally and physically for this first-ever buying trip. The bales of weed had all looked the same to Jimmy until the Chief took the time to educate his friend on the numerous varieties and grades.

There was the legendary Santa Marta Gold, which yielded a luxurious, long-lasting buzz. The fertile *llano*, or grasslands region to the east, produced a rich variety of herb once commonly called Lowland Colombian, until its fan base renamed it Panama Red, for its rich, red-brown hues. Further to the south in the Cali hills, Puna Roja, a darker variety of cannabis with red streaks, has a THC content so concentrated it is known to cause hallucinogenic effects. Then there's Colombia Green, which is actually more black than green. Either way, it's Wacky Weed that renders smokers, well, wacky.

The U.S. Drug Enforcement Administration (DEA) estimates that Americans in the early 1970s were consuming upwards of thirty-five thousand pounds of marijuana per day. By the time the decade drew to a close, *Time* magazine reported in a January 29, 1979, investigative story headlined "The Colombian Connection" that reefers had become "the most widely accepted illegal indulgence since drinking during Prohibition."

As the DEA sought to explain it, because marijuana was not considered a high priority for law enforcement agencies, many Americans believed they were free to use the drug as if they were lighting a cigarette or filling a tobacco pipe. Whatever the reason, the Colombians were more than happy to be supplying roughly two-thirds of the pot being smoked by the U.S. population.

"We finally arrived to this farm, which was more like a ranch," Jimmy recalls. "It had everything, acres and acres of property, and there were armed guards all around the perimeter. Two trucks pulled in ahead of us, another one or two behind us, and here I am riding in the middle—the whole nine yards, just like you see in the movies. And this caravan arrives at a large warehouse stacked with weed, top to bottom, every type of grass imaginable."

Flaco took it upon himself to provide the Bahamian with at least a nickel tour of the warehouse, sensing that his visitor didn't expect or require anything more. Either way, if not before, Jimmy was now the center of everybody's attention.

"I was telling myself, 'This is cool; I can live with this,' that sort of thing. I mean, these guys looked tough, and they were, but so was I, you know? They had to do their job; I had to do mine. I went into the warehouse with my instructions from the Chief to pick the bales with three particular stripes because they were the best. There was the cheaper weed, which had one stripe; the mediocre weed with two stripes; and three stripes was tops. I was looking for a red stripe across the burlap, with two blue stripes on each side. That's what I was supposed to get loaded onto the trawler."

A simple formality, it turned out. With Flaco standing beside him the entire time—and better yet, he spoke his language—Jimmy simply pointed to the red-and-blue-striped bales and told the drug lord that was the weed he wanted. At which point Flaco snapped his bony fingers several times, spouting instructions loudly in Spanish to several of the workers in the warehouse, who quickly leaped into motion. The tour leader next drove Jimmy to several of the nearby hemp fields, where thick, bushy cannabis plants, most taller than his head, filled the landscape for as far as the eye could see. Flaco and Jimmy climbed out of the Jeep more than once to inspect the varieties of plants—the Bahamian turned down several polite offers from the kingpin to sample some recent harvests—as if he were traipsing through a prize vineyard with the proud vintner. Soon, the time came for Jimmy to be introduced as the Cardinals' honored guest.

"There was the ranch house, and next to it they had this buffet set up where the food didn't stop—all the fresh fruits and meats you could ever want. And if they didn't have the meat you wanted, they'd go out and kill it for you fresh. And if they couldn't do that, they would have it imported for your next trip. It was better than the food in a five-star hotel. And you talk about pretty girls—oh, the girls were fabulous, and they were everywhere."

The way it worked, the Chief would secure his weed purchases through the cartel's compound in one of Miami's wealthiest neighborhoods. It was then up to the Colombians in Florida to arrange the logistics until such time the boats were loaded outside Santa Marta.

Flaco didn't bother to watch the early morning loading of Jimmy's weed selection. He never did. It was beneath his stature as head of the several-hundred-man cartel to be concerned with the manual labor. Plus, given the risky nature of the business, it was safer for the kingpin to stay out of sight anyway.

"It wasn't that he was worried about the authorities," Jimmy says. "The police and military were the least of his concerns, because they were all in his pocket. They were worried about the rebels—worried about the rebels either taking their product or taking one of them. It's big money if you get kidnapped. We didn't talk about that; everything was on a need-to-know basis. But they appreciated me coming. We were obviously important to their operation. Weed that just sits in a warehouse is of no value to them. Flaco often referred to the Chief as 'God's pocket,' because the Chief never lost a single seed. Every time the weed got loaded onto one of his boats, Flaco said it was like placing it into God's pocket. Colombians are strange like that. Once they have your trust, you're family, no problem. When the weed is out of their hands, then it's your responsibility to get it into the States. If something happens along the way, they understand that. But they don't want to hear any stories they can't verify. They have people everywhere. I knew people in the business who got busted, and when they went to jail, they actually wanted details of their arrests to be in the newspapers. That was cool with the Colombians; they understand stuff happens. They'd just replace the weed, cut their losses, no big deal. But if you *bs* them, something will happen. Somebody could die."

Weed loaded and bound for the Bahamas, Jimmy was provided another armed escort from the remote coastline above Santa Marta back to the airport. The Cardinals could not have been more hospitable.

"So they knew me now," Jimmy says.

That said, if Flaco had somehow known that in a few years' time his young nephew (whose biggest concerns on this day were finishing school and playing soccer) would wind up on the wrong end of a gun pulled by the Bahamian, the send-off would not have been so polite.

—
—
—

More than one U.S. Immigration officer was awaiting Jimmy's arrival. They were curious, for starters, about Jimmy's quick turnaround in Colombia. Not to mention the fact that he had made the journey to South America with barely a toothbrush in his leather carry-on bag—which took U.S. Customs officers all of two seconds to inspect. It was obvious that, given the few personal articles in his possession, whatever evidence the authorities were going to obtain from Jimmy would have to spill from his mouth, and that wasn't likely.

What was the purpose of your trip to Barranquilla?

To visit a friend.

So it was a vacation?

No, it wasn't long enough to be a vacation.

So it was a . . . ?

It wasn't a vacation.

Jimmy never took to kowtowing. But the Chief was right, Jimmy told himself, when finally allowed entry into the United States: always have a reason for being there. The Chief's excuse for sailing the ocean in his oversized freighter was to transport cases of Coca-Cola, representatives of which were based in the United States, which could explain his presence in Florida. In other words, it wasn't unusual for him to be in one of several places. Next time, Jimmy would be sure to carry home several cases of Colombian coffee. If nothing else, it would give the Customs officers something to open.

Sorry, Jimmy. I didn't think they'd harass you on your first trip out of the gate.

No problem, Chief. I'll be ready on my next trip.

<hr>

The sixty-five-foot trawler dropped anchor near Spanish Wells, a fisherman's village found on Charles Island, which sits off the extreme northern coast of Eleuthera. Unlike the rest of the Bahamas, Spanish Wells's population is almost entirely Caucasian—a census the islanders are proud of and not about to change. Whites settled the small island in the mid-1600s, and, apart from an influx of loyalists during the American Revolution, the population has promoted zero mingling with outsiders— some argue to the island's detriment. From the time he was a little boy, Jimmy heard the tales of inbreeding in Spanish Wells, where everybody was rumored to share the same last name.

"It's a strange community," Jimmy agrees. "They've become a breed among themselves. But they are very, very honest people. They're all fishermen and farmers; that's what they've done their entire lives. They moved there to escape religious persecution, wanting to live according to the Bible. It's a dry island; no liquor is sold there—the only beer you can drink is root beer. So in the big picture, they accomplished what they set out to do. But the gene pool got a little tainted along the way."

Pretty Pat and Bicycle Joe, two of the Chief's crew from Fort Lauderdale, had piloted the trawler from Nassau to Turks and Caicos, unloaded the usual fix of Coca-Colas—never too many cases, so there would always be a demand and thus a reason for the Chief's boat to be out on the water. They then proceeded south to Aruba to pick up van Gogh, until finally sailing into Colombian waters to load Jimmy's forty-thousand-pound purchase. Now the mother ship was anchored off of Spanish Wells, waiting to be off-loaded by a crew of local white boys. In one way, at least, the Spanish Wells fishermen were no different from their black fellow countrymen—they were always willing to earn an extra buck or two, far more than a boatload of grouper could ever bring in.

"Every island," Jimmy explains, "including Spanish Wells,

had their little crew: Mayaguana, Inagua, Ragged Island, Long Island, Exuma, Berry Islands, Andros, Acklins, Grand Bahama, Bimini—every island had the guys who were willing to do the work. Bimini was the most notorious of the islands because it was only thirty-eight miles from Miami. Biminites run anything that needs running into Florida. We were the 'weed people'; that's all we moved, no other drugs. But from Bimini they ran it all—cocaine, people, anything that needed going to the States."

The Spanish Wells boys pulled up alongside the mother ship in their large fishing boats, off-loaded the bales, and proceeded to the "weed line"—an offshore meeting place where a flotilla of smaller boats from South Florida, each equipped to carry at least two thousand pounds of contraband concealed in custom-built compartments—took the stash the rest of the way.

As it turned out, every bit of the forty thousand pounds of blue-and-red-striped ganja that Jimmy plucked from the Colombian warehouse arrived one week later in the United States. And for that one load, the Chief would pay the Bahamian six hundred thousand dollars. Not only did Jimmy have his first million; he was on his way to two.

Not that there weren't glitches here and there. The Chief was forever worried about Pretty Pat, one of the crew's captains who, despite having a large mouth and ego, could never quite dot the i's and cross the t's.

"Pretty Pat came from Ohio, and he wasn't so pretty," Jimmy recalls between laughs. "He actually looked like a Mexican. He was one of our boat captains, but whenever he was in charge, you'd be pulling flies from the ointment. What is it, Murphy's Law? If something can go wrong it did with Pretty Pat."

On the other hand, the Chief, who was the equivalent of a drug kingpin by Fort Lauderdale standards, could not be everywhere at once, and therefore had to rely on each and every member of the crew, a human conveyor belt of sorts moving a product worth tens of millions of dollars. And that was why he was so relieved to have Jimmy on board, his top lieutenant in the operation. The Chief handled all the purchases, and Jimmy all the logistics.

≡

"Bicycle Joe was one of the coolest guys you could ever meet," Jimmy says.

Blond, muscular, and in his early twenties, "Bicycle," as he was called for short, hailed from Australia and, like Jimmy, literally stumbled into drug smuggling. His nickname perfectly suited his simple lifestyle: his only possessions consisted of a red bicycle and whatever he could stuff into his backpack, including his prize belonging—a backgammon set. He had no fixed address, no driver's license, and no bank account. Any piece of paper with a number affixed to it he avoided like the plague. The way he figured it, with no official documents to pore over, law enforcement investigators would have no paper trail to follow and therefore could never catch up with him. For all intents and purposes, Bicycle Joe didn't exist.

"This guy would ride his bicycle everywhere—right up the boat ramp," Jimmy recalls. "He'd go right to work and then get paid; that's how he operated. And Bicycle didn't do drugs either. He just loved to play backgammon, no matter where we were, on the boat or sitting around the house. Bicycle used to always say that as quickly as he made his first million, he was going home to Australia to buy the ranch he always wanted."

Growing up Down Under, Bicycle had always wanted to tour America—see the Grand Canyon, Rocky Mountains, and Statue of Liberty. While he was participating in spring break in Florida, a friend of a friend of the Chief's told him how he could go on a free boat ride to Colombia, and Bicycle took him up on the offer. He got paid more money from the one trip than he'd ever seen in his life.

Bicycle Joe and Pretty Pat were two of the Chief's motley crew on a ten-or-so-person totem pole. There was Digger ("Despite being dyslexic, he was one heck of a boat captain," Jimmy says); Ghost ("A big guy prone to seasickness, but like stealth, he could disappear and reappear whenever he needed to"); Gook ("A little Japanese girl, she captained our smaller boats and had balls bigger than most of the guys"); Blondie ("Clint Eastwood and Robert Redford rolled into one—fabulous blue eyes and blond hair, drove the girls wild"); Crazy Charlie ("He used to be a high school track coach in the Bahamas—went from coaching kids to poaching lobsters to trafficking weed"); Dave ("A ranch cowhand from Davie, Florida, he was as redneck as they come—wanted to earn enough money to put Astroturf in his living room"); and Ride Sally Ride ("She was always anxious and willing to get behind the wheel of a van and drive the weed wherever it needed going").

"We kept it as a family; we kept it tight, just a bunch of friends," Jimmy explains. "All told, you're dealing every day with several hundred people—Colombians, the loaders in their canoes, ship captains, local islanders, dealers in the States.

Then again, we purposely worked it so the left hand didn't know what the right hand was doing. That way nobody ever knew too much about an operation. It was safer that way—you can't tell somebody what you don't know, you see?

"I remember all of us cowboys were having dinner one night at a nice restaurant in Miami and discussing the new RICO [Racketeer Influenced and Corrupt Organizations] Act they came up with [in 1970] to go after organized crime. And I commented, 'Well, it ain't gonna work against us, because we've never been organized in our life. I'll be the first one to stand up in court and tell them that: you all can charge us with something else, but never for being organized.'"

ELEVEN

WHEN CHARON WALKED OUT THE DOOR, SHE AND THE child she was carrying kept going. And Jimmy couldn't blame her.

As he puts it, he was now "single, free, and disengaged." He wasted no time moving to Fort Lauderdale, where he coordinated round-the-clock smuggling operations and supervised the distribution of tons of excess weed stored, more often than not, in the compound's stash house that remained under the twenty-four-hour protection of the neighborhood crime watch.

Concerned about falling into a routine that inevitably would attract the attention of local and federal law enforcement officials, the Chief and Jimmy were forever mixing things up. The cowboys were already worth millions of dollars anyway, much of it wired by friendly, none-too-naive bankers in Miami and Fort Lauderdale into foreign accounts that stretched from the Bahamas and Cayman Islands to Switzerland and Lichtenstein. Thus, the Chief decided the time had come to drastically scale back the number of freighters he was sending to Colombia, and instead rely on Flaco and his Cardinals to bring their product to him—the way coffee distributors operated.

"Everything changed, and suddenly instead of smugglers we became off-loaders," Jimmy explains. "The Colombians, who were always anxious to sell their weed, would send up a mother ship to the Bahamas and we'd run out and off-load onto our trawlers, which the Chief registered under a company named 'Family Island Charters.'"

The Chief launched this particular phase of the operation by purchasing two almost identical ships—"You could float them side by side and hardly tell them apart," Jimmy notes. Each trawler was manned by a small crew who resembled your typical island vacationers: yellow slicker rain hats down to white Sperry Top-Siders. The overdone outfits made it appear as if the boats were island-hopping charters, carrying loads of landlubbers from Milwaukee and Cincinnati to paradise. Of course, nothing was farther from the truth. With twenty thousand pounds of contraband stored in each hold, the ships wasted no time reaching the weed lines, where several of the crew's forty-two-foot Sports Fisherman, each specially equipped to hold three thousand pounds of contraband, had been filling their boat coolers with king mackerel, black-fin tuna, and, if the trolling was good, a mighty amberjack or two.

"We'd move fifteen thousand pounds of weed like this every night, which was a huge amount," Jimmy recalls. "Bicycle Joe, Blondie, Digger, the Gook—they all captained the fishing boats. Apart from all the fresh fish they could eat, they pocketed twenty-five thousand dollars for each run into Florida. You do the math, but figuring the amount of weed we were bringing in, you can imagine the profit margin. Don't forget, we were buying from the Colombians at a fairly cheap price, and the second it got off-loaded from the mother ship, the value would quadruple, and from there it grew considerably more expensive for the buyer on the street."

One of the biggest headaches for Jimmy was storing leftover weed. Given the frequency of the shipments, there were always several thousand pounds lying in limbo, whether it be in the holds of fishing boats docked in the various marinas, inside box trucks, or piled in the Fort Lauderdale stash house that Jimmy kept a watchful eye over from his bedroom window. The main pieces of furniture in the stash house were mere props—a sofa, a few chairs and lamps—that were visible through the living room window. Otherwise, if the stash house ever became full, the garage of the house that Jimmy shared with the Chief took the surplus.

"One day we had a garage filled with weed—and I mean it was full; you could smell it everywhere—and I'm sitting there waiting for 'Pat Boone' to arrive from Tallahassee. He was a great kid, with pretty white teeth, which is how he got his nickname. Without fail, Pat Boone would sell a thousand pounds of weed per week—every seed sold on the campus of Florida State University. We had a fleet of white vans, extra shocks, nondescript—even the scrapes on the sides were identical—and we always had one van in the garage ready to roll for him. He'd drive down empty in one van and drive home loaded in another van once per week like clockwork.

"So on this particular day I was sitting around in my boxers, expecting Pat Boone to arrive at any minute, and there was a knock on the door. And when I got up and looked through the peephole, all I saw was blue and white. I told myself, 'Oh well, I might as well grab a nice pair of pants, because I'm going to be arrested, and I ought to at least look good on TV.' So I told them to hold on while I threw on some pants, and then I opened the door to find three Fort Lauderdale policemen standing there with their police cars pulled up next to the crime-watch sign sticking out of the lawn."

Good afternoon, sir. We are hoping that you might be of some assistance.

Really? Of course, officers.

Confidentially, if you don't mind, we've reason to believe that some people who live in one of the houses across the canal from you are involved in some illegal activity.

Drugs?

That's what we'd like to find out.

Are they smugglers?

We're not sure at this point, sir.

So they might be bringing drugs into our neighborhood?

Well, with your permission we'd like to surveil their house and determine if that's the case. But again, we really don't know at this point.

Sure, that's fine by me.

We would need only one room to set up our equipment.

In this house?

Yes, if that's okay with you.

Uh, sure. Fine by me. When do you want to do this?

We have it on good authority that a sailboat is arriving tonight, so we'd like to be in place this evening before it gets dark. We will need a rear room of your house, preferably on the second floor, with a good view of the canal. All we ask is that you and your family—

Actually, it's just me and my roommate. He's the head of the neighborhood crime watch.

Yes, we were aware that somebody here holds that position. Which makes this house all the more convenient. All we ask is that you go about your normal routine—even use the back deck if you want— just go about your daily lives as if we're not here.

Right, no problem, officers. We're glad to do our part.

"And here I have a garage full of weed—three thousand pounds—and I have to get rid of it by six o'clock," Jimmy says. "On top of that, I've got boats coming in—twelve thousand pounds being off-loaded that very night in two marinas where we own slips. I mean, my heart was beating and beating fast."

Jimmy called every member of the crew who wasn't out fishing the weed line and told them to burn whatever rubber that rolled to the compound and evacuate a ton or more of particularly fragrant grass—to where he didn't care; just get it out. Sure enough, Ghost was the first to appear, loaded up a large truck, and disappeared before the next crew member arrived.

"So we eventually got it all packed up and moved," Jimmy says. "And I'm sweeping the garage floor and I'm scrubbing the floor and I'm running around spraying room deodorizer in the air—dropping cat litter to absorb as much of the scent as possible—and then I'm sweeping again. The Chief, meanwhile, wasn't even breaking a sweat. In fact, while I was playing maid, he was making a grocery list.

"Remember, he's an internationally renowned chef, and his specialty happens to be chateaubriand. 'You know, Jimmy,' he said, 'these cops can't ever afford a good meal, so I'm going to prepare a smorgasbord for them tonight. Don't worry. All they'll be smelling when they walk through that front door is tenderloin.' And when the policemen arrived at six o'clock, they got their equipment all set up upstairs, and then the Chief served them a five-star meal, complete with candles. Of course, before they arrived at the house, we had to tell the people across the canal what was happening. That goes without saying. We don't want activity of that kind in our neighborhood, you know?"

After three days of almost round-the-clock surveillance, involving numerous shift changes, and several additional gourmet meals, not a single sailboat sailed into the police video.

If you see any unusual activity, please be sure to give us a call. Otherwise, the department appreciates your cooperation. And please thank your roommate again for the dinners. If there's anything we can ever do for you in return, don't hesitate to ask.

Jimmy thought about requesting one of those special police badges, the kind presented to worthy citizens at civic ceremonies. But he knew better than to ask.

Without a doubt, gentlemen, we will call you in a heartbeat.

———

Easter Sunday of 1974 was fast approaching, and, as with other religious holidays, the drug smuggling ceased, if only for a few days, so that the Cardinals and ocean cowboys could spend time with their families or on their knees. Jimmy hopped over to Nassau to surprise Olive and touch base with his pregnant ex-wife, although he was also long overdue for a visit to Long Island, where his mother still surprised everybody by clinging to life. Time after time, for as long as he could remember, Olive would whisper to him at the breakfast table or when he came home from school that the end was close at hand. Perline, however, saw it another way, cheating death so often that in Jimmy's mind she'd now become immortal. If somebody could only have told him that she'd be gone in the space of a few weeks.

From a two-block distance, Jimmy spotted his stepmother standing large at one of her construction sites, clad in her signature floral muumuu dress. It was impossible for her not to recognize Jimmy as well, given he was flashing his now-customary Rolex watch and gold chains. If a person were to ask Olive, she would tell them that her youngest son was a boatbuilder in Florida, although she was the only person on Kemp Road who was in denial. Not that anybody would ever have the nerve to ask her. They'd tried that too many times before.

Who's knockin'?

Police, Miss Olive.

What you want at this hour?

We need to know where Jimmy was last night.

What do you mean where he was? He was in bed since nine o'clock. Why you ask?

It's about those rental cars down at the pier, Miss Olive. You know, they all got pushed into the harbor.

Yeah, I heard. What's that got to do with my family?
We need to ask Jimmy what he knows about it.
Jimmy don't know nothin'.
How do you know?
I know Jimmy, that's how I know.

—
—

If Olive had known Jimmy was a drug smuggler, "she would have just took me," he says. "And I'd have probably worked for her company the rest of her life, at least. She had her way of drawing the line. I remember the time I wanted to get my ear pierced. All the boys on Kemp Road were getting their ears pierced—just like the pirates did. That was the thing to do. So I thought before I made this move that I should go ahead and consult her."

You know, Mom, the latest thing now is for guys to get an ear pierced.
Yeah?
I think I would like to do it too.
Well, it's up to you; it's your ear.
Thank you, Mom.
But if you should put an earring in your ear, I will cut it off.
What?
I said if you put an earring in your ear, I will cut it off.
The earring?
The ear.

"And you know, the thing about it is I was at the stage in my life that if I wanted to try something, I would usually do it, but this time I didn't have the balls. Because in the back of my mind, I knew she would actually cut off my ear while I was sleeping—I would wake up in the morning and my ear would be gone."

TWELVE

ONE DAY AFTER WATCHING THE FUTURE GANG OF Kemp Road hunt for Easter eggs, Jimmy's phone rang. It had suddenly dawned on the Chief that Spanish Wells was a far shorter distance from Nassau than Fort Lauderdale.

Jimmy, Zeke needs our help.

What's the problem?

He's got a small load that needs to be moved off the island.

It seems Zeke had off-loaded onto his boat and then got burned by some no-shows up the coast. The bales sat in his hold over Easter, but he had to get back to fishing now and had stashed the weed somewhere near the marina. The Chief wasn't sure where.

I know it's of little value to us, but Zeke's helped us through plenty of binds. You feel like taking a boat ride?

Zeke was one of the more reliable locals that the crew worked with. He'd often run his big lobster boat out to a mother ship, off-load, hook up with smaller boats at the weed line, and then spend the rest of the day harvesting his crustaceans—albeit with an extra-large wad of cash in his pocket. There was little risk to fishermen like Zeke of ever getting busted in the hundred thousand square miles of Bahamian seas. Generally speaking, sophisticated law enforcement virtually did not exist beyond the twelve nautical miles the United States claimed as its territorial waters. And even if the few Bahamian patrol boats that floated came this far east, they'd pay little attention to Zeke. The lobsterman, after all, had more reason than anybody else for his boat being out on the water. That's how he earned his living. Jimmy, on the other hand, was always looking for an alibi.

I appreciate you coming over.

No problem, Zeke. How much weed you got?

One thousand pounds.

What, you keeping the rest for yourself?

I wish. I didn't want to dump it over the side. I'd rather get some money for it.

I can carry twelve hundred. Let's get her loaded. I want to leave by sunset at the latest.

No problem. Stay here and I'll be right back.

More than one hour passed, and there was still no sign of Zeke. Bored with pacing back and forth on the slimy dock, Jimmy was more agitated than worried. If something fishy went on in Spanish Wells, whatever police presence there was here would never confront Zeke. Not only was he a hardworking family man and respected member of the community, but, as Jimmy used to tease the lobsterman, all of the cops on Spanish Wells were related to him anyway.

I thought you got lost, Zeke.

I can't get to it.

What does that mean?

Church hasn't let out.

So?

So I stashed it under the church.

You did what?

I had to hide it somewhere, and the crawl space of the church was the closest place to my boat. So after my wife and kids went to bed last night, I came down here, and that's where I put it.

Oh, Lord.

Oh, Lord is right. It didn't occur to me that there'd be an Easter Monday service too. And if I try to grab it now, the entire congregation is going to see me. And I don't need to tell you that everybody in there knows me.

This ain't good for my schedule, Zeke. When does church let out?

About nine o'clock, or so I was told by Mrs. Pinder in the vestibule.

Jimmy almost burst out laughing. If there was one prevalent name in the Spanish Wells phone book, it was Pinder. But he was in no mood to joke. Instead, he and Zeke now paced back and forth in the church parking lot, Jimmy staring the whole time at his Rolex. When the pews didn't empty by 9:30, he all but physically pushed Zeke inside the house of worship to find out when they might get around to it.

Welcome, Brother Zeke. Nice to see you this evening. And I see you brought a visitor with you. Praise God, friend, you are always welcome here, this Easter season or at any time of the year. We are just wrapping up our Easter "singspiration," so Zeke, if you and your friend would please join hands and bow your heads in prayer. O God, who for our redemption gave Your only begotten Son to death on the cross, and by His glorious resurrection has delivered us from the power of our enemy, grant that we who celebrate with You the day of our Lord's resurrection may be raised from the death of sin by Your life-giving Spirit. And to our island fishermen, reach out Thy hand when we tremble in storm and gale, and cast out Thy net to carry us safely home. Amen. Now, sisters and brothers, let us rejoice in song.

From the pew where he was seated, Jimmy could smell the weed—a rich, moist aroma rising up from the darkness below, through the sacred floorboards and into the hallowed sanctuary. As far as the smuggler was concerned, the entire flock was stoned.

At ten o'clock, seemingly out of nowhere, the church ladies, dressed in their lavender and pink dresses, produced platters of fried chicken and deviled eggs. "Munchies," Jimmy whispered to Zeke, as Mrs. Pinder poured everybody cups of Kool-Aid.

≡

Instead of making a beeline toward the flickering lights of Fort Lauderdale and relying on the red and green flashers that marked the Port Everglades Inlet, Jimmy stared through his dark sunglasses into the bright reflection of the morning sun, zigzagging his way in no distinct pattern across the Straits of Florida.

"Going in I always run zigzag—different angles, back and

forth, up and down," he explains. "Sometimes I will slip into the lee of a cruise ship and automatically disappear from radar."

Before he'd left Spanish Wells, Jimmy had Zeke throw whatever discarded fish he could find at that ungodly hour into his boat's built-in cooler, to make it appear as if Jimmy had been out fishing the Florida coastline before dawn.

"Other than being exhausted, everything seemed cool," he says. "I lowered my bandanna from my face, went straight into Port Everglades, hung a right, and headed for the compound's canal. I was just going along, minding the no-wake speed limit, enjoying the crisp morning air, looking forward to catching some z's, and out of the blue I heard this bullhorn that made me practically jump out of the boat."

The gentleman in the white open fisherman, proceed to this dock. I repeat, the skipper of the white open fisherman, proceed to this dock.

Jimmy cut back on the throttle and almost soiled his pants in one motion. He turned the bow of the boat toward the shore and slowly crept in—no hurry, obviously, to get there. He could see only two police cars parked near the bulkhead, yet there was a lot of commotion. Enough activity, at least, that nobody appeared to be looking in his direction, so he quickly opened the cooler and washed his hands in fish juice, running his fingers through his thick black hair for good measure. For the first time, he took his finger and poked one of the blackfin tuna that an unimpressed fisherman had tossed out in Spanish Wells. Sure enough, it was hard as a rock. "Definitely not good," he said out loud, dropping the lid.

"I was just idling in, because I had way too much going on in my mind: *Oh man, I am in big trouble here, big trouble. Not only am I in big trouble, but what an embarrassment. If I go to jail for one thousand pounds of weed, I'm not going to have anything to brag about, that's for sure.* I could already hear it: 'What you get busted for, man?' And I would say, 'A thousand pounds of weed.' It's almost a disgrace. I mean, here we smuggled hundreds of thousands of pounds of weed into the States, and I'm going up the river for doing a Spanish Wells guy a favor."

As if he needed a reinforcement of reality, the bullhorn sounded again, this time the voice more demanding, reverberating ripples of sound up and down the peaceful canals and straight into the compound, where the Chief right about now would be waking up and wondering what had become of Jimmy.

I repeat, the gentleman in the white fisherman, get your craft to shore now!

"Already tied up to the seawall were two boats, and I pulled in right behind them and shut it down," Jimmy says. "On the boat directly in front of me is this Cuban-American woman, and let me tell you she was not pleased to have gotten pulled over. She was cursing up a storm, calling these two officers—one of them a woman—everything but a child of God. She was cursing them in English, she was cursing them in Spanish, and she was cursing their dog—for whatever reason. And I was sitting there listening to all this while watching the police dog sniff the entire length of her boat, inside and out. I mean, this dog was so thorough I told myself right then it was all over.

"So this young cop—he was practically a kid—he hopped on board and asked for my identification, which I gave him. And he asked me for my boat papers, which I gave him. And he went back to his squad car and ran everything through dispatch. And then he came back and peered into my cooler. I was shaking like a leaf by then."

You don't have many fish.

No, I didn't have the tide working with me this morning. But I got the biggest one biting, you know?

How far out were you?

Dropped over the shelf and came back.

"Fortunately, he had simple questions, and I gave him simple answers, being as polite as possible. But I could feel the sweat trickling down my body. If I ever needed a drink in my life, this was the time. So while the woman officer and her dog stayed with the Cuban lady's boat, the cop and I went all through my boat. He opened up all the holds that you normally find on these boats, and then he took this little probe and stuck it down into my gas tank—I assume he's looking for a false tank—and he wanted to know how much fuel I have on board. So I tell him how much gas I have, and I tell him all about the boat, and I tell him where the boat was built—it was a Whitewater, made right there in Miami.

"He might not have known whether a fish was fresh or not, but he was quite knowledgeable about boats. He was curious why I had the extra tank in the front. And I told him that I go fishing a lot, and I've yet to see a gas station out there— something to lighten the atmosphere, you know?"

The way it is, Officer, I know I have a hundred and eighty gallons up front. And I know if I run out of gas two times, I can still come home—no matter how far out I am, I can make it to a pump.

"So the female cop finished being abused by the Cuban woman and climbed off her boat with the dog, and sure as there's a God this German shepherd starts doing circles—

going round and round, around the officer's legs, between her legs, every direction a dog's legs can go while attached to a leash, they went. And if it wasn't over before, it was now. That cop was being pulled by the dog right toward me, and I could see that she was not in a good mood to begin with. She got right up alongside my boat, and the dog was going crazy. And right then it crossed my mind to start running—until I looked at that dog's teeth, and I didn't dare."

What do we have here?

Everything is in order. This gentleman has been out fishing; lives right up the canal a ways.

As Jimmy recalls, the officer and her dog were seconds away from jumping aboard—"They were in midair almost, I could almost see the foot coming down"—when suddenly the dispatcher summoned the woman officer to her cruiser. The drug-sniffing canine, meanwhile, didn't want to budge, barking out loud that Jimmy's boat was loaded to its deck screws with contraband.

We have a possible hit at the other marina. They need me to get the dog over there.

Should I stay here with this gentleman until you come back?

Did you already check the compartments?

Yes, checked every one. It's clean.

Let's wrap this one up, then.

Sir, thanks for your patience. I'll remember you and try not to stop you next time. Have a nice day, and enjoy those fish; they look delicious.

Jimmy just stood there, toes trembling in fish juice that dripped down his entire body. He waited for the two police cruisers to drive out of sight, and then he fell to his knees, opened the cooler, grabbed the Spanish Wells rejects—now more stiff than his boat's cutting board—and threw them over the side for the crabs to dissect.

Next time, he told himself, he had to come up with a better reason for being there.

THIRTEEN

FOR EIGHT MONTHS, SPRING AND SUMMER THROUGH autumn—if indeed there are seasons in the tropics—it was business as usual for the ocean cowboys. Mother ship after mother ship was safely off-loaded, never twice in the same watery place. Prior to each weed transfer, the Chief would unroll a nautical chart stored in his mahogany chest, remove a parallel ruler and divider from their wooden case, and pinpoint for the Colombian captains new coordinates, as well as recommended bearings for the ships to follow into and out of the Bahamian waters that he knew like the back of his hand.

One such rendezvous took place just days before Christmas,

after the Chief placed a special order for forty thousand pounds of extra-prime weed—what with all the partying Americans like to do around the holidays.

"So we ran out with our large trawler, the *Grand Celeste*, which carried twenty-five thousand pounds, and then several of our smaller boats. We had it all covered," Jimmy recalls. "We pulled up alongside the mother, and we were immediately told by the captain that he was holding a hundred thousand pounds of weed, which is a huge amount. Without going into detail, he complained that something had gone wrong along the way—the buyer got spooked; the coordinates got mixed up; it could have been one of several things. So we went ahead and off-loaded our share, filling up all of our compartments, and even then the mother sat low in the water—she had *weed* written all over her. I felt bad for the captain because he knew he wasn't going to find anybody to take the rest of the load, especially two days before Christmas. And he was as anxious to get home as everybody else to celebrate the holiday and what have you. Either way, the Colombians offered the Chief the deal of the century if we would take some surplus off their hands, which would make for a faster and a far safer trip back home for them."

For once the Chief was perplexed. Here he was being offered the opportunity of a drug smuggler's lifetime—and at a cut-rate price. Sixty thousand pounds of pure Colombian Gold, floating here at his fingertips, but his six boats were already full. The thought crossed his mind to try and round up some of the local fishermen from the neighboring islands, but it was almost Christmas, and their wives had the seldom-seen husbands decking the halls anyway. The Chief was telling the boat captain no thanks in Spanish, when Jimmy spoke up with his grand scheme.

Let's take all the weed right now and not worry about concealing it.

What are you getting at, besides lunacy?

Why not off-load the bales right onto the deck of the trawler and take them straight to an uninhabited cay? There are plenty between here and Freeport.

Do you know how big a sixty-thousand-pound stack is, Jimmy? If we're not arrested for having it piled on the deck, somebody would surely see it and even try to steal it from the island. There are too many boats passing the Abaco chain.

I'll stay with the weed until you come back for me. Nobody's going to mess with me; trust me.

And what if the defense forces spot you?

At Christmastime? We'll hide the weed under the trees. Trust me, it will work. Just make sure to come back and get me.

Do you understand how long that might take?

I have no yuletide plans other than sitting around Fort Lauderdale, watching you party. Just round up all the food and water on the boats and give me the cooler and I'll be fine.

The Chief was always intrigued by a plan of genius that he didn't come up with first, even a crazy one such as this. Apart from the several-million-dollar profit the crew stood to gain from the original purchase, it now would earn a multimillion-dollar bonus, quadruple the original amount—all because of the cartel's predicament. In other words, Bicycle Joe could go home tomorrow and buy his Australian spread just from this one snafu. What had seemed impossible one minute ago, Jimmy suddenly made doable.

And so it was agreed that the small boat captains would proceed as scheduled to the respective Florida berths and the *Grand Celeste* would follow in their wake with its original twenty-five thousand pounds—but only after delivering the many tons of excess bales to the uninhabited cay of Jimmy's choosing. Since he was the one volunteering to spend Christmas there, the least the Chief could do was give him a choice of views.

"It was the early morning hours of Christmas Eve when we finally got it all unloaded," Jimmy says. "Everybody just wanted to get home, enjoy the holiday, and I was standing there in the dark, waving good-bye to shadows as they climbed back aboard the trawler. That's when the guilt got to Crazy Charlie, the former basketball coach. He suddenly announced to the Chief that he was staying too. It was quite a gesture on his part. So now it was two of us standing there in the surf, waving good-bye. And when the outline of the *Grand Celeste* disappeared, it hit us. We were like the Skipper and Gilligan. And it was Christmas Eve, of all days. But we had everything we needed. The Chief left us with the big cooler from the trawler, and we had a supply of slam bam [sausage and bread] sandwiches, cheese and fruit, sodas—even some beer for Charlie."

Instead of the hammocks that magically appeared on *Gilligan's Island*, the real-life castaways built their beds with the most expensive cushions Mother Nature could provide. They figured each mattress was worth a million dollars on the street, although on this unnamed cay—unless you smoked pot—its only value was measured by a good night's sleep. Jimmy didn't stop with the bed. His youthful spirit took over, and he built himself a multimillion-dollar grass mansion.

"I built my own hut out of bales," he explains. "And then I

cut some of the island's pine branches and laid them across the top for my roof. It was like building a fort on Kemp Road—it was really, really cool."

———

Christmas morning dawned sunny and mild. "No white Christmas," Jimmy announced to Crazy Charlie, stirring the cowboy awake before kneeling for a Christmas prayer in the pink powdery sand, which gets its unique color from pulverized coral and shells. After morning grace the Bahamian went straight to the cooler and fetched a breakfast of slam bams and bruised bananas, washed down with ice-cold cans of 7-Up.

Merry Christmas, Charlie. Don't say I didn't get you anything.

Thanks, Jimbo. Merry Christmas to you. These sandwiches don't look half-bad. I'll buy your dinner tonight; how's that? I still can't believe we're out here—and on Christmas day no less. I was thinking last night, let's make a little wager on when the Chief will return—if ever.

You're on. He'll be back sooner than later, I bet. But this much weed is probably going to take two trips unless he rounds up enough locals. Then again, that would cut into our profit.

I just hope he remembers where he dropped us. It was awful dark when we got here.

Trust me: with all the money we're sitting on, you don't have to worry about the Chief leaving us here to rot. Even if he forgets where he left us, he'd spend the rest of his days searching.

Jimmy was right. This tiny, empty cay in the middle of nowhere—its only imprint of man being the assorted litter washed up on the beach—went overnight from having a gross domestic product (GDP) of zero to somewhere around forty million dollars.

It took the Bahamian all of ten minutes to walk the island's perimeter, albeit he was walking at a fast clip for fear that an airplane or distant ship might catch a glimpse of a marooned sailor and send out an SOS—"Save Our Soul" instead of "Save Our Ship." Then again, the chances of anybody spotting the pair of cowboys was extremely remote.

Jimmy amused himself by inspecting the scattered debris on the beach. He recalled reading in *Reader's Digest* about a fun competition held in a Scandinavian country where beachcombers were assigned the task of finding the most unique and farthest-traveled objects that had washed up on shore. Among the more unusual items in that contest were a garden gnome and a sun-bleached toupee, which the finder guessed had blown off the scalp of a poor soul down on his knees on the deck of a cruise ship, proposing to his sweetheart. On the beach of his cay, Jimmy mostly found soda cans, cigarette filters, and several feet of yellow polypropylene rope half buried in the sand. His more unusual conversation pieces consisted of a tennis shoe, an empty shotgun shell, and a plastic toilet seat—the prize find that he would place between two bales and stick in the hut Crazy Charlie built for himself.

It had taken the *Grand Celeste*'s crew of five (the Ghost, when he wasn't seasick, accomplished the work of two men), including Jimmy and Charlie, more than two hours to drag the marijuana into the middle of the cay, concealed by a canopy of pine trees. Forests of pine grow thick throughout the Bahamas, and at one time two of the country's largest islands supported commercial logging operations. The first sawmill, built in 1905 on nearby Abaco, churned out highly sought-after and sturdy Abaco Pine for decades until a hurricane blew the entire operation off the map in 1964. By that time, however, most of the country's logging had moved to Grand Bahama to the west, where the production continued into the 1970s.

For the Christmas dinner menu, Jimmy announced that it would be similar to breakfast, save bruised apples instead of bruised bananas. The castaways didn't dare build a fire any time of the day or night for fear the smoke or flames would attract unwanted attention. But not having a campfire didn't prevent the men from waxing eloquently into the night, spooky stories or otherwise.

I used to have American teachers like you—Catholic nuns, mostly. What brought you to the islands?

Truth be told, I got myself into a bit of trouble in Miami.

Yeah?

Got mixed up with a student not quite eighteen. It was only one time; happened off of school property. She was a wild thing, let me tell you. I decided to split before anything serious went down and took whatever tenure I had to Nassau.

What did you coach here in the Bahamas?

Track mostly. And let me tell you, if the kids I coached in Nassau ever had the opportunity to compete against the kids in Miami, the Americans would be left in the dust.

Yeah, we could never catch up with some of the black kids on Kemp Road.

So do you believe in God, Jimmy?

Why you ask?

I saw you praying this morning.

I always pray, but not so much to the Christian God.

Then to whom do you pray?

I think there's something greater than the God who Christians created in their minds. Given what Christians believe, how could God be a Christian? In other words, if He were a Christian, He wouldn't allow all the bad stuff to happen that's going on around the world. You see what I mean?

Yeah, I never looked at it that way, I guess.

I still send money to Jimmy Swaggart, though.

You're kidding!

I figure it's like the lottery—maybe the guy can bring me some luck.

Surprisingly comfortable on their cannabis cots, the pair talked on and off about myriad subjects until the illuminated dials of their waterproof watches—the only lights on the island—reached ten o'clock and they nodded off.

Jimmy, Jimmy, wake up—wake up, man!

What?

Come outside, quick!

What's wrong?

The Coast Guard has a spotlight on us!

"I stumbled out of my hut, expecting to be blinded by a beacon with a machine gun pointed in my face. And I look one way, and then I look the other way—I mean, the island is tiny, right? And all I can see is a bright moon just rising up out of the ocean."

Charlie, you dumb fool. That's the moon coming up! I should shoot you.

═
═

Jimmy knew how Ernest Shackleton's crew must have felt when, after four agonizing months of being stranded in the Antarctic cold, the Chilean tugboat *Yelcho* broke through the ice encasing Elephant Island and rescued them. It was only four days ago that he and Crazy Charlie were cast away from civilization. Finally, on December 28, as he peered out from under the tree branches with his large pair of binoculars, Jimmy spotted a ship on the horizon: a fishing boat, from what he could tell, outfitted for trolling. He carefully tracked the vessel's progress and concluded that if the captain wasn't steering for their cay, then the stiff morning breeze was pushing it easterly in their direction. Soon, another fishing boat came into view, sliding up the channel on the same windblown course. He aimed his lenses farther south. Sure enough, three or more miles behind the lead boats, there she was. He knew it was the *Grand Celeste* after zeroing in on the Chief's telltale red flag flapping in the breeze—a martini glass and olive.

They're coming, Charlie, they're coming! The crop is saved! The crop is saved!

Or half of it, at least. The Chief would have required twice the number of boats to haul away the entire thirty tons. And once half that amount was dragged back onto the beach and stashed in the crew's boats, and nobody else volunteered to house-sit the island's hemp huts, Jimmy and Crazy Charlie stubbornly agreed to dig in their heels for another few days. But not before being offered larger cuts of the proceeds. In addition, the Chief presented the castaways with a generous care package containing vacuum-packed delicacies from the States: meatballs in homemade gravy—"Place them in the afternoon sun, and they'll be perfect by dinnertime," the chef instructed—Colorado smoked rainbow trout, and bacon-wrapped barbecued shrimp. For dessert, the Chief's catering company in Nassau had boxed up some chocolate-covered strawberries, oatmeal and coconut cookies, and an entire pink wedding cake that the bride never got to slice because her careless groom woke up with more than a hangover just hours before they were to exchange their vows. The crew broke into hysterics when Jimmy held up the cake toppers—two grooms, compliments of the Chief.

"I figured you and Crazy Charlie got lonely out here," the Chief laughed.

There was a bottle of champagne for the coach to uncork on New Year's Eve and sparkling cider for Jimmy. Bicycle Joe surely struggled with the gesture, but he loaned the pair his backgammon set in its worn leather case, which the castaways could play day or night now that they had battery-operated lanterns to switch on inside the huts. And to keep the men entertained, the Chief left them in the company of his three favorite poets: John Keats, Robert Seymour Bridges, and Rudyard Kipling:

Wasted my substance, I know I did,
On riotous living, so I did,
But there's nothing on record to show I did
Worse than my betters have done.
They talk of the money I spent out there—
They hint at the pace that I went out there—
But they all forget I was sent out there
Alone as a rich man's son.

The Kipling passage haunted Jimmy every time he heard it recited, as if it was penned by the Chief himself, who now tried telling Jimmy that he was envious of his island sentry duty—that if he didn't carry the license to pilot the trawler, he would gladly volunteer to remain on the cay. But his friend knew better. There was nothing on a deserted island of any use to the Chief—even the best weed Colombia had to offer.

"By this time the Chief was partying more and more," Jimmy explains. "It wasn't just alcohol and dope; he had really gotten into cocaine and the lifestyle that comes with it. We were making way more money than we ever had before. Like somebody in the crew said one time, we were making more money than the Beatles. So everybody was happy, but some were more in control than others. The guys who did the coke had all the powder they wanted. The guys who drank liquor had all the rum they wanted. The beer drinkers had cases and kegs—they had their own refrigerator in the compound, the beer guys did. And I had my refrigerator too, filled with regular and Diet Coke.

"There were always impromptu parties at the compound, always girls hanging around the house at all hours. And you could watch the Chief and see that he was becoming more distant; he was becoming paranoid. In this business, that was dangerous for everybody. I stayed away from the partying— did my own thing, worked out in the gym, read a lot. That's why I didn't mind staying on the cay. It was a relaxing change of pace—longer than I anticipated, yes, but once we got the care packages, I actually enjoyed it. But I had to second-guess every smuggling operation from this point."

There was no specific place or time that the Chief relin-quished authority and told Jimmy the operation was his now to lead. Then again, everybody from Barranquilla to Nassau to Tallahassee knew already that they had to deal with Jimmy Divine.

≡

Glancing at his watch like all anxious Americans do on New Year's Eve, Crazy Charlie managed to keep awake by adding up in his head all the cash he would earn for being marooned. By volunteering to work both holidays, so to speak, he announced into the darkness that he would soon have enough money to buy the waterfront home he'd always dreamed of owning in the Florida Keys. Better yet, there would be enough spare change to tie a new forty-foot Viking to his dock, which he planned to christen *Rising Tide*. Jimmy skirted the question when Charlie asked him what he would do with his share of the loot—triple or more his fellow cowboy's cut, likely. Jimmy had more money (just how much he didn't know) than he could ever spend, given his lifestyle. He had a dresser drawer full of watches already. And he was only getting started.

FOURTEEN

IN 1960, BARELY FOUR MILLION AMERICANS WERE experimenting with illegal drugs. And very few of them lived in the retirement mecca of south Florida, where Harvey Wallbangers and Lucky Strikes were the vices of choice. This made life easier for the federal law enforcement officers based out of Miami, who had a far bigger fish to fry.

A massive wave of Cuban immigrants was crashing into the Sunshine State, fleeing political upheaval created when a young revolutionist named Fidel Castro overthrew Cuba's de facto military leader Fulgencio Batista on the final calendar day of 1958. If Batista wasn't scary enough, President Dwight D.

Eisenhower warned his Cabinet that the United States suddenly had a bearded monster on its hands.

Ten years down the road, having survived a Bay of Pigs invasion and Cuban missile crisis, Castro continued to pose problems for the U.S. government. But something far more sinister was also beginning to rear its ugly head throughout the Caribbean: "International drug trafficking syndicates," as they were classified by Uncle Sam, operating unhampered and feverishly, for the most part, to quench America's insatiable appetite for a popular new high. In other words, the baby boomers were coming of age, and their drug of choice was marijuana.

In response to America's growing narcotics problem, President Richard Nixon declared the country's first-of-its-kind war on drugs, labeling the illicit substances "public enemy number one." Meanwhile, at the president's urging, the U.S. Congress in 1970 passed the Controlled Substances Act—Title II of the Comprehensive Drug Abuse Prevention and Control Act. Replacing more than fifty separate pieces of drug legislation, the sweeping law went into effect on May 1, 1971, and was enforced by the Bureau of Narcotics and Dangerous Drugs—the Drug Enforcement Administration's (DEA) predecessor agency.

"This law, along with its implementing regulations, established a single system of control for both narcotic and psychotropic drugs for the first time in U.S. history," the DEA wrote in a history of its agency during the 1970s.

The law established five schedules that classified controlled substances according to their danger and potential for abuse and addiction. Marijuana was placed on Schedule 1 of the controlled-substances list, meaning it was considered extremely dangerous. By the time an executive order created the DEA in 1973 to establish a "single unified command" to combat illegal narcotics, America was "already beginning to see signs of the drug and crime epidemic that lay ahead," the DEA recalled. "The problem was sufficiently serious to warrant a serious response."

Whereas the former altar boy from Kemp Road would be the last person to classify himself as the kingpin of an "international drug trafficking syndicate," the Justice Department in Washington knew of no bigger catch than Jimmy and his ilk—at least north of the Colombian grass fields. And with the sweeping new laws and unprecedented crime-fighting tools at their disposal, the U.S. drug enforcement agents were out to round up any traffickers they could find from Florida south. Whether it was farmers, cartels, traffickers, or dealers, the attorney general of the United States declared that all operators of the Caribbean drug trade would be pursued by land, sea, and air—from the lush mountains and coastline of Colombia, to the empty channels and beaches of the Bahamas, to the busy marinas and highways of Florida, where on any given day, in all three places, one could find Jimmy or one of his cowboys.

Fortunately, for the "weed people" at least, President Gerald Ford replaced Nixon in the White House, and while Jimmy and his crew didn't know it at the time, the new president immediately pulled drug enforcement resources out of the Caribbean region and concentrated them elsewhere. He accomplished this maneuver after he had created the Domestic Council Drug Abuse Task Force, which he asked Vice President Nelson Rockefeller to chair. According to the DEA, Rockefeller was tasked with assessing the extent of drug abuse in America and making recommendations to bring it under control. His final report maintained that "all drugs are not equally dangerous. Enforcement efforts should therefore concentrate on drugs which have a high addiction potential."

"This report deemed marijuana a minor problem and declared that cocaine was not a problem," the DEA explained in the history. Indeed, the White House report concluded: "Cocaine is not physically addictive . . . and usually does not result in serious social consequences, such as crime, hospital emergency room admissions, or death."

Rockefeller, rather, recommended that the "priority in both supply and demand reduction should be directed toward those drugs which inherently pose a greater risk—heroin, amphetamines . . . and mixed barbiturates."

"Specifically, the panel recommended that the DEA and U.S. Customs Service de-emphasize investigations of marijuana and cocaine smuggling and give higher priority to heroin trafficking," continued the DEA, which, thanks in part to Ford's misleading White House report, would not be able to open an office in Nassau for another four years.

"This policy shifted enforcement efforts, resources and manpower away from cocaine cases towards heroin," stated the DEA. "The report recommended that agents focus on Mexico, a source of both heroin and dangerous drugs, rather than on domestic posts such as Miami, where they are more likely to 'make a cocaine or marijuana case.'"

So it was "government policy makers," as the DEA described the paper pushers in Washington, who became more concerned with heroin, while marijuana, the drug-fighting agency continues, was considered "a harmless recreational drug, typically used by college students, and cocaine wasn't considered a serious drug problem. This lack of emphasis on marijuana and cocaine meant that the marijuana smugglers from Colombia and cocaine traffickers faced minimal law enforcement opposition. Moreover, it allowed the traffickers from Colombia to lay the foundations for what would become the powerful Medell'n and Cali drug cartels. . . . Having already established marijuana distribution networks along the East Coast, they were easily able to add cocaine to their illegal shipments."

≡

As a child growing up in the islands, Jimmy would often look to the sky whenever he heard the sound of a plane or helicopter. Aircraft of any shape and size were rare, even over the more populated islands like New Providence. Now as an adult, every time he off-loaded, the Bahamian smuggler would scan the horizon for approaching ships and always make certain to keep one eye on the sky, straining to hear the distant hum of an approaching aircraft. But they never came—no planes, no helicopters.

When they did eventually fly into the smuggling world, and he knew it was only a matter of time before they did, the Bahamian would be smart enough to realize they wouldn't be up there sightseeing.

"When we started smuggling, we set our courses and hid out in the open," Jimmy says. "We didn't do any strange routes. You always took the maritime routes, and you always pulled right into port. There was little reason to worry, because we always looked the part, always tried to have a reason for being there. We were proud to be smugglers. And we weren't violent. The cowboys used to say that if Jimmy Divine ever held a gun, the safest place to be is in front of it. Truthfully, we didn't think we were doing anything wrong, and we didn't think we were hurting anybody. The Pat Boone kid was selling a thousand pounds of weed a week—I thought that was a lot of weed. So I asked him about it one day, and he explained that he lived two blocks from the university campus and sold every seed of it to college students. I thought it must not be hurting too many people, because everybody was graduating. Even our fleet of vans never encountered a problem. I mean, we couldn't get caught if we tried, even when we were being flamboyant. The Chief used to send me out to buy ten or fifteen Rolex watches at a time—the Gold Presidential was seventy-nine hundred dollars for the male, and the female was fifty-five hundred, and he would pass them out to his guests during the dinners he hosted. If he thought you were interesting and that you had injected some stimulating conversation into the evening, then when you got up to leave, he would hand you a little gift. And you'd open it up and it would be a Rolex. If we weren't drawing attention to ourselves, I don't know who was. As I said, we always were hiding out in the open. Somebody might see us toting a bale of weed up the dock and say, 'Nobody would be stupid enough to take a bale of weed off a boat in a marina in the middle of the day.' But that's how bold we were—so brazen that people wouldn't look at us twice.

"I guess we were blessed, I don't know. I had the crew laughing at dinner one night when I told them the only thing left for us to do is have bumper stickers made up and put on the back of all of our vehicles: 'We Transport Drugs and Stop at All Railroad Crossings.'"

===

Gerald Ford would disappear as fast as he appeared. And in early 1976, Chicago native Peter Bensinger became the new administrator of the DEA. He was streetwise and tough for a Yale graduate, having been the first-ever director of the Illinois Department of Corrections—in charge of all state penitentiaries, reformatories, parole supervision, and jail inspections. He'd seen just about everything a criminal could throw at a law enforcement officer, and then some. Immediately he started to focus the DEA's investigations from a statistical emphasis on seizure totals to arresting major drug kingpins and traffickers.

"We realized we had to stay one step ahead of the authorities, so we were always coming up with foolproof ways to bring in the weed," Jimmy recalls. "While the Bahamas were free and clear for the most part, the Coast Guard, Customs, and what have you became like flies in the Intracoastal, pulling over any boat that remotely looked suspicious. One thing we did to throw them off was to have one of our boats be in distress. It was a good setup while it lasted—we just did it one too many times.

"We'd have two boats out fishing the weed line, and once both were loaded up with weed, one of the captains would get on the radio and inform the Coast Guard that his boat was having mechanical problems and needed a tow. And then the other boat captain next to him would jump on the radio and tell the Coast Guard that he was in the same vicinity as the boat in distress and that he would gladly respond. He'd then hook up to the other boat, and the whole time while they were coming in, the captain towing the other boat would be talking to the Coast Guard on the radio saying, 'Don't worry, I've got the broken-down boat in tow—there's a leak in its fuel line, so I'm taking it in for repairs.' And the whole time the Coast Guard would be thanking the captain. I mean, with all the Coast Guard has to do, the last thing they want to bother with is some joker's fuel line, right? We're saving them time and money. But more important for us, the last thing the Coast Guard or anybody else would do is pull us over once we reached the Intracoastal. They didn't want to have anything to do with us.

"Well, the same thing happened one evening, and I was in the tow boat, which, thankfully, was clean for once. I had gotten a call from one of the crew that the police boats were every-where in the waterway and he didn't want to chance coming in. So I went out and I'm pulling this fully loaded fisherman into the Lake Worth boatyard where it was supposed to unload. Except this time I come around the edge of the dock, and I mean you could read the jackets waiting for us—DEA, FBI, every law enforcement jacket made in America was in the boat-yard that night. And I should have known better, because it had become more obvious that they were getting clever on us.

"So there was nowhere to go—we floated right into their trap. All eyes were on me, and all I could do was slide up to the dock. And this gentleman in a DEA jacket leaned down and actually told me that the boat I was towing fit the descrip-tion of a boat involved in some smuggling."

No, really?

We'll soon find out.

You know, sir, I was supposed to be in at six o'clock, and I'm going to need to call my wife, who is really nervous right about now. Do you happen to have a dime I could borrow?

Uh, yeah, sure.

Great, I see the phone is right up there. I'm just gonna call her and let her know that I'm running late because I had to rescue this fool who had a problem with his boat.

I'm going to need to see your paperwork first.

Sure, it's all right there in the console next to the radio. Help yourself. Feel free to look around if you want. Just don't drink my last soda.

"So I walked to that telephone, dropped the dime in, and looked back, only to realize none of the eyes were on me. And you talk about a brother who can run when he has to—I took two strides and I was out of the boatyard and tearing up the road in my bare feet. I ran as fast and as far as I could for several blocks, and then I spotted a taxicab and flagged it down."

My man, where are you running off to so fast?

Nassau!

There's no bridge to Nassau, brother.

Then get me to the closest point. I'll make it worth your while. How about MIA?

You got a deal. But stop so I can buy a pair of flip-flops, will you?

Jimmy barely felt guilty for abandoning the two crew members, neither of whom ranked a notch on the totem pole. The pair had been mainly deckhands of Pretty Pat's, but they were always looking to earn some extra cash whenever they could. But nobody would blame Jimmy for fleeing either. He was, arguably, the top cowboy and certainly the brains behind the operation, given the cocaine-induced deterioration of the Chief.

Which is the exact reason Jimmy did not dare have the taxi driver take him to the compound. For all he knew, the place was swarming with cops and the Chief was in cuffs.

Jimmy had long since become disenchanted with the living arrangements in Fort Lauderdale. He relished the camaraderie, obviously, and the opportunity to live in the United States—sitting on the fifty-yard line for the Miami Dolphins' football games, flying to Las Vegas for world-title boxing matches. He looked forward to every extravagant five-star dinner, when everybody got to show off their Rolexes and gold chains—"All the gold there was in the world," he says—and the inevitable wisecracks every time he ordered his trademark Shirley Temple.

But the compound had become party central, which was not only taking a physical toll on the Chief, but also on Jimmy, who more often than not locked himself in his bedroom with *Reader's Digest* and *Popular Mechanics* while listening to music through his headphones.

"I did enjoy going out to dinner. That was always a big deal. We entertained a lot in the compound too, but dinners on the town were a big part of our lifestyle. We ate at all the best restaurants, and with the Chief being a chef, he expected the finest food and service. Again, at this stage of the game, money was no object. And he always picked up the check—never, ever allowed anybody to pay for anything. He used to order Dom Pérignon by the six-pack. And if it wasn't the right temperature, he would send it back. But everybody knew him at these places, and they appreciated his business. I'll never forget the night we were at the Forge in Miami—there were eight or nine of us, a typical evening, which meant that I would be ordering my usual Chateaubriand, and the Chief was ordering the best wines off the list. He loved Château Lafite Rothschild, and ordered the oldest bottles they had in stock. Anyway, we had a little 'sweet' as our waiter—I don't know if *sweet* is politically correct; *homosexual* is the right word—and the Chief was giving him everybody's orders, as he normally does. Many times he would call the chef out of the kitchen and have him explain to the table how each meal would be prepared. And the Chief and the chef would converse in French about the age of the meat, about the seafood, and everything that goes along with the pomp and pageantry of being the boss and a chef at the same time. After the Chief and the chef finished their French dialogue, the little waiter came swishing back to the table with all the drink orders, including one glass loaded with extra cherries. And he announced with one of those cute giggles, 'I see somebody's having a Shirley Temple.' And the Chief looked at the waiter and raised his hand and said, 'It's me.'

"Without fail, we always closed the restaurants down. We stayed there and we talked so much foolishness, and our waiters would have to stand there to the side the whole time, obviously anxious to leave, but at the same time they knew from previous experience that the Chief made it worth their while not to show it. And the bill that night might have been two or three thousand dollars—could have been more, I don't remember. And the Chief pulled out his credit card and actually wrote the waiter a tip for twenty-five cents. Then we walked out. And there was nothing this poor guy could do."

When the Chief got into his cocaine years, as Jimmy calls

them, he would ask his friend to recite some of his poetry, hoping the entire time to jar his memory back to its prior strength and charm. "And he could never do it," Jimmy says. "And I'd say, 'See? You're losing your mind, you fool.' And he'd always answer, 'Jimmy, having access to cocaine is an attribute. It's no different than being tall, dark, and handsome, or having a lot of money.' But the poetry was gone. All the days and nights spent at sea on the *South Wind*, when there was time set aside for Bicycle Joe's backgammon tournaments, they were always followed by the Chief's poetry. He recited everything under the sun. He once explained to me that he'd been very lonely while in school in London, so that's when he memorized all the classics. That was his thing even after he had become a chef; he never forgot his poets. He brought them all to the Bahamas with him."

The Chief used to prepare wonderful meals on his trawlers, cooking up the best of everything—the finest meats money could buy, as Jimmy describes them. Chicken is chicken, the Chief would say, so instead he would provide the cowboys with steaks, pork chops, and lamb. He'd find out everybody's favorite dish, how he liked it prepared, and he would overstock the ingredients just to make everybody happy—and full.

"For whatever reason, I always had to cook the rice; every time the Chief would put rice in a pan of boiling water, out would come a ball of wax. And this guy's suppose had to be a chef? One and a half cups of water to a cup of rice, how hard is that? I guess it came down to the fact that the executive chef of a five-star European hotel never had to cook the rice—a simple task left to the assistant chef. So he never really learned how. But my favorite thing he used to prepare when we were out at sea was toasted bread and fried onions, sautéed in olive oil. And when we'd get back to shore, every time I smelled onions frying, I would think of the Chief."

If he ever needed a better reason than now to pick up his life and move it back to Nassau, Jimmy didn't want to stick around and see it unfold. Somehow he had escaped the DEA's dragnet at the Florida marina, but there was the one agent who had looked him dead in the eye, seen every feature of the Bahamian's sun-tanned, goateed face. That narcotics agent was probably being interviewed by a police sketch artist at that very instant. And in a few minutes' time, when Jimmy's taxi rolled up to the main terminal of Miami International Airport (MIA)—only after it stopped for his flip-flops—they'd probably be weighing the two thousand pounds of choice Colombian herb that Pat Boone anticipated selling in Tallahassee by midnight.

Jimmy had left his Bahamian driver's license, which really serves no official purpose in the United States, in his dresser drawer in Fort Lauderdale. And he wasn't about to show his mug at the compound to retrieve it. It was probably now in the possession of law enforcement anyway. But he wouldn't need it to enter the Bahamas either. He never did.

Whereas Jimmy had grown up to be a drug smuggler, several of his classmates had become Bahamian Immigration officers. Odds were one of them, as usual, would be standing by at the arrival gate.

Citizenship papers?

Could you grab my friend John over there; we went to school together and—

Jimbo, what's up?

I had to leave the States in a hurry, John, and I have no ID.

Come through, Jimbo; we know you. Be sure to tell Miss Olive hello for me.

FIFTEEN

THE HIDDEN COMPARTMENTS THE CHIEF AND JIMMY had custom-built into their fleet of fishing boats were unparalleled—so meticulously designed, crafted, and positioned, they were undetectable to the naked eye of a badge-carrying officer, even though each held a ton or more of marijuana. The Coast Guard and drug enforcement officers were professionally trained to locate contraband secreted inside water tanks, fuel tanks, and other unusual hiding places. But when the cowboys had a hold carved beneath the fiberglass deck of a vessel, to find it somebody would have to either disassemble the entire boat—marine bolt by marine nut by marine screw—or else cut the craft completely in half. And anybody pulling over one of the crew's fishing boats wasn't equipped to do that—not yet, at least.

"Here is what is absolutely amazing," Jimmy says. "The two guys on the boat that I towed to the Lake Worth boatyard didn't say a word to the authorities about knowing me. They just said their boat broke down, that they called for assistance, and had no idea who I was when I showed up to tow them in. I'm not sure if the authorities believed them or not, but here's the real strange thing: the DEA never found the stash in the boat. Can you believe it? They didn't drill in those days, and they didn't cut your boats up. The guys had one bale that wouldn't fit in the hold, so like idiots they put it in their cooler, and that's all the DEA found. If they had been smart enough to throw it over the side, they would have walked away that day. And you want to hear something really bizarre? The Chief got the boat back with all two thousand pounds intact, still down in the hold. They never found the weed. The two guys were charged with possession of one bale of marijuana, which they argued they had found floating in the Florida Straits while they were fishing. The Chief got our attorney to represent them, and all they got was a slap on the wrist."

Jimmy enjoyed several days of visiting his family and friends in Nassau. The time he didn't spend with his young daughter, born to Charon, he spent with Olive. And one afternoon he even picked up a hammer and helped Kirkwood bang a few nails at one of his stepmother's construction sites. Otherwise, he took it upon himself to purchase a bucket of aqua paint and paid a neighborhood kid good money to touch up the Kemp Road house. He also stocked Olive's refrigerator with meat and vegetables and treated his family to a steak-and-lobster dinner on the town—yes, lobster had suddenly become quite the trendy menu item, if you could even afford it. For the first time, Jimmy had noticed that age was taking its toll on his stepparents, which reminded him to promise Olive that he would soon pay another visit to Jacob on Long Island, and an extended one at that. What Jimmy could not tell her is that because U.S. and Bahamian authorities were stepping up searches of maritime vessels making their way north through the Great Bahama Bank, his crew of weed people were switching job titles again—they were loaders now, instead of off-loaders. And fortunately for Jimmy, Long Island was one of the newly chosen work sites. Instead of hooking up with mother ships that sat like ducks in the open water amid the increased law enforcement presence, they would now be looking to the sky for their dope shipments. And not a moment too soon, as far as Jimmy was concerned.

While lying low in Nassau, Jimmy had received an early morning phone call from the Chief, updating him on the legal proceedings of the two crew members who'd been nabbed by the DEA and charged with possession of the single bale of herb. And, the Chief added as if suddenly remembering, a fellow drug trafficker out of Cape Canaveral named Mark was in need of some very urgent assistance. Bicycle Joe, Crazy Pat, Digger, and Ghost, he explained, were presently en route to the north coast of Abaco to off-load a mother ship precariously anchored for two days with a tremendous load of marijuana in her hold.

"Mark had called the Chief to say he was in a big jam, that his off-load boats were stuck in the canals somewhere up there, and they couldn't make it out to the mother. He stood to lose millions of dollars," Jimmy recalls. "So we did the guy a huge favor and ran everybody out to off-load, and they returned safely and fully loaded to our marinas. The crew was waiting at the compound for further instructions—and for our cut of the pie—when my phone rang. It was Mark, and he was fuming, having gotten nowhere talking to the Chief."

What happened to your guys?

What do you mean?

Where are they?

They're back in Lauderdale.

No way, Jimmy. They never hooked up with the mother ship.

Yes, they did, I just spoke to them ten minutes ago. They're all back at the compound, playing cards. The weed is sitting in the boats waiting for you.

Jimmy, my Colombian contacts are still calling me. The mother's still out there with my weed that I've already paid for, and they ain't waiting any longer.

For the first time since Jimmy had become a drug smuggler, the wrong mother ship had gotten unloaded. In other words, there was so much weed being smuggled into the United States that not one, but two big Colombian freighters were anchored off the coast of the same Bahamian island—their holds spilling over with weed. And whereas one Colombian captain was relieved to have gotten rid of his fifteen thousand pounds of contraband, there was another Colombian captain who was cursing to high heaven in Spanish.

"There was another mother out there in almost the same spot," Jimmy explains. "The Colombian captains liked to use these Roman and Greek names to establish contact with their hookups: Romulus, Spartacus, Remus, Tiberius, what have you.

So when Bicycle got on the horn to establish contact with Romulus, Remus answered with a confirmation, and his coordinates, and the ocean cowboys pulled up alongside Remus and off-loaded. I guess the captain, whose load was already paid for, figured one Roman name was as good as any: 'Let's go ahead and load up these guys. They're here, after all.'"

Suffice it to say, drug smuggling was a risky business, and it was understood by everybody involved in the trade that you had to be prepared to lose millions of dollars in contraband or cash at any given moment. It went with the territory. Certainly the cartels and buyers sought to make reparations after every botched job, but it wasn't unheard-of that somebody went home unsatisfied with the outcome—if he ever went home.

As Jimmy describes it, weed smuggling got easy again once the ocean cowboys became affiliated with an American pilot named Terry Lowe. A military veteran, Terry was married to a Colombian, and they lived next door to her farmer parents in South America. A native of Illinois, the short, stocky pilot with bright red hair and freckles was the quintessential aviator, right down to his brown leather jacket.

"He got to know several of the growers in northern Colombia, and he would get this primo weed—fabulous, fabulous weed, the best the country produced. And he'd fly it up and do drops for us two or three times a week. And it was simple, because we had four identical boats at the time—two we'd keep in Florida and two in the Bahamas. We'd snatch the bales right out of the water, each wrapped in burlap and then plastic, and head straight for the weed line, where we'd switch boats with the two boats arriving from the States. In other words, they would jump on the loaded boats, and we'd jump on the empty boats; they'd go one way and we'd go the other. We never had to transfer the weed a second time, so it went real fast, you know?"

Talk about turning a profit. The high-quality cannabis flown north by Terry was in such high demand it was fetching twelve hundred to fourteen hundred dollars a pound in Florida.

<hr/>

Although Jimmy would return occasionally to the Fort Lauderdale compound, he was now spending the majority of his time in the Bahamas, particularly on Andros, the country's largest and least explored island. To the delight of scuba divers and fishermen alike, Andros is blessed with the second-largest barrier reef in the Northern Hemisphere. The island is also considered the bonefish capital of the world. Better yet for Terry, it was the very first Bahamian island beyond Cuba, which made it a cinch to reach from Colombia. Most often, he would drop his load—two thousand quality pounds—just off the island's northwest coast near the village of Red Bay. Treasure hunters to this day still frequent the area between Red Bay and Morgan's Bluff, searching for a huge bounty of treasure that history suggests the notorious pirate Sir Henry Morgan buried there.

Otherwise, Andros is arguably the most unusual of all the settlements in the Bahamian archipelago. Right about the time Jimmy was plying his illegal trade, the descendants of an ancient tribe, along with their chief, were actually discovered living in the wilds of the island—not terribly far from modern Miami—devotedly following their original customs and rituals.

During the mid- to late 1970s, Jimmy never encountered the indigenous tribal people, although they looked a lot like the natives he'd seen in the pages of *National Geographic*. But he did know plenty of other unique inhabitants of Andros.

"You know when you enter a church, the altar and pulpit are usually at the far end looking out onto the pews, right? Well, in Red Bay they turned it around so that now when you come in the front door, the altar and pulpit are right there. And there's a good reason for that. What happened is that Reverend Banks—he was a great old guy—he was preaching one day to the congregation, and in midsentence he looked out the window across the bay and he saw a bale drop out of the air—*splash!* He kept on preaching and then he saw a second bale drop—*splash!* And then a third bale—*splash!* And in between preaching he still watched carefully, and he never saw a boat come into view.

"So as the story was told to me, he turned and said, 'Brother Mackey, can you lead the congregation in prayer?' And one good thing about Brother Mackey was that he always prayed long. And Reverend Banks slipped right out the door, but not before tapping his son on the leg and telling him to get their Whaler started. And in no time the father and son were speeding into the bay and collecting the weed that had been dropped—they pulled in seven hundred pounds. Now, what usually happened in a situation like this is whoever was supposed to pick up the bales had not shown up yet, and the pilot had no choice but to drop the load in the prearranged place because he couldn't keep circling or fly home heavy, you see?

"So Reverend Banks collected all this weed and he put it in his house for safekeeping. And when I showed up on my rounds one day, he sought me out."

You know, son, I found some of those bales floating around here.

You did?

I don't want any money for myself, you understand. But the church could use some new benches.

I'll handle it for you, Reverend. I'll also get you the finest benches money can buy; does that work?

Jimmy loaded all the marijuana Reverend Banks had plucked from the ocean and sold every stem of it in the name of the Church of God. More important, he kept his promise to the preacher.

"I went to the finest woodworker in Fort Lauderdale— some old German guy—and he made all new benches for the church, along with a beautiful pulpit and three chairs that were fit for a king and his court—one tall chair and two shorter ones for each side, everything made out of solid mahogany. And they have a beautiful church in the bays now, thanks to that one airdrop."

Despite Andros's small population and few roads, planted as it is between Nassau and the Florida Keys, it had became one of the busier locales in the world of drug smuggling. And unless they were walking around with buckets over their heads, a majority of the islanders were not only aware of the illegal trafficking; they condoned it.

"It was a really big business in Andros, especially in Red Bay and Lowe Sound. There was an airstrip at an old farm down in Twin Lakes where the pilots would land. So Andros was a hot, hot place. Everybody knew what everybody was doing, but nobody hurt anybody, nobody stole from anybody, and nobody ever told on anybody. Which brings me to the rest of the story: the congregation knew what the reverend was up to, and when I delivered the new pulpit and benches, these old church ladies had the pulpit turned around so that it didn't look out over the water anymore. Instead, the people sitting on the benches had the nice view of the bay. So whenever bales were dropped from that point on, the reverend couldn't see it happening. The congregation got their new benches, and for that they praised Jesus, but as far as they were concerned, nothing like that was gonna ever happen again."

One day Jimmy was waiting for a drop to come down, and he struck up a conversation with Reverend Banks, who always made a point of saying hello when the Conchy Joe came into town.

I hope the church is enjoying the benches.

We are very much. Thank you again for all that you did, son.

Does it bother you, Reverend, that something illegal made it all possible?

Son, God made it, Solomon smoked it, so I must can sell it.

SIXTEEN

JUST AS ROBIN HOOD ROBBED THE RICH TO PROVIDE for the poor, so, too, one might argue, did Jimmy Divine, who finally figured out how to put his fortune to good use. What cash the crew didn't deposit in numerous overseas bank accounts, lock in fire-resistant safes, and wire home to loved ones, they stashed in canvas sail bags handmade by Mr. Albie in Abaco. He stitched and sold sail bags by the dozens to the smugglers without ever knowing why.

Approaching the worn and splintered dock, Jimmy was pleased to see the seagulls diving into the small hold of Jacob's fishing boat, a sure sign of a good day's catch, when more meat and less scraps are left for the birds. It was just past noon according to Jimmy's Rolex, and by the smell of things, his father was outside in the kitchen, frying up a fresh whole grouper—usually still gasping for air when slapped on the frying pan. He was long overdue for a visit, but the wayfarer breathing in Jacob wouldn't demand an explanation from his youngest son—the one born with the gold letters in his head. He was more than pleased that Jimmy was doing all right for himself in Nassau, where the latest *sip-sip* to reach Long Island put Olive more than under the weather. Jacob figured something was afoot if his big-boned sister wasn't charging out of bed in the morning and taking the bull—and everything else that blocked her path—by the horns. But he would hardly ask his son for an update on Olive's well-being. He couldn't take any more bad news. He was already lonely enough without Perline in the kitchen, God rest her soul, and the days of sailing to Cuba were long since over.

Nor was Jimmy about to tell his father that Olive, strong and powerful as she once was, was suddenly reduced to skin and bones. It had reached a point where Jimmy could no longer bring himself to visit her in Nassau. The pain he had felt was too much for him to bear.

Jimmy reached into the side compartment of his Sport Fisherman to retrieve a black duffel bag, which held a bottle of Barbados rum for his father, a box of manila envelopes, two handfuls of elastic bands, and enough hundred-dollar bills to make it heavy to lift. It was the dead of summer, he was reminded while walking toward the pink house, given nothing edible was growing on the five hundred acres that this time of year were sole property of lazy sheep and Jacob's horse—standing still as a statue, as equines often are, oblivious to the heat. And then he saw it, parked next to the peeling sun-bleached house: Jacob's first and only link to the twentieth century. Jimmy could also see that his father had brushed the Volkswagen Beetle convertible a chartreuse yellow, using regular house paint.

"That night Jacob insisted on driving me to the neighbors, because he was still in charge," Jimmy explains. "That was important for him. I had to laugh because he refused to turn on the car lights for fear of drawing down the battery. I tried to explain to him that every car has an alternator, which charges the battery while the car is running. Well, I couldn't get that across to him. He had it in his head that if he turned on the lights, it was going to drain the battery, and we'd be stuck in the middle of the island. Long Island has no lights—it is pitch-dark—and so here he was, driving down the road to Ma Miller's house with no lights."

Jimmy, you've gone from big to grown-up. Perline would be proud to see you. Evening, Jacob. Come in from outside. What brings the both of you out tonight? Is Olive not well?

Everything be fine in Nassau, Ma. I just wanted to let you know you'll be seeing a lot more of me. My job will allow me to be around here from time to time, keeping Jacob company and doin' a little fishing, you know? I also have something here for you, Ma. And this one is for you, Mr. John.

What is it, boy?

Something for a hot day when the fish ain't bitin'.

The reaction was the same behind every weather-beaten door Jimmy and Jacob knocked paint chips off that night—except at the home of the Farrells, who couldn't speak through all their tears.

"Each envelope contained five thousand dollars—all in hundred-dollar bills, wrapped tight with elastic bands. I'd give one to the woman in the house, and another to the man. That way the husband couldn't take it all and do whatever he wanted with it. And talk about dancing with joy—they would hug me, hug each other, kiss me, kiss each other, shoutin' and hollerin'—it was fabulous to see how happy they were. And when I told them I had to be going, every family said the same thing: 'Are you going to be here tomorrow?' And I said, 'Yes, I'll be fishing with Jacob tomorrow.'"

The very next day, Jacob and Jimmy cruised back to the dock to find all of their Long Island neighbors—fathers and mothers, children and grandchildren, aunts and uncles—awaiting their arrival with platters of roasted mutton, salted fish, corn, grits, watermelons—everything they didn't know they even had the day before was now being served in generous quantities.

More than anybody else on Long Island, Ma Miller would never forget Jimmy's generosity. In fact, one day in the not-too-distant future, the eighty-plus-year-old woman would single-handedly see to it that whatever military the Bahamian government was outfitting at the time did not get around to nabbing him.

=

Once a smuggler's paradise, Andros soon became too risky for Jimmy's comfort level. Bahamian ministry officials, the police, and defense forces were all under increasing pressure from Uncle Sam to clamp down on any and all operatives in the drug trade, including local accomplices. The time was now,

Jimmy told the cowboys, to move the airdrop operations southeast to Long Island, which meant slightly shorter flights for Terry and his fellow pilots flying the contraband, but longer boat rides for Blondie and Bicycle Joe to reach the U.S. mainland. Otherwise, there were few reasons for Jimmy to check in with the Chief, who was becoming a regular at the VIP lounges of Miami and Fort Lauderdale.

Ever since the cowboys turned to airdrop deliveries, Jimmy had been coordinating each and every shipment via a two-man—both Americans, understood by the Bahamian to be ex-U.S. military—communications base set up in Nassau.

"We communicated via two-meter radio, with a single band, or side band, I think they called it, which provided the needed lift into Colombia. These guys worked for Terry out of a house they shared in Nassau, and they handled all of our airdrops. They would know at all times where Terry was, they'd know where our crew was, and they'd relay any updates or change of plans. The knowledge of these guys was impressive, and that's why everybody assumed they were military-trained. These were the guys who taught me how to use the loran long range navigation radio system, which they understood completely. This was a few years before the GPS (global positioning system) came onto the scene."

Before Jimmy evacuated Andros, he had arranged for a planeload of potent weed to be flown into the old Twin Lakes airstrip—its runway running south to north for the pilots arriving from Colombia, smack in the center of the marshy island. Twin Lakes was once a farm by the same name, and even had the beginnings of a town during the 1940s, until it was abandoned. The road leading to it, however—one of the very few on the island—was still passable and transformed the ghost town into an ideal rendezvous point for the dealers and smugglers who were flying in their cargoes of grass. Jimmy borrowed the biggest truck he could find on the island, parked it next to the airstrip, and waited for Terry's pilots to touch down.

"And you talk about hilarious, although I wasn't laughing," he says. "These two clowns, Americans, decided to smoke some of the pot on the way up, and when they landed, they actually forgot to lower the landing gear. I was sitting there thinking, *They're gonna die!* But they just came skipping along the runway—*bup-bup-bup-bup-bup*—and finally ground to a halt. I still don't know how they didn't flip the plane. But it was a perfect landing, given they weren't using wheels. And when they stepped out of the plane, I was expecting to see them all shaken up, but they were just as high as kites. They walked over to me sounding like they were Cheech and Chong: 'Oh, hey man, was there some sort of problem?' It turns out they had been smoking the weed the entire trip. It's unbelievable some of the fools you run into in this business."

The Chief, wherever he happened to be that week, wasn't behaving much better. Especially when he was in the company of Winslow, the wealthy son of a nationally known ice-cream maker in the United States. Jimmy couldn't stand to be around Winslow, who was about thirty. He always seemed to be hanging around the Fort Lauderdale compound whenever Jimmy slept over, pulling up each time in a red convertible sports car, usually with one or more bikini-clad women sharing the passenger seat.

"I never had a good feeling about this guy. He and the Chief were cocaine buddies," Jimmy says. "They'd snort coke with the girls from the strip clubs; that's all they would do. But remember, that was just the Chief. You had Bicycle and Blondie and the others, and we would always go to the gym, work out, keep a healthy lifestyle, you know? But there would be those guys who were staying up all night, partying with the girls. As long as the coke didn't stop, the women didn't stop coming. I finally put a steel bar across the door of the hallway to separate the living room and dining room from my side of the house. I would go in and out through the back door and garden gate, which I used to lock. That way I could go to sleep at night.

"I remember I once accompanied the Chief to the West Coast. We stopped by Winslow's family estate in Los Angeles, and he had a basement that he'd turned into a disco with a valuable art collection. The place basically resembled a nightclub. I had been to one or two museums in my life, and it dawned on me that he had these very expensive paintings hanging next to cheap and ugly prints."

Winslow, I'm curious. Why do you have these priceless paintings hanging next to these dime-store prints?

It's just like my life, Jimmy. The people I surround myself with—some are real, some are not.

Jimmy didn't like the cocky tone of Winslow's voice, uncertain whether the spoiled American might have been purposely insulting him. It wouldn't be until the Bahamian's last-ever drug run, unprecedented in scope, that he would understand what Winslow meant.

SEVENTEEN

FLACO WANTED TO SHOW HIS APPRECIATION IN PERSON after Jimmy, of all the bizarre coincidences, personally saved the lives of two of the Colombian's fellow cartel members and countrymen. And the Bahamian accepted his invitation, although one might argue that both men had ulterior motives.

In his previous journeys into Colombia, Jimmy had never met any of the farmers, the peasant growers who supplied Terry Lowe with his planeloads of "jolly green"—as the pilot liked to call marijuana. Given his own background, Jimmy had always felt more of a bond with the pot growers than he did with the kingpin he was en route to meet. So on this trip, unbeknownst to Flaco, he would meet with those planters whom Terry not only dealt with, but treated as if they were his own brothers. What the American pilot had done—successfully so far, since he was still alive—was bypass Colombia's powerful drug lords, who more often than not put farmers on their payrolls, for whatever that was worth. The pilot was dealing with growers outside the cartel's turf, their smaller fields scattered throughout northern Colombia. And while their plots were small, their harvests, in the potency category, were high-test.

"Expect a visit soon from a high priest who is being sent by the pope himself," the pilot teased the growers prior to Jimmy's arrival. "He will be wearing robes of purple, gold, and red. He is coming to bless your crops."

For this priestly pilgrimage to Colombia, Terry warned Jimmy in advance that he would eventually be clutching a machete instead of his Bible. "Where we're headed, no Bible will protect you," he said.

Flaco, meanwhile, was preparing to host his second all-Jimmy-can-eat feast of Latin food and ladies, his unspoken priority to pressure the Bahamian into buying his weed solely from the cartel again—or at a minimum, returning to the crew's purchase levels before Terry flew into the picture. But the physical backdrop of the Cardinals' lobbying effort would be to raise a toast to Jimmy for having rescued a marooned pair of cartel members based in the Colombians' Miami compound.

"I was taking one of our boats back to the States to be serviced, as was often the case," Jimmy explains, "and I was cruising past the Berry Islands—a small string of cays between Andros and Abaco. I was taking my time, just enjoying the day, and I happened to glance over my shoulder at Bonds Cay, when it struck me that there were no houses on that island. So

I slowed down and circled around a couple of times, and I saw this wall of burlap. So I put the bow into the beach, and these two gentlemen come running towards me, shouting in Spanish: '*La-la-la-la-la-la—yakka-lakka-yakka-lakka-yakka-lakka.*'"

Hold on, slow down!

Miami! Miami! Miami!

Yes, I am going to Miami.

Miami! Miami! Miami!

Relax, gentlemen. Tell me what's going on here.

"I came to find out that they were observing an off-load off the coast of one of the islands and there was a lot of weed left over," Jimmy says. "So the purchaser talked them into staying on Bonds Cay with the extra ten thousand pounds, promising he would be back for the weed and them. He probably offered them some extra money; who knows? Well, he didn't come back. When I found them, they'd been there for almost two weeks—their food was gone, and they didn't have too many swallows of water left. I mean, these guys were all but dying. There was one small Colombian, about five feet four, who I eventually nicknamed Chipmunk. He's my friend to this day—he looks just like a little Chipmunk. He kept saying, 'Miami! Miami! Miami!'"

Miami's fine. I'll get you to Miami, no problem. What about your weed?

Yours! Yours! Yours!

How am I going to take it?

You take it!

I have an idea. You stay here, and I will come back for you. Stay here.

No! No! No! Please, señor, no leave us. We die!

Okay, get on board. Nobody's going to find this weed anyway.

Within thirty minutes of backing out of Bonds Cay with his relieved passengers, Jimmy swung his boat into Little Whale Cay, a breathtaking ninety-three-acre private island with a two-thousand-foot airstrip. The tiny cay, some 150 miles southeast of Fort Lauderdale, was purchased in the 1930s by Wallace Groves, who created a first-of-its-kind Bahamian sanctuary for exotic birds, butterflies, turtles, and a handful of vacationers who could afford the slice of secluded paradise.

"I knew the caretakers, a father and son who were members of a respected family in Nassau, and I would always be welcome to bring my daughter up there to see the flamingos and peacocks. It was a special getaway, a wonderful place to spend the weekend," Jimmy remembers.

Greetings, Mr. L.

Long time, Jimbo. How are you?

Been a gin up, Mr. L—found these two gentlemen stranded on Bonds. They're hungry and thirsty, and I'm taking them on to Miami, but I'm in a bit of a bind. I've got almost ten thousand pounds of weed they're giving me.

It's in there?

No, Mr. L, too much weight for this boat. It's stacked over on Bonds.

Take Junior and go get it, no problem.

Mr. L, I can't put weed on this boat. The dogs in America will be barkin' up a storm, you know? I don't need none of that, especially with these foreigners on board. Plus, they've been sleeping on the weed for two weeks, so they stink.

You and Junior take the Whalers. And spend the night here. We'll wash their clothes and eat something.

After this slight but profitable detour for everybody involved, Jimmy saw the Colombians safely to Miami, where they immediately made contact with the cartel's top lieutenants in Barranquilla. Jimmy guessed these guys wasted no time ordering a not-so-polite visit be paid to the party responsible for leaving the two men for dead. "When it comes to drug trafficking," Jimmy explains, "the Colombians always played fairly until such time as they'd been crossed, at which point they would track the offending party all the way to Alaska if required. If their demands still weren't met, the pursued had better have his or her affairs in order, or enter the Federal Witness Protection Program."

When Jimmy was a student at Sacred Heart in Nassau, his school won a nationwide sports competition. Because he scored the most points among his classmates—winning both the 100- and 200-meter dashes—he was handed the honor of accepting the school's trophy. And it was presented, no less, by none other than Bahamian bishop Paul Leonard Haggerty, who, in the Catholic tradition, was appointed by the Holy See himself.

"The only problem was the nuns told me that I had to kiss his ring," Jimmy recalls. "And that wasn't sitting well with me. Sure enough, after I received the trophy, the bishop stuck this giant ring in my face with an ugly old stone in the middle. I wouldn't kiss it. I didn't even want to get close to it, thinking about all the places that ring had been. So I turned my head, and the nuns gasped. I never forgot what that ring looked like."

Before he donned his priestly garb—a mishmash of every-day, choir, and liturgical dress—for his short flight to Colombia, during which he carried a counterfeit Bahamian passport iden-tifying him as Father Jerome Constantakis, Jimmy stopped by a Miami arcade and won the largest, chunkiest, ugliest ring displayed behind the counter. During his previous journeys into Colombia as a holy imposter, he could feel the eyes star-ing at his naked ring finger. Now, as far as he was concerned, his ecclesiastical costume was complete.

"It was amazing—when I would stroll up to a Colombian immigration or customs officer, he wouldn't even check me," he says. "He never asked me if I was bringing anything into the country, or taking anything out. The entire time I was in Colombia, it would be free admission wherever I went. Go buy a train ticket, no charge. Go into a restaurant, everything's on the house—breakfast, lunch, and dinner. That's why I always made a point of blessing each and every immigration and cus-toms officer for letting me in: 'Bless you, my son.'"

As quickly as Colombia's drug revenues grew during the 1970s, with more than a dozen of the largest cartels like Flaco's amassing huge amounts of money and influence, so, too, were leftist rebel groups on a rise to power: the Revolutionary Armed Forces of Colombia (FARC), the May 19th Movement (M-19), and the National Liberation Army (ELN). The ELN, Jimmy knew, actually had Catholic priests—genuine men of the cloth—in leadership posts, due to their purported cam-paign for social justice and human rights. So he wasn't overly concerned about encountering any of these particular combat-ants. Otherwise, he was saying his prayers that any FARC or M-19 guerillas who might be dressed in peasant garb wouldn't bother kidnapping and holding for ransom a member of the clergy. After all, nobody from the Vatican would miss him, and certainly would not buy his freedom. Still, he couldn't help but wonder, as his train chugged north through the green country-side toward the Sierra Nevada de Santa Marta mountain range, why Terry kept saying he would require a machete to reach the fertile cannabis fields. Was the vegetation so thick they'd have to hack their way through?

The pot pilot grew tired waiting in the empty depot near the end of the line for the lone train that departed Bogotá late that scorching day, when the sun burnt gray through a haze of humidity that made the drooping tongues of the local pack of dogs look all the more rabid—or so Jimmy thought when he finally jumped off the train. Keeping a wary eye on the under-nourished creatures, he retrieved from the deep pockets of his vestments prickly pears, plantains, and mangos—gifts of fruit from appreciative peasants—and threw them over the heads of the canines so that he would have a running start to Terry's rusty pickup truck parked beneath the depot's lone tree. Otherwise, he was relieved to escape the confines of the train, the curiosity and clawing that followed his "performing" the sacrament of anointing the sick—or in this case the deceased.

The snoozing pilot, his eyes shaded by a straw hat, climbed out from behind the steering wheel of his truck and erupted in laughter at the sight of Jimmy being so divinely adorned, if not ordained. He normally saw the bobbing Bahamian from the cockpit of his plane—just sunglasses and a bandanna star-ing up at him.

Where's your staff, Saint Peter?
Get me away from these dogs.

They won't hurt you. The mean ones have already been shot and eaten.

I should have saved them the chicken I just gave away.

Boiled or fried?

Breathing, but that's another story for another time. So what's this about me needing a machete?

You'll see when we reach the base of the mountain.

So it's dangerous?

It could be, especially in that Halloween outfit of yours.

So they don't like priests?

Who are they?

The guerrillas.

Guerrillas? It's donkeys you have to worry about up here, padre, not guerrillas.

"The roads were rough enough, and where the pavement ended, we had to get out and walk up the side of this mountain," Jimmy says. "And when it got too steep to walk is when we got on these little donkeys. I must have looked like I was riding out of the book of Zechariah. We rode these two donkeys, both of them guided by local children with ropes, right up the side of the mountain. And the entire time we were on the edge of these cliffs looking straight down. And like Terry, I had a machete in my hand. He had explained to me, 'If your guide suddenly slips off the side of the mountain, just chop off his hand—whatever you do, don't let him pull you and your donkey over the cliff with him. Just chop off his hand if he should start falling.'"

Jimmy didn't know whether Terry was kidding him or not, "but the whole time I made sure I kept one eye on my guide's feet and the other on his hand."

EIGHTEEN

IT WAS HOT BY LONG ISLAND STANDARDS. SO MISERABLE that nobody in his right mind stirred the eighty miles from Cape Santa Maria in the north—Christopher Columbus's third "discovery" after San Salvador and Rum Cay—to Cape Verde in the south. Nobody except Ma Miller, the last soul anybody would expect to see join the lizards under the sweltering sun.

Good God, woman, did you come all this way on foot?

Afternoon, Jacob, I need to talk to Jimmy if he's home.

Rest here by the gate and I'll fetch him—and you a glass of water.

Don't ask me why, Jimmy, but Ma Miller is down at the gate;

says she needs to talk to you. Woman must have walked two or more miles. When you're done talking, tell her to stay put, and I'll run her home. She's about wilted.

Ma Miller, what's happening?

You know my oldest daughter, Denae?

Yes, I know Denae.

She's married to that defense force fellow.

Yes, I know that.

Well, she said if you were down here to be sure to tell you that they're down here too.

Denae and her husband are down here?

No, the defense force is down here. She said you would know what she means.

Oh, okay, Ma. I appreciate your coming all this way to tell me that. And be sure to tell Denae that I said thank you. But you might better wait until her husband's not around.

You don't need to be thanking nobody, Jimmy. I don't know what my family would have amounted to without you. You saw to my children's future—Denae is married and working because of you. And plenty of others up and down the island like her. You did your family, Jacob and Perline, proud. Now Olive, God rest her soul. You've got two mothers looking down on you, Jimmy.

"And that's what it was all about, making a difference in people's lives," Jimmy says. "We weren't hurting anybody; we weren't killing anybody. Yes, we were breaking the law, but we weren't bad people. We were just weed people."

Jacob pulled up his faded yellow Bug to the gate and poured a jug of water on the vinyl seat to cool it down before Ma Miller climbed in. He never asked the old lady about the urgency to see his son—what could have been so important to walk all that distance in the heat—mainly because he wanted her to think he already knew the reason. Rest assured, Jacob drove back home faster than he had driven to Ma Miller's, discovering Jimmy in his fishing boat. Without knowing why, the father jumped on board and steered his son in the direction of a nameless cay, where for more than one uninterrupted year Terry Lowe and his pilots had air-dropped with little concern the world's finest strains of cannabis into Jimmy's waiting arms.

As his fishing boat approached the cay, Jimmy thought about everything Ma Miller had just told him. To tell the truth, he would be proud of his country's small defense force—several hundred marines at most, equipped with zero airplanes and fewer than a handful of patrol boats—if somehow they had gathered enough intelligence not only to deploy to lonely Long Island but descend on the very empty cay that Jimmy owned by squatter's rights.

"We swung around the cay and there they sat—two of the most beautiful new defense force vessels you've ever seen in your life," Jimmy recalls. "Anchored right there, waiting for something to happen—waiting for Terry's plane to come in. 'No worries,' I tell Jacob. 'I'm just going to pull up alongside and talk to them a bit.'"

Good day, gentlemen. Nice boats you have.

Whatchu up to?

Checking a few of our traps, you know?

This time of day, are you?

Grabbing some lobster for supper. What brings you defense boys all the way down here?

Jimmy snatched the two biggest lobsters from the first trap

he pulled, and then he and Jacob made a wide turn and slowly headed for home—just in case they were being watched, which he knew they were. Jacob remained silent, as he had done for more than a year now while Jimmy went boating by himself. The aging father was happy just to have his son at his side; that was all he needed at this stage of his life. But as quickly as the boat reached the dock, Jimmy radioed Nassau, while Jacob carried the lobsters to the kitchen.

Cancel the drop! We've got company!

Repeat that, Divine?

Cancel the drop. Under no circumstances make today's delivery, do you read?

Got it. Anything else we need to know?

Tell our contact there will be no delivery Tuesday either. I will explain everything when we talk this weekend.

Once Terry was turned back—shortly after his takeoff from Colombia—Jimmy got on the ship's radio and reached Blondie and Bicycle Joe. They were en route to Long Island from Nassau—lucrative trips the cowboys had made at least twice a week for the past thirteen months—and told them to make U-turns and enjoy their time off. Jimmy spent the next several days at his father's house, trying to assess the situation, keeping a casual eye the entire time on the defense force boats that never strayed far from the Deadmans Cay and Grays area of the island—Jimmy's stretch of backyard since he'd been born. By the time the weekend rolled around, he was huddling with the crew in Fort Lauderdale.

The operation's been compromised; it's that simple. How much they know about us, I have no idea.

Are you sure they were anchored there because of us, Jimmy?

Who else is working out of Long Island? All you have to do is look where they were anchored—behind the very cay where Terry makes his drops. That's no coincidence. Trust me and an old lady on this one, they know what we're doing.

Not that Jimmy was surprised. He'd come close to getting nabbed in a joint U.S.-Bahamian operation one year earlier off Abaco, where, needless to say, Sarge was no longer in charge. Instead, Jimmy's police friend had been promoted and transferred to Nassau, where he was rumored to be climbing up the ranks.

"After Andros became too dangerous, and before we moved everything to Long Island, we thought we'd give Abaco a try," he says. "I was sitting off Spanish Cay, north of the island, and I was in contact with one of Terry's pilots a few minutes before he was scheduled to make his drop. It was a beautiful evening, calm seas, just before sunset."

Where are you?

Still in the plane.

You're funny.

I see you, little brother. I'm coming right at you.

You and somebody else. Are we doing a double drop this evening?

I don't know anything about a double, Divine.

Check it out—there's a plane almost right on top of you!

"There were two planes coming in—our plane was on the bottom, and just behind him was a DEA plane, no mistaking it. We didn't have any planes like that in the Bahamas," Jimmy points out.

Tell me right now what you want me to do. I drop it now or I drop it someplace else, because I'm not taking it home.

His heart racing for once, Jimmy did a quick check of the

water around him. Nothing was stirring except a large school of bonefish in the green shallows.

Drop it! Drop it!

And out the bales came in one fell swoop, smacking the surface of the water like torpedoes fired from their tubes—*Pop! Pop! Pop! Pop! Pop!* Jimmy had never seen an entire planeload of weed floating so close together, which made for a speedy recovery for the Bahamian and his first-time loader—a Cuban national named Tony.

Not for the first time in his smuggling career, Jimmy overcame the threat that lurked around him by concentrating on the task at hand. On the outside, at least, he appeared as calm as that evening's ocean. Weed pulled aboard, he was only slightly concerned about Terry's pilot, who had now flown out of sight—as Jimmy expected, with the DEA trailing him—and more likely than not would arrive safely back in Colombia on schedule in his million-dollar turboprop equipped with extra fuel tanks. The DEA pilot and his passenger, who no doubt filmed the drop, would tail the pilot until they were ordered to back off. Plus, as Jimmy had known for some time, the DEA now had its own squadron of pilots based in Colombia, their duty to patrol the airspace along the country's coastline and relay positions of suspect vessels and aircraft to the DEA's El Paso Intelligence Center in Texas. The crew there relied on both U.S. Navy satellites and the U.S. Air Force's new AWAC (Airborne Warning and Control System) planes to track possible shipments of contraband, with coordinates radioed to both the U.S. Coast Guard and U.S. Customs for interdiction purposes. The DEA Air Wing, as it was called, was comprised of thirty-eight pilots across the United States, many of them veteran fighter pilots from Vietnam and even World War II. One of the four Air Wing divisions, the Eastern region, was based in Miami.

That said, what a difference a decade had made in the U.S.-led war on drugs: the U.S. military was now providing the use of its space-based satellites to hone in on the likes of van Gogh as he stood on the bow of a freighter and signaled the F—owes to row out from under the trees in their long canoes crammed with enough marijuana to flood an entire college campus in Florida.

This was one reason these natives in their canoes were now mostly retired from transporting drugs, and pilots like Terry Lowe were in high demand. Cocaine pilots, who took a far greater risk than those flying weed, were even in higher demand, earning up to half a million dollars per flight that took off from one of two dozen or more clay runways scattered throughout the foothills of northern Colombia.

———

"Tony was Cuban, and he weighed more than three hundred pounds. He was so big I made him stand in the middle of the boat. He was living in Nassau, and he wanted to come along for the ride—and he got the ride of a lifetime," Jimmy recalls. "After Terry's plane disappeared and the DEA plane after it, we snatched up all the bales and got them on board. I was running it full throttle to Treasure Cay, and I heard this *whoop-whoop-whoop-whoop-whoop*—it was a DEA chopper, and out of the blue it was on my tail. I mean, it was on top of my engines, looking down Tony's shirt. I didn't have time to throw the weed overboard. I didn't have time to think. I didn't have time to do anything. And Tony was screaming at me that they were going to shoot us, but I knew that wasn't going to happen. They don't shoot at you unless you start shooting at them. You have to engage them before they respond in kind.

"Otherwise, I was in one of the worst places you can get—I couldn't outrun the chopper, and I couldn't dump the weed; therefore I knew I was in big trouble. And then the golden letters started arranging in my head: *Let's go toward Coopers Town*. And in no time I was speeding along the shore in Coopers Town, the chopper still on me, and I could see ten people running out onto the dock there. And I made one wide swing, just like you see in the movies, and came around again, and now there were twenty people running around the dock. I kid you not, by the time I made my third swing, the dock was swarming with people, all of them rushing down to the water's edge to see what all the commotion was about. They quickly knew what was going on. Some of them were running along the beach, waving their arms at me. I was giving them one heck of a show, let me tell you. And then I started yelling to Tony."

Listen to me. I'm going to do one more swing, and then I'm going to come along the shore, and when I do, you start tossing out bales. And you keep tossing them, you got it?

Won't I get in trouble for that?

You're already in the most trouble you're ever going to be in your life—get rid of it!

Tony was scared, Jimmy remembers, wondering what he'd gotten himself into. His huge body literally shaking, he turned around and stared almost pleadingly into the determined, if not smiling, faces of a DEA pilot and Royal Bahamian policeman, who shared the cockpit for the joint government operation. Tony then reached down with his tremendous arms and started heaving bale after bale overboard until the boat was clean. Whatever grass might have remained on the deck blew out of the back when Jimmy spun the wheel and headed full bore toward Treasure Cay, gold letters still talking to his brain.

"The guys in the chopper must have been pissed," Jimmy says. "I gave them a choice: either they go after the people in Coopers Town, who are now collecting enough weed to keep everybody on Abaco stoned for a year, or they come after me. I guess they wanted me, because they didn't leave my tail, not for one second. And I was booking it."

The helicopter pursued Jimmy across the broad sound, passing Nunjack Channel, Crab Cay, Green Turtle Cay—where the famous eighteenth-century pirate Charles Vane fled before his capture and death by hanging—Noname Cay, and then straight into the inlet leading to Treasure Cay.

"I threw it into neutral, slammed hard into the sand, and I took off running," Jimmy says. "I knew there was no way Tony was going to run anywhere, given his size. Sure enough, I heard later, some of the defense force guys riding in the back of a truck grabbed him by the shirt—he'd basically already thrown his hands up to surrender—rolled him into the bed of the truck, and drove off to the Coopers Town jail, where all of this started in the first place. I was running faster than I ever ran before—well, at least as fast as I ran in Lauderdale— while the helicopter was landing in the resort's parking lot. I made it to the boatel before they even climbed out of the cockpit, opened the first door I came to, and was face-to-face with this beautiful young American lady sitting on the end of the bed, drying her hair. I think she might have been on her honeymoon. Can you imagine?"

This is drug related. Don't say a word.

Oh my God!

Please, keep quiet. Nobody's going to get hurt; just a little misunderstanding.

My husband is in the shower.

Then go into the bathroom and tell your husband that I'm out here, but tell him that everything is okay. Nothing's going to happen to anybody; you have my word.

Honey, there's a man in our room, but he says everything is okay and nobody's going to get hurt.

What do you want? Who are you?

Look, I'm not armed; I'm not dangerous. I'm going to level with you. A little weed deal went bad, that's all, and I'm being chased as we speak. I feel real bad that I'm in your room, I swear. But I could use your help.

All right, man. What do you need?

I need you to please walk to the end of this unit and ask for a maid named Gaylene, spelled G-A-Y-L-E-N-E. When you find Gaylene, please tell her that Jimmy is in your room and to come and get me with her basket.

Her basket?

You know, the rolling basket they put dirty sheets and towels in.

Jimmy had known Gaylene from the days he and his wife had worked at the resort, and he would always try to stop by and say hello to her when he was on Abaco. She was Treasure Cay's chief housekeeper, tasked with hiring, training, and supervising all the maids; arranging work schedules, planning the budget, filing damage reports, maintaining inventories, and ordering supplies. Fortunately for Jimmy, she was also responsible for the distribution of laundry.

Maid service!

Gaylene, thank God. You got to get me out of here, baby.

You better not get me fired, Jimmy. You scared that couple half to death, and who knows where they're headed right now? They'll never come back to this island again, I can tell you that right now, the poor things.

I'm sorry. I was cool with them. Talk to them for me, please. Tell them I used to teach scuba diving here; maybe that will help. Tell them I'll be leaving them a honeymoon present, anything they want.

How's Charon?

She's fine.

Your daughter?

She's fine too, thanks.

You tell Charon to get in touch with me, you hear?

Gaylene, you got to get me out of here.

Go on and get in—and curl up, or you'll make the sides bulge. Get down under the towels more, I can see your blue head scarf.

It's a bandanna, not a scarf.

What'chou wear it for?

To protect me from the sun.

You do what you do for a living and you're worried about the sun getting you? Where am I taking you, anyway?

Take me to any empty villa. Just get me someplace fast.

I better not get in no trouble because of you, Jimmy.

Don't worry; just act normal.

I can't hear what you're saying, so shut up.

Okay.

Oh, they're everywhere, Jimmy. Oh, they're everywhere, honey. I've never seen so many policemen before. Oh, they're everywhere. And to think they're all here because of you.

Like every other day—although perhaps a bit earlier in the day than normal since most of the resort's guests weren't back from the beach yet with their dirty towels—Gaylene hooked the laundry basket to the hitch of one of the resort's white golf carts and pulled Jimmy and every sheet and towel she could pile on top of him in the direction of the laundry room. Fortunately the facility was adjacent to the boatel's original three-story wing of guest rooms that overlooked the beach and marina. As more than a dozen law enforcement and defense force officials branched out to search for Jimmy, going so far as to pull a magazine off the face of one sleeping sunbather on the beach, and checking inside the cabins of every luxury yacht in the marina, Gaylene inserted her master key into the lock of room 301, which, luckily for Jimmy, had a leak in the ceiling directly above the mattress that nobody in the maintenance department had been in a hurry to patch.

Enjoy your stay with us, sir. You can tell me later what you did— unless I hear about it first from the police. How long you planning on staying?

I don't know—a few days maybe, at least until I know the coast is clear. Do you mind bringing me something to eat, Gaylene?

In time, child, in time. You have Charon call me, you hear?

Jimmy didn't dare crank on the air conditioner, and he made certain the curtains were shut tightly before he removed his trunks and climbed into bed. The sun wouldn't set for several more hours, but there was nothing else to do. And that concerned him, almost as much as his unscheduled flight from the authorities. He had no choice now but to think of Olive, which he'd somehow been able to avoid until now.

"We'd been out on a run," he recalls, "and when I returned I got word that Olive was near death. She'd been dying for a while, was losing a lot of weight, but now her condition had grown worse. I rushed to Nassau and for three days while she was in the hospital I stayed at her side. Then the doctor walked in and told my family that she had only a few hours to live. And that's when I left. I prefer to remember people how I knew them, you know? When they're just lying there like that, that's not really them. So I kissed her on the cheek and told her good-bye. And then I left for Lauderdale—had to get out of Nassau. I couldn't even come back for the funeral—only the dead bury the dead anyway.

"I guess I was hurting more than I ever knew at the time. But the funeral was huge, held at the Church of God, people overflowing into the aisles."

NINETEEN

THERE WILL NEVER BE ANOTHER HURRICANE DAVID. The 1979 storm was so big, so mean, and so deadly that its name was officially retired, replaced by Danny. In fact, between David and another coming storm in the Caribbean—this one a crackdown on drug runners initiated by Ronald Reagan—Jimmy would be lucky to escape alive.

David was a monster Category 5, clocking winds of 172 miles per hour at the ungodly hour of one o'clock in the morning, when it threw waves as high as four-story buildings onto the Dominican Republic. More than two thousand people in its path would not live to see the sun rise, including

430 Dominicans who squeezed into two churches inundated by floodwaters.

Several hundred miles to the northwest, Jimmy and his more-than-comfortable cowboys, who were making fewer and fewer drug runs these days, had something seemingly as large as the hurricane on their hands: twenty thousand pounds of "gungeon," the most potent leaf grown in Jamaica.

"Colombia had become too far to travel, too hectic, too dangerous, and on top of that, some of the Colombians we'd been dealing with switched over to cocaine. And under no circumstances were we going to go there," Jimmy says. "Jamaica, by then, had established itself as having some pretty incredible weed, and I had hooked up with a guy down there named Fast Eddie. He had his own airplane and airstrip on his property, and he would deliver a few thousand pounds at a time on the back side of Andros."

In fact, Jamaica was so close to the southern Bahamian island that Fast Eddie would sometimes fly up a load in the morning and another one at dusk if there were a demand. "It was a dream operation, a piece of cake," Jimmy says.

"I will never forget Fast Eddie's house up in the Jamaican mountains. It was unbelievable. It was a plantation-style house with a wraparound deck all made of Jamaican mahogany and teak. And he built this house right on the river—I don't mean near the river, or next to the river, I mean he built his house right *over* the river, like a bridge. It was absolutely fabulous. You could be sitting there and whatever fruit the local Jamaicans up there had picked for themselves in the trees—bananas, mangos, guavas, all the citrus you can think of—they would put on these little bamboo rafts and float it down the river, because it would be easier than carrying it all the way down, you see? But the fruit would have to pass under Fast Eddie's house—pass through his house. We'd be sitting in his living room about two feet above the water, and we would just reach down and grab the fruit as it passed beneath on its way down the mountain and plop it into our mouths. And the whole time we were surrounded by this magnificent scenery. Jamaica is truly a beautiful, beautiful country."

A Rastafarian named Israel supervised the ganja operation for Fast Eddie, and he was the exact opposite of somebody like van Gogh.

"Israel was a Rasta, and he was big and well built—right out of the heart of Africa," Jimmy recalls. "He was one of the Jamaican Maroons—the famous descendants of runaway slaves who lived up in those mountains there and fought the British. These people weren't born to bow; they were born to stand. And if you drew a picture, or chiseled a statue of someone who was confident and self-assured, you'd end up with Israel. He had all the dreadlocks, all the little Rasta children. He took pride in being the best, and he was the best. He was in charge."

Israel would press the Jamaican weed, which usually sold for fifteen hundred dollars a pound in the United States, into what Jimmy calls bibles—"about the size of a Gideon Bible"—and stick them together until he'd created a manageable forty-pound bale, which was then wrapped in plastic.

"It was perfect, because Fast Eddie would toss these bales out of the plane, and we'd stash them right under the center console—bible after bible of specialty weed. I mean, this stuff was good; we couldn't get it fast enough. As quickly as we got it to the States, it was gone—they were lining up to haul it away. Pat Boone was like, 'Oh, man, I've died and gone to heaven.'"

Jimmy smuggled much of the Jamaican gungeon into West Palm Beach, which had a much smaller law enforcement presence than Miami and Fort Lauderdale. In almost a decade of smuggling, the cowboys had never so much as experienced a minor successful bust, excluding a bale or two here and there. All of which was more reason for Jimmy to make sure every cooler in his fleet was always stocked with fresh fish—a few with hooks still lodged in their cheeks for good measure. He was older now, extremely wealthy, and he had been looking forward, of late, to the day when he could sit back and enjoy the fruits of his labor—illegal harvest that it was.

≡

As Jimmy describes Digger, outwardly he wasn't the sharpest tool in the shed, suffering as he did from dyslexia, but he was one heck of a boat captain.

"One time we tied up to a boat to off-load and, careful as he was, Digger checked the radar to make sure we didn't have any company," Jimmy remembers. "And he got all excited."

Jimbo! Jimbo! They're coming down on us!

Where?

Check the radar!

I don't see nothing but wide-open water.

See it right there?

You fool, you're seeing the boat we're tied up to! I ought to slap the taste out of your mouth for being so stupid, Digger.

One thing about Digger, no matter where he was in the archipelago, asleep or awake, he'd be wearing a four-inch strobe light he kept tied around his neck. Fortunately, the only time he ever turned it on in ten years was when he tested the batteries or else searched for something in the dark, like a backgammon die that fell onto the deck of the boat. From the day the dyslexic cowboy was first introduced to Jimmy, he pleaded with the Bahamian—as well as every other crew member—to invest in the lifesaving contraptions, which cost all of ten dollars.

If I get you one, will you wear it?

Too big and too ugly, Digger. I like wearing gold instead.

Gold doesn't do you a bit of good when you fall overboard or your boat sinks.

That's when I start swimming.

Blondie wouldn't be caught alive wearing one of the strobes either. If he wasn't vain, he cared enough about his appearance to not have an orange flashlight dangling around his neck.

"He was the best-looking guy in the crew, yet he really never knew how handsome he was," Jimmy says of Blondie. "I'd sit in a restaurant and time after time watch the women just swarm around the guy. All he had to do was sit there. It took me a long time to figure out that I could use him for bait, and it worked wonders for me."

Any seasoned sailor would have taken one look at the wind-whipped whitecaps off the eastern coast of Andros—a wide channel of deep water labeled on the map as the Tongue of the Ocean—and duck into the nearest watering hole. But Jimmy didn't drink. Furthermore, he had twenty thousand pounds of Jamaican bud concealed in four brand-new Midnight Express fiberglass go-fast boats that he and Digger, Blondie, and Bicycle Joe were scheduled to have docked and unloaded in Florida before the sun rose. Jimmy was buoyed by news that Hurricane David, after its deadly landfall in the Dominican Republic, had lost so much of its strength that it had been downgraded to a tropical storm by the time it reached eastern Cuba. Otherwise, the Bahamian needed two hands to count the number of tropical depressions and storms he'd sailed into in his lifetime—and through the infamous Bermuda Triangle, no less.

Since even the most knowledgeable hurricane forecaster in Miami could not have accurately predicted that David, after reaching Cuba and fizzling, would suddenly veer north out into the open waters of the Windward Passage and re-intensify into a Category 2 hurricane, how was Jimmy supposed to?

"We had everything loaded and ready to go," Jimmy says. "The water was extremely choppy, so you can imagine Digger by this time. Even on the nights when the seas were calm, he would say, 'Put this light around your neck / put this light around your neck / put this light around your neck'—I mean, he was like a nagging wife, you know? So this time to shut him up, I said, 'Give me your damn flashlight.' For once I made him happy. So I told the crew, 'Let's hop on and do it!' and we started the engines.

"Our Midnights had three engines on the back—some were actually outfitted with four or five. And these babies moved. They were made to outrun any boat the feds had—

Blue Thunders or anything else. So we headed out, and at first it wasn't too terribly bad. But then the waves grew bigger and bigger, and by now we were committed, right? And keep in mind it was dark—pitch-dark—and the winds were now howling tropical force. We were on a loran course that took us a short distance north from Nicholl's Town [on Andros] to Chub Cay in the Berry Islands, then northwest to West Palm Beach. We figured if worse came to worse, we could at least make Chub Cay.

"Well, when we reached the middle of the Tongue, the waves must have been twenty to thirty feet—they were big. All of us were struggling, cutting way back on the throttles, and I was riding up this giant wave, like everybody else was doing, except when I came down I heard a loud *thump*. I rose up on the next wave, and when I came down, I heard a *crash*. And up again I went, and when I came down this time, I heard a *boom*. And in a split second my boat was broken in half—split right in two; can you imagine? Here I was, in the deepest part of the ocean. I couldn't see two feet in front of me. Waves were crashing all around me, I was swallowing rainwater and salt water in intervals, and all I had to hang on to was this little light tied around my neck. Fortunately, I'm an excellent swimmer, and as I was treading water, I grabbed the light and started shining it all around me, trying to get the attention of the other boat captains."

Ten minutes passed and there was not a sight or sound of the other boats and captains, just the terrifying roar of the hurricane as its strengthening winds slammed into the giant walls of waves that similarly grew bigger and more unpredictable. Not that Jimmy could see a very far distance in front of him, although were it not for the beacon of light, he would have seen absolutely nothing.

"And that's when I started to get a little worried," he says. "Maybe fifteen minutes passed and I was being beaten by the waves. If the storm didn't get me, I figured maybe the sharks would, if they were even out in this weather. It seemed like an eternity, and I was all but exhausted—and who knows how far the currents had taken me away from the loran course. But I was still holding my little light up in the air the best I could, hoping that one of the other captains would see it. And then I actually heard something, strained to hear what sounded like a boat's engines, and it was getting louder and louder—*bladda-bladda-bleedee-bladda-bladda-bleedee*. All of a sudden I rose up on the crest of this huge wave and saw a bright light. And I shone my little light at the bright light, and the next thing I knew I was literally lifted by my shirt out of the water and dropped onto the deck of one of the Midnights, foam everywhere. It looked like I was in a washing machine.

"It was Digger, who had been following my running lights through the storm until he noticed they suddenly weren't there anymore. They just disappeared. And for that entire amount of time he'd been searching for me, searching for my little light. That's how rough it was out there. But he continued to circle, risking his own life for sure with the wind and waves, hoping he'd catch a glimpse of the light that he'd made me wear around my neck. I was lucky that night. We lost two boats within two hours—both split in half."

Blondie was the other lucky captain to survive the stormy night, plucked out of the ocean's Tongue almost immediately after his boat was pounded in half by the massive waves.

It didn't go unnoticed by the fortunate Bahamian that his trusty dyslexic companion—who avoided all occasions when he would have to demonstrate his handwriting, what with his backward and irregularly shaped letters, and who hesitated jumping on the marine radio unless absolutely necessary to warn that a "hekalopter" was on the horizon—had not only saved the lives of two of his fellow cowboys, but he had demonstrated above everything else that apart from being a caring person, he was modest to boot.

"He never once said, 'I told you so,' or 'Aren't you glad you were wearing the light?' He just went about his business, as if nothing had happened," Jimmy says, "although he did bear-hug me a few times."

Blondie wasn't wearing one of the strobes when he was rescued, but from that trip forward he made sure one adorned his leather necklace right next to his prized great white shark's tooth. And if any women should ask him about the unusual neck attire, he would tell them how a mighty hurricane named David was so mean and nasty that it snapped in two a brand-new, top-of-the-line offshore fiberglass go-fast boat—like a saltine cracker.

Thinking back to that horrific night, Jimmy remembers being too busy trying to stay afloat—too intent on staying alive—to pray.

"There was no time to pray," he insists. "But if I had, it would have been no different than when my uncle Mattie once prayed. You ever hear that story of Uncle Mattie? He was digging a well, and they used to put dynamite down in the hole. They'd dig way down, put in the dynamite, light a long fuse, and climb out as fast as they could. Well, one time Uncle

Mattie was digging this well, and he got down so far that when he lit the dynamite and tried climbing up on the rope, it popped. So he started praying, 'Oh Jesus, oh God, oh Lord, you get me out of this and I promise to do this, and I promise to do that.' At that point, one of the other diggers looked down into the well and shouted, 'Mattie, pull the wick out, you fool.' And Uncle Mattie pulled the wick out, then looked up into the light streaming down into the well, and said, 'God, I got out of this one by myself. Save all those promises for another time.'"

≡

Jimmy and the other captains later read in the Nassau news-paper that winds in excess of ninety miles per hour had raked Andros that night, although where the Bahamian and Blondie were struggling for their lives—northeast of the eye, which is always the strongest part of a hurricane—the gusts were much higher. Ironically, David made its first U.S. landfall just a few miles north of West Palm Beach—as if it was following the same loran course as the cowboys. From West Palm it briefly moved back out into the ocean, ran parallel to the Florida coastline, and made landfall again near Savannah, Georgia, eventually impacting the entire Atlantic seaboard. Downgraded to a tropical storm, David flooded the city of Norfolk, Virginia, raised Cain in Philadelphia and New York City, and continued on its northerly path into New England and Canada. All told, it caused more than $1.5 billion in damage and turned out to be the strongest hurricane to strike the Dominican Republic in the twentieth century.

TWENTY

JIMMY WAS ONE LUCKY CONCHY JOE. FOR MORE TIMES than he cared to remember, he had outsmarted, outmaneuvered, and outrun law enforcement and the military alike—federal and local, black and white, operating joint and solo. And now, somehow, he had dogpaddled his way through one of the deadliest hurricanes ever to blow through the Caribbean. And yet he took none of his good fortune for granted. He told Bicycle Joe as much while playing a two-person backgammon tournament with the Australian cowboy, while relaxing dockside in Nassau.

I don't know about you, Bicycle, but I'm getting tired.

I'm with you, mate. It's been a long ride, but ace all the way. I'm ready to go home, be near my rellies again—give Mum and Pop some of this jake to spend however they want. I'll be expecting you to lob in, Jimmy. I'm building you your own bedroom with a gorgeous view and lots of privacy. The Chief and his yobbos won't disturb you there.

Frankly, I don't think the Chief could travel Down Under if he wanted to.

Not the full quid he once was, that's for sure. I'll never forget my maiden voyage with him to Baranquilla. I learned more poetry in that one week than during any year of schooling. I hate to see the bloke lose it. He would dig Australia—a lot more than he did England. Two different worlds. You know what a 'roo bar is, Jimmy?

Yeah, it's a vegetable.

Not rhubarb. A 'roo bar is an iron bar that we Australians affix to the front of our cars so that when you run into a kangaroo, it doesn't come crashing through the windshield and land on your lap. It's a different world, all right. You think we have sharks here in the Bahamas? You haven't seen a shark until you've seen a great white, mate. They're huge, which is a blessing in disguise, because you want to see them coming. Australian surfers tell the proverb, "The shark that gets you is the one you never saw." When you come down I'll take you to the prettiest coastline you've ever seen. We'll swim the reefs, the finest in the world.

That's what I hear. That would be nice, Bicycle. You got some pretty women down there, right?

They blanket the beaches. I'll introduce you to the woman of your dreams; you'll never leave.

You've already sold me, Bicycle. I'll lob in, as you say.

Spiffy. After the week you've had, you could use a change of scenery. I'll even have my pop teach you how to shoot a gun.

All week long Jimmy had been the butt of the crew's jokes:

"If Jimmy's holding a gun, the safest place to be is in front of the barrel," and so on and so forth. The Bahamian took each barb in good stride, but he wasn't laughing. He was too shell-shocked to even smile. Whatever demonism had poured out of him when he huddled with the Colombians at their luxurious Miami compound he hoped never possessed him again. Then again, he might have saved his life by pulling a .38 caliber snub-nosed revolver from his breast pocket—a gun he initially didn't want to have anything to do with—and dotting the designer threads worn by Flaco's nephew in bullet holes.

It all started when he had hesitantly taken what would turn out to be his last buying trip to Colombia, and like his inaugural run eight years earlier, it was by trawler. He was accompanied by Pretty Pat and the Gook, for a change of personalities, and they were to pick up twenty-five thousand pounds of primo pot from the Cardinals. For several months now, Flaco's nephew Carlos, who had recently celebrated his twenty-first birthday, had been anxious, like other young climbers his age, to enter the workforce with a bang—in his case, rising as rapidly as he could through the cartel's ranks and impressing his powerful uncle in the process. It was Carlos whom Flaco assigned to supervise Jimmy's purchase, allowing his nephew to select the weed from the Cardinals' warehouse and oversee its loading onto the cowboys' trawler off the Colombian coast near Santa Marta.

"Twenty-five thousand pounds was put on board," Jimmy recalls. "But for whatever reason, Carlos went back to Flaco and told him they had put thirty-five thousand pounds on board, which was impossible. And I said as much to Flaco one week later when he was demanding more money. I told him his nephew was mistaken, and as far as I was concerned, that was the end of it. The next thing I knew, Flaco had flown to his Miami compound on Star Island and dragged Carlos with him, to teach his nephew a lesson, I assumed. So Flaco called the Chief and requested a face-to-face meeting on their turf. I tried talking to him one more time on the phone, but you can only say so much for fear that somebody is tapping the line."

Flaco, you've known me for a long time. We're talking ten thousand pounds here. I'll pay you the money if it makes you happy. It's no big deal.

That's not what it's about, Jimmy. My nephew said he put thirty-five thousand pounds on your boat, and either he's lying or you are. I can't believe this is even happening.

It didn't happen, Flaco; that's what I'm telling you. The boat only holds twenty-five thousand pounds no matter how you stack it. And it was your people who stacked it!

The next morning the Chief called Jimmy.

He wants to meet with you tomorrow.

Why?

He says there's still a problem with the count.

Their count isn't right. I've already told him more times than I care to. And I don't feel comfortable going to their compound so I can tell him again.

Jimmy, it's Star Island, not Colombia. Nothing's going to happen to you in the middle of Miami's nicest neighborhood.

The Bahamian wasn't so sure. He knew the ways of the cartels, how they settle unsettling matters like this one. He'd heard gruesome details of countless abductions, beatings, bombings, and killings—mostly in Colombia, the majority never prosecuted because the drug lords had bought the entire government, or whoever was left breathing in it. They weren't afraid to take on the U.S. government, either superpower that it was. In 1976, just a few days before Christmas, DEA agent Octavio Gonzalez, the agency's country attaché stationed in Bogotá, was gunned down while sitting in his office. He'd been assassinated by an American, no less, Thomas C. Coley. As if it wasn't already aware, the DEA had a deadly drug war—international in scope, and personal in nature—on its hands. But with limited manpower it wouldn't be until 1981 that the U.S. drug-fighting agency could open two strategic field offices in the Colombian hot spots of Cali and Medellín. Even then, American agents risking their lives on the frontlines were unable to inquire about the cartels without the cartels knowing about it.

Jimmy had sensed a change in Flaco's demeanor several years earlier, after he had taken his weed purchases elsewhere. He understood that he had insulted the Colombian, and he knew the day would come when he would have to make amends. How Terry Lowe survived as long as he had, operating in direct competition with the Cardinals and the other cartels, Jimmy would never understand. Maybe it was luck.

Against his better judgment, the Bahamian finally gave in and agreed to show up at the cartel's waterfront mansion, one of thirty-five luxury residences on lozenge-shaped Star Island, a dredged-up mound of sand in Biscayne Bay directly between downtown Miami and South Beach. But before he stepped foot into Colombian territory, Jimmy contacted a close American friend and fellow martial-arts competitor who lived in Orlando.

Alan was ten years Jimmy's junior, and every kickboxing move the Floridian knew was compliments of his Bahamian friend. Between the two of them, Jimmy realized they could break every Colombian neck in the compound with the soles of their flip-flops.

I've got to meet with some Colombians in Miami, and I've got a bad feeling about it. I need you to cover my back.

No sweat, Pops. I'll be down.

"He's a professional kickboxer," Jimmy explains. "He grew up in the rough part of Miami—Overtown, although he used to call it 'Colored Town.' This guy knows the ins and outs of everything. Not only did he drive down that evening; he showed up carrying two pieces."

Alan, what am I supposed to do with this?

I was thinking about what you told me. I don't like going into nobody's private residence either, especially a drug lord who you say ain't happy with you to begin with. You take this thirty-eight, and I'll pack the bigger one.

Oh, man, I don't even know how to use one of these. I've never held a gun in my life.

You don't have guns on your boats?

No weapons. Not even slingshots.

Don't worry, Pops, you won't have to use it. But if you do, it's easy to operate—just aim it and pull the trigger. But don't do it now; it's loaded.

I don't know, Alan. This can't be good.

Jimmy climbed out of his shorts into his fanciest beige suit, accented with enough gold around his neck, arms, and hands to sink a steel ship. Given they were almost the exact same build—and knowing Flaco would be wearing his trademark Mark Twain–like threads—Jimmy dressed Alan in a bright white suit and tie, just for effect. The Bahamian had never seen his friend in a collared shirt, and both men stood staring into the mirror, highly impressed with their transformations. The way Jimmy saw it, not even a Colombian hit man would waste two guys who were dressed so dapper.

To further err on the side of caution, rather than driving over the two-lane bridge that leads to Star Island, and later discovering their car inoperable behind a locked gate, Jimmy lined up a getaway driver, so to speak. Bicycle Joe volunteered to steer one of the cowboys' go-fasts to South Beach, while Jimmy and Alan remained neatly combed and pressed by driving the Chief's silver Ferrari 308 GTB to South Pointe Park, parking it less than one block from where the Australian had tied the boat to a seawall to watch a pair of Cuban escapees play chess. The two men in their expensive duds then jumped on board the speed boat and in less than ten minutes were deposited on the cartel's modern dock, Bicycle squeezing the crew's go-fast between the Colombians' Hatteras 58 Yachtfish, which sleeps eight, and a shimmering white thirty-six-foot cigarette boat—polka-dotted bikini tops dangling from the throttle. *Flaco's fingerprints are all over this party vessel,* Jimmy thought, looking over the boat. Three cartel members who had been leaning against a white Mercedes and white BMW parked on the pebble driveway—no doubt awaiting Jimmy's arrival behind the compound's tall iron gates—stamped out their cigarettes and rushed down to the dock as soon as they saw the three securing their boat. While one Colombian stood with a foot resting on the creosoted seawall—where he could keep an eye on Bicycle Joe—the other pair of Cardinals escorted Jimmy and Alan along the neatly landscaped garden's winding stone path, past lush tropical plants and gurgling waterfalls feeding into a blue mosaic-tiled swimming pool. Whoever had been lounging on the still-dampened towels spread out across the pool's recliners—and, for that matter, who probably belonged to the bikini tops abandoned in the white cigarette boat—were now nowhere to be seen. The four men walked beneath an almost-too-perfect canopy of royal palms separating the pool from the guesthouse, through a series of Spanish-style columns and arches, and into the thirteen-bedroom mansion to participate in the "business meeting" called by Flaco.

The Bahamian was too cautious to be impressed with the gourmet brick kitchen, where the Chief had told Jimmy he'd once cooked dinner during a friendlier visit, when scantily clothed women outnumbered the men two to one. Nor did he notice that the library walls were draped in maroon silk, since the Colombians didn't do much reading. Somewhere a floor beneath him, the Chief had happily picked his way through a ten-thousand-bottle wine cellar, which was directly adjacent to a walk-in gun safe that Flaco had once boasted could equip an entire army.

"We were led into a formal dining room, which had a beautiful mahogany table with chairs enough for, say, sixteen people. A large crystal chandelier above the table filled the place with light," Jimmy remembers. Flaco was seated at the head of the table, and next to him on his right side was his nephew. Jimmy sat to Flaco's left, directly across from Carlos, and Alan took the seat next to his Bahamian friend. Six or seven other Colombians occupied various positions in the room, either seated around the chair railing or standing in the doorways.

As I said, it's no big deal.

Well, Jimmy, it is a big deal, because I never thought the day would come that anybody would steal from me. And that's what I've come here to find out. Believe me, I have better things to do; I think you know that.

Your guys loaded twenty-five thousand pounds—that's all the trawler holds.

I've questioned Carlos over and over again about this missing marijuana until I'm tired of talking. You can ask him; he will tell.

I understand.

Do you? My nephew says thirty-five thousand pounds were put on your boat. And now that the two of you are sitting down at the same table, I am confident we can learn the truth and put this unfortunate misunderstanding behind us.

Look, as I told you before, I will pay you for the ten thousand. How much do you want?

It's not a matter of money; it's the principle.

What's the principle here, Flaco?

The principle is that Carlos, my sister's son, says without a doubt he counted thirty-five thousand pounds loaded onto your trawler. My people also recall that thirty-five thousand pounds left the warehouse that morning with my nephew. So somebody here has a poor memory.

If you're suggesting I stole from you, I don't do that—I don't need to do that. That's not who I am, and after all these years, you should realize that.

All of these years? Do I need to remind you, Jimmy, that we've barely heard from you for the last, what, two or three years?

And then from the other side of the table, the first words from Carlos's mouth shot across the polished table and penetrated the Bahamian like the barb of a stingray.

How old is your daughter now, Jimmy?

"I don't know what happened at that point," the Bahamian says. "In a split second, I reached underneath my jacket, pulled out the gun, and started shooting at this punk—*Boom! Boom! Boom! Boom! Boom! Boom!* I emptied the gun, although I think I was still pulling the trigger. But here's the amazing thing: somehow, and I don't know how, I didn't hit the fool with a single bullet. I was sitting there, waiting for his wide-eyed skull to come crashing down onto the table, and he just sat there, white as a ghost."

As Jimmy tries to describe the parabolic path between the barrel and his target, the explanation seems to be this: the first bullet must have lodged in the table, and Carlos's immediate instinct was to leap up from his chair, which is when the next slug passed directly through his unbuttoned jacket.

"His suit jacket had holes—you could actually see the light coming through them."

For whatever reason, Jimmy and his companion were still alive. (Later, safely aboard their go-fast boat piloted by a relieved Bicycle Joe back to South Beach, Alan told Jimmy that the thought had crossed his mind to reach for his own gun and start blasting away, but he admitted that, like everybody else around the table, he was frozen in his chair.) Dumbfounded, Flaco immediately screamed out loud in Spanish, ripping open Carlos's cotton jacket and sticking his pinky finger through the shredded holes. Still, he wasn't half as astonished as Jimmy that none of the slugs had torn through his nephew's flesh. All told, there were apparently three bullets, miraculously enough, that passed through the young man's baggy clothing, one or more of them splintering an arm of the mahogany chair where Carlos had sat. The three remaining rounds lodged in the dining room wall behind the Colombian, one defacing somebody's oil-based grandfather hanging in an intricate gold-leaf frame.

When Flaco calmed down enough to speak in English, Jimmy couldn't believe his ears. He announced to everybody in the room that if the Bahamian insisted only twenty-five thousand pounds of marijuana was loaded onto the trawler, he would take him at his word.

"And it ended right there," Jimmy says. "But it was the only time during my eight years of dealing with the Cardinals that there had been a discrepancy on the count. And it was all because of this little fool. The first time he was in charge of the count, we had a problem. What I think happened is Carlos sold the ten thousand pounds to somebody else, somebody in Colombia more than likely, and he tried to stick it on me. Seriously, I believe they were planning to take me out—they were going to ice me, weight me down, and dump me in the Intracoastal. Turn me into fish food, you know?"

Pops, I'm proud of you.

I'm glad to be alive, Alan. Bicycle, let's get out of here in a hurry before Flaco spots the brown stain on his white velvet chair and changes his mind.

You should have seen Pops, Bicycle; you'd have been proud of him. I figured us good as dead when you started firing, but you caught those skinny foreign bastards off guard—they had no idea you had it in you. Especially that Flaco dude.

Yeah, I thought it was all over when he started cursing up a storm in Spanish.

Cursing? Pops, he wasn't cursing. Flaco was warning his dudes not to make a move, saying that in his entire life he'd never seen anybody handle a gun as expertly as you—able to shoot and miss the way you did just to make your point. No, he wasn't cussing—he was telling them not to mess with you. What was he calling you—oh yeah, he was calling you a lizard slayer.

"That's the sad part," Jimmy says. "I was trying to hit the fool."

TWENTY-ONE

NASSAU WASN'T THE SAME WITHOUT OLIVE POUNDING the pavement in her colorful muumuus. If Long Island had offered a decent-sized city with a suitable gym and restaurants that served something other than grouper and grits, Jimmy would probably have moved there to be closer to Jacob. But even his sober lifestyle required electricity, and the island of his ancestors didn't provide near enough juice.

As far as retirement living goes, rather than buying a place in Nassau in which to settle down, Jimmy decided he would build one. If a heaven did exist—and Olive spent her entire life teaching Jimmy that it surely did—then she would be looking down on her stepson with approval. And rather than wasting sweat equity on a single residence, the Bahamian drew up plans for an entire apartment building, reserving the most luxurious unit for himself and putting the other three up for rent. The construction would take him just over a year to complete, and to meet that schedule, an aging Kirkwood showed up to supply whatever assistance he could, although his weak hand could no longer grip the hammer he had swung for Olive.

Jimmy kept loosely in touch with the Chief, who, after hosting an infamous retirement party in Nassau two years earlier, was now dividing his time between New Providence and Florida. There, in the latter, he had moved into a more high-priced place, where he was no longer in charge of the neighborhood crime-watch program.

"The Chief threw a huge party at his home in Montague Heights, a nice place with a swimming pool in a quiet neighborhood of Nassau," Jimmy recalls. "But let me tell you how bold this fool was: he sent invitations to the U.S. ambassador and to the DEA's top guy in the Bahamas; can you imagine? Granted, the Chief had associated with these types of people when he lived in Europe, but it was clear to everybody that he was thumbing his nose in their faces because of the fact they could never catch him."

Perhaps he had outsmarted the authorities, or perhaps luck was the reason the Chief and his cowboys were never busted. Just weeks before his retirement party, an unprecedented joint DEA/FBI task force in Miami immobilized the Black Tuna Gang,—"Competition," Jimmy confirms, "but we were much smarter than they were"—a major marijuana smuggling ring responsible for bringing five hundred tons of marijuana from the same Santa Marta region of Colombia into the United

States during one sixteen-month period. The gang, whose members wore solid-gold medallions bearing a black tuna emblem, had operated in part from a suite in Miami Beach's Fontainebleau Hotel, according to the DEA. Like the cowboys, the Black Tuna Gang had its own fleet of specialized boats and was affiliated with one of the owners of a Fort Lauderdale yacht brokerage. Similarly, they also owned several stash houses in posh neighborhoods of the coastal city.

"And now the Chief was retiring from the business, and he had the nerve to send the authorities invitations to his retirement party, basically saying: 'It's over, and you all didn't catch me.' I said, 'Chief, I think you should have waited seven years before you sent out the invitations'—statute of limitations, right? And when I say he had a huge party, you would not believe where these people came from: the United States, Colombia, Venezuela, Brazil, Saint Croix, Caymans, the Grenadines, practically every island in the Caribbean. And in the middle of the swimming pool, there was a model of the *Flying Swan*, with straw bales on the deck with three stripes on them. He was so out of his mind that floating around the boat were money bags from the Royal Bank of Canada, where we had stuck a lot of our money.

"I'll never forget the Chief invited our lawyer from Miami, Bill, to the party, and he asked us to pick him up at the Nassau airport. Knowing us all too well, Bill said he hoped we would be keeping a low profile when we arrived. Well, the Chief and I drove up to the airport in this Cadillac convertible, and I was sporting ten Rolex watches up and down my arms and more chains than Mr. T. The Chief must have been wearing nine watches on each arm, and chains everywhere—you couldn't see his chest or mine. And I'm not talking fool's gold either. You should have seen Bill, who is a close friend of mine to this day. When he walked out of the terminal, I'll never forget the look on his face. It was like he saw Jesus."

Not surprisingly, neither U.S. ambassador William B. Schwartz Jr., who was appointed to the Nassau diplomatic post by President Jimmy Carter, nor anybody from the DEA's Nassau field office or Miami division, bothered to RSVP for the bash. But rest assured, the outrageous invitation more than got their attention.

"And what did the Chief do? He had his entire party videotaped, and everybody who attended, as well as all of the insiders who couldn't make it, received copies. Unfortunately— or fortunately, as it turned out—several of the big cocaine dealers were among the guests. Not that we had anything to do with them, but at one time they were weed people like us. The coke business became far more lucrative than moving weed, and in certain ways easier, so they made the switch. So we had these acquaintances of the crew who were now on the other side. And that was it—when the retirement party was over, it was over. I went my way, and everyone else went their way."

Indeed, the very day after the party, Bicycle Joe handed his salt-encrusted bicycle to a friendly Nassau boy, who was always hanging around the docks and thought the world of the Australian and his two wheels. He shoved his backgammon board one last time into his backpack, caught one of the daily puddle-jumpers to Miami, and flew home to build his ranch among the kangaroos. Ride Sally Ride had landed a job in Florida, driving limousines for VIPs, many of them South Beach partiers, stocking the long rides with more than mints and booze if the clients so desired. Pretty Pat never, ever considered returning to Columbus, Ohio—not enough water. The last Jimmy heard, he had answered an ad in a Puerto Rico marine magazine for a charter-boat captain to sail barefoot vacationers as far south as Trinidad and Tobago. Crazy Charlie shook the Chief's and Jimmy's hands one last time and motorboated to the Florida Keys to buy his waterfront house—"I want a place where I can sit in my underwear on the porch of my home and watch the sun rise and set over the water," he said. Digger wasn't sure what he was going to do with his life, but he was dyslexic, after all—"A rich dyslexic," Jimmy points out. The Ghost, not surprisingly, was the one guest at the Chief's retirement party who escaped the intrusive lens of the video camera. He disappeared before Jimmy could say good-bye, but the Bahamian knew his giant friend would be appearing again when he least expected it, "like stealth," Jimmy commented, time and time again. Dave, the chain-smoking redneck from central Florida, was the token person on the weed boats whom everybody had constantly picked on. He was never mailed an invitation to the Chief's party because nobody cared to discover his whereabouts. Jimmy says after he made his million dollars, he went back to the fields of Florida and wrapped everything but the roof of his ranch house in Astroturf. The Gook, in all her natural beauty, made an appearance, and every Latin man in attendance adored her and extended invitations to join their cartels. She wasn't biting, but at the same time never bothered to say where she was going. Blondie, given his constant fear of commitment, or what he called the C-word, was the one member of the crew who decided to stay in the trafficking business, albeit on his terms.

Besides his good looks, he was also worth more money than several Fortune 500 CEOs. The more glamorous women at the retirement party—single and attached—gave Blondie one last try, catering to his every need and desire, to no avail. He told Jimmy that if he ever needed to find him—and Jimmy eventually would—to search in a hammock on Bimini, unless he happened to be running contraband into Florida that day.

It had been two years—since the retirement party—that Jimmy had seen any of the cowboys other than the Chief, who had become a recluse, for the most part, while snorting his life away. And then one day, Jimmy's phone rang. It was his old friend, rebounding—and extending the invitation of a lifetime.

<hr />

At an early age, resentment had grown inside Jimmy and every one of his friends on Kemp Road—for the royal family in England.

"The queen would routinely appear on the movie screen in Nassau, I guess to instill in our little heads who and what we belonged to," Jimmy says. "It would always be footage of her coronation, when she was walking up the aisle to get crowned. And they showed this over and over and over again at the beginning of every movie. I never forgot her visits to the Bahamas. She seemed to pick the hottest days to come here, when there wasn't a cloud in the sky, blue as blue could be. And the nuns would make us stand outside all day long, waving these little Union Jacks under the blazing sun—parched us half to death waiting for the queen to come driving by. And then we'd have to go back inside the school and write an essay on what it was like to have seen her. Whenever the queen appeared on the movie screen, we would throw tomatoes at her—throw tomatoes at the screen. Because when you went to the movies, you had to stand up too—and sing 'God Save the Queen.' It wasn't until after we messed up a couple of these big screens that the theater finally stopped showing her coronation."

And to think that the Chief all these years later was now calling to invite Jimmy to be one of the queen's honored guests at the fairy-tale wedding of her son, Prince Charles, and his future bride, Princess Diana, at St. Paul's Cathedral in London. The Bahamian, who had just walked in the door from fishing, wondered if the Chief had gotten hold of some bad powder. He did recall seeing a photograph on the front page of the Nassau newspaper of the spectacular engagement ring that had been given to Lady Di—an oval sapphire surrounded by fourteen brilliant diamonds. The accompanying story described the upcoming ceremony as the wedding of the century, when residents from Nassau to Nottingham would be taking a holiday to celebrate. And now Jimmy was being invited by the Chief, of all the kingdom's deserters, to be among the carefully chosen congregation of 3,500 that would crowd like sardines into the church—leaving an estimated 750 million people around the world to watch on their tellics.

To think Jimmy was impressed when the Chief scored ringside seats to see Sugar Ray Leonard and Roberto Duran exchange punches at the Superdome in New Orleans!

So where did you find these tickets?

Tickets! These aren't tickets. This is an invitation from the king and queen.

Come on!

Remember when I worked at the Dorchester and climbed up through the kitchen? Well, one of my chefs ended up cooking for the royal family, and he and his wife were invited to the wedding. But since he's in their company day in and day out, the last thing he wants to do is watch the prince get married. He already poaches the kid's eggs every morning. So he's talked to the palace guards or whoever's in charge over there, and he's getting the invites transferred to my name. I'm letting his family stay at my place for the week, and they can use my car and boat. So are you in?

The pair flew first-class on British Airways, and unbeknownst to Jimmy, the Chief had booked the finest of the three rooftop suites at the Dorchester, which overlooks Hyde Park. Often called "the Harlequin," the Dorchester is where Elizabeth Taylor was awakened from a nap with news of her record-breaking contract to star in *Cleopatra*. The Chief and Jimmy would be staying in Taylor's suite. In fact, the hotel's former chef told Jimmy that the pink-marble bathroom attached to the second bedroom in the suite was installed solely for the actress.

"The Chief threw a party in the suite every night we were there," Jimmy recalls. "All his friends he had known and worked with in Europe were there. He wasn't showing off; it was just his last hurrah—and he knew that was the case more than anybody else."

On the morning of the wedding day, the two Bahamians put on their "gray morning suits, with the top hat, the whole nine yards," Jimmy says. A black stretch limousine pulled up to the Dorchester and transported them in style to as close to the cathedral as a limo could get on this festive day, when Londoners crowded the streets, intersections, and pubs.

Winding their way on foot through a maze of barricades, the pair was required to present their invitations at several security checkpoints before they were permitted to join the final queue and entered the magnificent baroque sanctuary, which had been built in 1675.

Jimmy might not have been a card-carrying member of the mother country fan club, but he watched in awe as Lady Diana Spencer made her nearly four-minute walk up the red-carpeted aisle, pulling a twenty-five-foot train of ivory taffeta and antique lace as she headed for the stiff arm of the Prince of Wales, who stood at attention in the full dress uniform of a naval commander. Jimmy's thoughts turned to his childhood on Kemp Road, sitting on the front porch every evening and listening to Olive and Kirkwood discuss the queen's family and their privileged lives. He glanced in the direction of Queen Elizabeth, who obviously was much older now than when she'd appeared week after week at the Nassau movie house—rerun after rerun of her coronation in 1953, when Jimmy wasn't yet a year old. He recalled the long-nosed British diplomat telling him to his face that he would never be an Englishman, but would be limited his entire life to the rank of British subject. He could hear the rejoicing and revelry in the streets all over again when the Bahamians finally won their independence, when he'd been so caught up in the euphoria he almost gave in and drank his first glass of champagne. And to think he was now sitting in a pew next to a lady and a lord, within easy tomato shot of Her Majesty.

He leaned over and whispered to the Chief, "Have I come full circle or what?"

TWENTY-TWO

"HE WAS KILLING HIMSELF. HIS MIND WAS ON THE WAY to being gone."

While that was Jimmy's assessment of the Chief, having closely observed his friend the week they'd spent together in England, surely the former kitchen staff of the hotel walked away from the Dorchester, whispering the same opinion. Jimmy guessed they were all shell-shocked to find the once burly Bahamian in such a deteriorated state.

"He was the definition of a cokehead. It was sad to see," Jimmy says. "He'd gotten married to a nice lady, but she couldn't turn him around. He was a mess, and they were headed for a divorce."

Winslow and his nose, on the other hand, never strayed far. And in a bizarre twist of circumstances, perhaps through his father's lofty connections, the well-heeled American was now affiliated with one of the intelligence arms of the U.S. government.

Jimmy, sorry to wake you up. I need to see you in Fort Lauderdale. When are you coming over next?

No time soon, Chief. I'm right in the middle of completing my apartments. What's up?

I'll tell you when I see you, but it's pretty important. I can explain everything when I see you.

It was ten o'clock at night when the Chief called Jimmy, the latter having just retired for the night, while it often took the former that long to start his day. Because of their friendship, Jimmy shut everything down and left the next afternoon for Florida.

Winslow needs us for what?

He's bringing in twenty thousand pounds of hashish.

Are you kidding me? I don't want nothing to do with it. There are plenty of people that can off-load it for him; he doesn't need me. Call Blondie; he'll get a Bimini crew together in no time. I've been out of this business for two years, and I'm not getting back into it as a favor to Winslow, that's for sure. You know I can't stand to be around the guy.

Jimmy, listen to me. It's completely safe.

Nothing's completely safe.

Believe it or not, he's working with the CIA on this run.

Are you serious?

Serious as a heart attack. That's why he needs us and nobody

else. He's waiting to hear from me today, and he'll explain every-
thing in detail, if you will agree to handle it.

What's the deal?

Thirty-five percent.

And why hashish? Where is that coming from?

Winslow did not arrive in Fort Lauderdale for another five
days, and by then Jimmy was not a happy camper. He'd flown
back to Nassau, worked for two days, put his construction
project back on hold, then flown back to Fort Lauderdale and
waited. With the crew scattered around the globe, there was
nothing for him to do except work out in the gym—and even
to do that he had to go out and buy all new athletic gear.
Otherwise, he sat in the Chief's air-conditioned house and
watched him rot away.

When Winslow finally showed up, he was accompanied by
a pair of military-style men introduced as Noah and Hutch.
They wore short-cropped hair, matching khaki trousers, and
tight white T-shirts that showed off their continuously flexed
muscles.

"I remained in Florida another couple of days to get a rundown on the operation," Jimmy says. "And talk about full of
themselves—I could see now why Winslow was so attracted to
these guys. At one point he remarked, 'Jimmy is a martial artist.' And Hutch says, 'You are, are you? I'm pretty good myself.
Do you train around here?' And I said, 'Yeah, when I'm in
town, I go to a little gym up the street here.' So he came along
with me that very afternoon, and while I was working out with
some weights, he went over to the boxing bag. He kept trying
to get my attention, to see if I was noticing his style, which I

guess he thought was advanced, but let me tell you, he was slow as Christmas. He wasn't in my league, that's for sure, but he didn't know that. He was all jabs—no cross, no hook, no uppercut. He definitely lacked the one-two combo. Anyway, before I went back to Nassau, the five of us were sitting on the back deck of the Chief's house, shooting the breeze, and Winslow made the mistake of opening his mouth too wide."

Hutch said he could take you.

Take me where?

Take you out.

Sorry, I don't date men.

He wants to spar with you, Jimmy.

No problem. Do you want to spar light or heavy, Hutch?

You tell me.

You want gloves or not?

Doesn't matter to me.

Fine, but let me explain something to you. I don't fight for free. I haven't since I was a kid learning how to fight in Nassau.

For once the Chief revealed some of his old enthusiam again, breaking into a wide grin, jumping to his feet, and throwing ten thousand dollars in cash on the patio table. "That's for the last man standing," he announced.

Forever trying to emulate the Chief, Winslow then proclaimed, "And I'll match it after I go to the bank."

Hutch, we can split this after I knock you cold, or I can knock you cold and keep all the money for myself. Your choice.

Or I can keep the entire amount after I knock you out.

Well, let's go to it, then. Winner takes all.

Jimmy and Hutch headed for the steps leading to the fenced yard and a grassy area that was almost identical in size to the boxing rings where Jimmy had fought professionally for much of his life. Winslow, of course, had paid little if any attention to the Chief when he had bragged about Jimmy being one of the top-ranked fighters of his kind in the country, but then again the Chief did much of his boasting when he was high on cocaine, which means Winslow would have been in the same boat. Hutch, in other words, never got the full story on Jimmy. Like anxious teenagers rushing out to the school playground to watch the bully box the jock, the three spectactors beat the two fighters down the stairs to the battleground. As Jimmy expected, Hutch immediately assumed a full upright stance—left arm and fist extended out front, to protect his rib cage and lower half of his body, while he kept his right fist clenched an inch or so in front of his nose. The defensive technique works well for professional boxers who can strike quickly with both hands, and it might have worked for Hutch, except Jimmy had no intention of taking lower body shots.

"It took me less than twenty seconds to knock the fool out," he says. "I threw something for him to block, and then I was going to hit him with my other fist, but he never blocked my first blow. It was over that fast. He went right down, staring up into the sun but out like a light. He reminded me of the cartoon character on TV—the guy who gets clobbered and you see stars floating around his head. You know which one I'm talking about? Noah looked ticked, or else he was disgusted with his other half. I think he realized then and there that the more muscular you become, the slower you become. These guys looked like they were in great shape, but they couldn't run two blocks if they had to. I just grabbed my money and laughed. Hutch didn't really come to until after I had finished packing. They had him sitting in the shade with a wet washcloth on his head, and when I went to say goodbye, he asked me what happened."

Well, there were two blows—the blow I hit you with, followed by the blow when you hit the ground.

———

Hutch phrased it at one point that he and his partner were intelligence "operatives," not that Jimmy hadn't already suspected as much. "They never showed me their IDs, obviously—I doubt they make IDs for those kinds of people. But you know what they say: if it looks like a rat, and smells like a rat, there's a good chance it's a rat."

Based on what Winslow had told the Chief, the Bahamian figured the pair was affiliated with one of the big U.S. intelligence agencies, probably the CIA, or else one of the special forces of the U.S. military. It wasn't so much their similar appearance, their mannerisms, or the sophisticated electronics gear they stored in the trunk of their car that blinked enough lights to land an airplane. It wasn't because of their intimate knowledge of a covert hashish operation that was said to be beyond the planning stage, proceeds of which, or so they hinted, would help supply arms to freedom fighters around the world, perhaps even the mujahideen fighters in Afghanistan, who were presently facing an invading Soviet Union army.

Rather, the clincher for Jimmy was the fact that Hutch and Noah had not so much as popped a beer can, rolled a joint, or snorted a line the entire seventy-two hours they were all together in Fort Lauderdale. Everybody else Jimmy had ever seen in Winslow's company was high as a kite. Come to think of it, unless he'd been retreating to the privacy of one of the Chief's several bathrooms, Winslow—for the first time the Bahamian could ever remember—didn't cut himself a single line either.

———

Judging from how jacked Noah and Hutch were that onetime California governor Ronald Reagan had replaced former Georgia governor Jimmy Carter as president in the White House, Jimmy concluded the dynamic duo—like Winslow and his ice cream–making father—were hard-core Republicans. Watching the Chief's television one day, the two had chided the former Democratic president for clobbering the country with high interest rates and then blaming Americans for suffering from malaise. They suggested that it was no coincidence that the 444-day Iranian hostage crisis, with its failed rescue mission that killed eight members of the U.S. armed forces, had ended literally minutes after Reagan took the oath of office. The pair explained to Jimmy that Carter even carried a telephone to Reagan's swearing-in ceremony at the U.S. Capitol, continuing negotiations to resolve the crisis right up until his last seconds in office. As it was, the newly inaugurated Republican was allowed the privilege of announcing the very afternoon of his first partial day in office that the fifty-two American hostages were finally coming home. And nice guy that he was, he appointed the Democrat he had defeated as his special emissary to West Germany to be the first American official to greet the hostages.

Although Americans had no way of knowing, Reagan had

assumed the reins of another secret operation launched by Carter, confirmed later by the latter's former national security adviser Zbigniew Brzezinski. The official timetable of this U.S. "intervention" ordered by Carter had it appear that CIA assistance to the mujahideen fighters began only after the Soviet Union had invaded Afghanistan, or more precisely December 24, 1979. But former CIA director Robert Gates later disclosed in his memoirs that the agency had, in fact, been providing extensive aid to the Afghan rebels some six months before the Soviets crossed the border to begin their demolition of the Islamic republic. Asked later about Gates's revelation, Brzezinski confirmed that on July 3, 1979, Carter had indeed signed a secret national security directive to funnel armaments and other assistance to the mujahideen resistance.

Having inherited the secret operation that Carter set into motion, Reagan would soon sign his own national security directive that drastically escalated the covert mission, to the extent that the bearded Afghan rebels—who, with their long, flowing robes and open-toed sandals, resembled fourteenth-century tribesmen—would soon be tapping into state-of-the-art reconnaissance and intelligence. It reached a point that, with the help of American intelligence operatives, the rebel fighters were tracking Communist troop movements via U.S. satellites and then pounding the invaders with long-range sniper rifles, wire-guided antitank missiles, shoulder-fired Stinger antiaircraft missiles, C-4 plastic explosives, and other modern weaponry that the CIA was said to be conveying to the front lines. All of which required money.

It had long been alleged, albeit hardly reported by U.S. news agencies, that to help raise funds for its myriad covert operations, the Virginia-based CIA turned a blind eye to the underworld, especially drug smuggling, which garnered enormous profits. Jimmy wasn't certain who was purchasing, peddling, and profiting from this particular cargo of hashish—a THC-rich resinous by-product of the cannabis plant collected, dried, and compressed into round, cookie-like sheets—and he didn't care to know. Whether the beneficiaries were the Afghans or the Israelis—as also was suggested by Hutch and Noah—didn't concern him. What did concern him, besides the fact that he was coming out of retirement for reasons that still bothered him, was that the unprecedented drug run would take him into the belly of the U.S. government—central Virginia—not terribly far from CIA headquarters and the White House.

"I was told that the 'agency' would see to everything working out, that there was nothing for me to worry about," Jimmy says. "But it was all too much for me. I'd never been that far north on a weed run—I'd never been north of Florida. I'm a little island boy, and I still couldn't figure out what they needed me for. I had a bad feeling—didn't like leaving my comfort zone."

═══

The nation of Israel was anything but a Mediterranean playground in 1981. Invisible though its operatives were, the CIA was never far away, keeping tabs on—and learning from—the Palestine Liberation Organization (PLO), which at the time was earning hundreds of millions of dollars from hashish trafficking. The illicit drug profits were even higher in Syria and

Lebanon to the north, where hashish was a major cash crop—more than one hundred thousand tons produced annually.

One Palestinian terrorist must have been stoned on hashish in 1981, when he hopped onto a windsurf board and glided under sail into Israel's seaport city of Acco, where he actually proceeded to take a hostage. Fortunately, the Israeli sunbather escaped when the kidnapper fell asleep. If that wasn't bizarre enough, one month later a hot air balloon manned by Palestinian terrorists floated above Israel, purportedly to cause mayhem and destruction. But the slow-moving balloon was easily brought down in Galilee, where the infiltrators were promptly dispatched.

Certainly the overall situation in Israel was far more serious and dangerous. Israeli troops that year had repeatedly attacked Syrian and Syrian-supported terrorist targets in southern Lebanon, while Israel's warplanes destroyed antiaircraft missile positions on the outskirts of Beirut. In addition, three months before Jimmy's scheduled rendezvous with the several tons of hashish, Tel Aviv had ordered an air strike that obliterated one of Iraq's nuclear reactors near Baghdad—never again to generate suspected weapons of mass destruction. Weeks later, the Palestinians started shelling the more populated regions of northern Israel, which resulted in Israel's bombing of PLO headquarters in Beirut.

Meanwhile, thousands of miles away, the Israeli government, supposedly with the assistance of the CIA, was rumored to be supplying light arms and shoulder-fire missiles to Nicaragua's Contra rebels, who were battling the Cuban- and Soviet-supported Sandinista government that had just ousted Nicaraguan president Anastasio Somoza Debayle.

It was all enough to make a Bahamian's head spin. Especially after it became obvious that the twenty thousand pounds of hashish that he was to off-load onto the trawler *Grand Celeste* exactly two hundred miles off the coast of Hog Island, Virginia, was cultivated and compressed in Afghanistan, where the processors were stamping the slabs with anti-Soviet slogans like "Crush the Kremlin" and "Smoke Russia Away."

Noah and Hutch were right. Jimmy would have to trust them for this run.

TWENTY-THREE

HE HAD SEEN BLUE HIS ENTIRE LIFE—NOTHING BUT sky and water. Now, in the space of six days and nine hundred miles, everything was green—flora, fields, and forests. Giant, towering trees, unlike any he'd ever laid eyes on before. Jimmy now understood why the English had chosen the lush banks of a river they christened the James to build their first permanent settlement in the Americas in 1607. They'd called it Jamestown.

President John Tyler also appreciated what he saw in the James, born fresh in Virginia's Allegheny Mountains, flowing brackish over Richmond's cobblestones, and emptying salty into Chesapeake Bay. The rebellious tenth president of the

United States, one of Virginia's sons who'd helped organize the Southern Confederacy, was so enchanted with the broad and lazy river that before he'd finished his one term in the White House, he purchased a previously owned eighteenth-century plantation and house along its tidal banks, renaming it Sherwood Forest after the president's outlaw hero—Robin Hood—who robbed the rich to provide for the poor. After Tyler and his second wife, Julia, completed several modern additions (the president, after all, would eventually have fifteen children, eight of them from his first marriage) to the circa 1720 house, including a huge ballroom and wings on each side, its frame facade became the widest in America, measuring more than three hundred feet.

When Hutch revealed the ultimate destination for the shipment of Asian hashish as being in the vicinity of Sherwood Forest, Jimmy smiled at the irony. Or was it serendipity—given the tens of thousands of dollars he had deposited in the cookie jars of Long Island?

"After I knocked out Hutch, he and I became friends—he had complete respect for me," Jimmy says. "No more Mr. Macho. He wouldn't even let me carry my bags. He barely left my side, kind of like a puppy dog. And he started to talk, suggesting what Winslow and the Chief had said—that it was a CIA operation. He was pretty knowledgeable, knew all the percentages of what everybody would make, and spoke about the various countries and groups that the CIA supported in the Middle East. He probably would have told me everything he knew, but I told him I didn't want to know."

Three boats slid out of south Florida bound for Virginia—the *Grand Celeste* and two of the Sport Fishermen the Chief hadn't purposely sunk, each requiring hours of elbow grease to remove the seagull droppings. "I told the Chief time and time again that he should have also sunk the *Grand Celeste*, because that boat would come back to haunt us," Jimmy notes.

As for the Chief, he was growing weaker and more paranoid by the day, and—as if anybody expected otherwise—he told Jimmy that he would be staying behind to monitor developments for this operation. The Chief actually relished the times he was left alone, when he wasn't expected to communicate—carry on a normal conversation—because communication now required too much thinking. Instead, he would shut his opaque curtains and sleep off the day. His house in Fort Lauderdale—or, more precisely, its food- and beverage-stained sofa—had become one of two comfort zones, his final resting places so to speak, as his big frame rotted away. The other was his house—or chaise lounge—in Nassau. Given his coke addiction, it became increasingly difficult for him to travel between his two homes, not an hour apart by private jet and limousine. In other words, the Chief had all the money in the world at his disposal, but no stamina to spend it.

All that Winslow relied on the Chief for these days was his next snort. Thus, it was Jimmy whom the American depended upon to assemble a trustworthy yet skeletal crew for the top-secret operation—although, as the Bahamian assured him, this drug run would frankly be no more clandestine than the others. As Jimmy told Winslow, every smuggling operation he'd orchestrated during his decade in the drug trade, while overt, he had to also be *covert*, or else he would have been locked up a long time ago.

≡

The Intracoastal Waterway isn't the continuous body of inland water that some suspect. Rather, it's a jumble of bays, sounds, rivers, inlets, swamps, canals, and ocean that stretches from Maine to Florida to Texas. Jimmy purchased navigational charts for the south Florida to Tidewater Virginia portion, and put them to use early one morning in September 1981 with his fellow skippers—Captain Dave, a seasoned sailor, smuggler, and longtime friend of the Chief's who took the big wheel of the *Grand Celeste*; and Blondie, who, as he promised Jimmy, was found swinging in a hammock in Bimini. Boat traffic was extremely heavy in the beginning, especially in Florida, as the snowbirds plied south and in every other wrong direction, making it all the more difficult to relax. But the congestion subsided dramatically by the time the flotilla floated into the dark and murky waters of the Great Dismal Swamp of North Carolina and Virginia, where in 1763 a young surveyor named George Washington had organized a land company that set out to drain the massive marsh and log its virgin cypress and white cedar—almost to its demise centuries later. Today, the mysterious swamp is spooky again, and practically impossible to reach on foot. For more than a hundred years, hundreds of runaway slaves concealed themselves in the swamp's thick muck—building rudimentary huts alongside the lizards, salamanders, and poisonous snakes. A wide-eyed Jimmy couldn't begin to absorb so much eerie scenery.

The Bahamian had no problem persuading Digger to sign

on as the first—and only—mate of the *Grand Celeste*. The dyslexic had not yet found honest work, not that he needed to anytime soon. He was delighted to hang his strobe around his neck again and be part of a crew. Like Winslow, Noah had mentioned to Jimmy the day they were introduced in Florida that the fewer the players for the clandestine operation, the better for everybody. At the same time, the operative assured the Bahamian that there would be sufficient manpower to off-load both the mother ship—in this case an absolutely gorgeous 140-foot triple-mast sailing schooner that Jimmy assumed was owned if not captained by a wealthy Arabian—as well as Jimmy's three boats once they slid onto the autumn shade of Virginia's Sherwood Forest.

"One of our Fishermen had some minor engine problems on the trip north, so we left it at a marina near the mouth of the James to get it repaired," Jimmy recalls. "Actually, we had more than a week to kill before the sailboat would get into position off the coast—we had to hurry up and wait, in other words. That's the one thing about the smuggling business: you have to hurry up and wait. So we went ahead and got our rooms in a little motel in colonial Williamsburg, and we played tourists. We rented a car and saw the Rockefeller house, visited William and Mary College, and then we drove north—Yorktown, Baltimore, Annapolis, Washington, D.C. We visited all the monuments, just four guys having fun, you know? And the whole time I would hop into telephone booths to stay in contact with Winslow, who was getting updates from Noah and Hutch on the schooner's progress. How they trusted him for an operation like this, I will never know."

The morning air was crisp and horizon clear when Jimmy and Blondie helped untie the *Grand Celeste* and waved good-bye to Captain Dave, who was now navigating the large trawler from the Chesapeake Bay into the Atlantic Ocean, where, two hundred miles off the sparsely populated Eastern Shore of Virginia, it would rendezvous with the tall sailing ship. Once the off-load was completed, the ship would hook up with the two smaller boats twenty-five miles offshore—a weed line well outside U.S. territorial waters. Way back in 1793, the United States had established a three-mile territorial limit that remained in the books until the 1980s, when Ronald Reagan cited national security concerns as one reason to increase the country's territorial waters to a dozen miles. Still, for the first time ever since he began smuggling contraband, Jimmy wasn't concerned about encountering federal law enforcement officials. The way he figured it, he was now working for them for once. He was worried, however, about the local harbor police or Fish and Game officers going about their duties, like a surprise inspection, perhaps, of one of Jimmy's three boats to make sure they were carrying sufficient life preservers or hadn't fished above the limit. Were that to happen, and the illegal cargo discovered, he knew that he and his crew would be the fall guys, CIA fingerprints or not. It wasn't like the arresting officers were going to believe a Bahamian national, his bearded face concealed like a pirate's behind a bandanna, baby-sitting a multimillion-dollar boatload of hashish, when he swore up and down on his stepmother's grave that he was smuggling drugs on behalf of the president of the United States. Jimmy could hear himself attempting in his island accent: "Don't worry, officers. Everything you see here is legitimate. This hashish is the property of the U.S. government, so go back to your fish counts and have a nice day." He would be better off arguing that he was the pope.

It was agreed by all parties that the valuable shipment would better be distributed onto three boats, as opposed to leaving the entire stash on the trawler. In addition, reentry into the Chesapeake would be staggered, so as to attract as little attention as possible. That way, if one of the boats got stopped and boarded by the authorities, the entire cargo of hashish would not be compromised—and there would be less chance of the drug scandal of the century unfolding in the press and sending shockwaves from Norfolk, Virginia, up the Potomac River, and into Washington.

"We decided that I would go in first," Jimmy recalls. Blondie's boat would follow several miles behind, with the *Grand Celeste* bringing up the rear—all three vessels remaining in constant VHF radio contact. It was agreed that Jimmy would check in with the other two boats every half hour, the signal that the operation was proceeding as planned. If the radio contact suddenly stopped and did not resume after a specified period of time, the other two boats were to turn around and head out to sea. Similarly, if Jimmy was to radio the other boats and one of the captains did not respond, he and the other vessel would follow the identical bailout plan, careful to steer clear of each other in the process. At that point, Noah and Hutch would be alerted via marine radio, which the pair of operatives would be monitoring from the shore, and the captains would await new instructions. If too much time passed and the boats were bobbing around in a watery limbo, Jimmy instructed his captains to dump their loads, head for home, and go into hiding if necessary.

"Actually, I wasn't nervous. I don't get nervous; it's just one of those things," Jimmy says. "The only thing that bothered me was Winslow telling me time and time again to make sure that I protected a white duffel bag that would be off-loaded with the hashish."

What's in it?

Something important for me.

Something important for you, huh?

I just want to make sure it gets delivered to me, Jimmy. I can't have it getting lost in the shuffle.

I'll see that it stays safe, don't worry.

Thanks. Remember, it's a white duffel bag.

Got it.

Passing through one of the several shipping channels created by the twenty-three-mile-long Chesapeake Bay Bridge-Tunnel connecting Virginia's Eastern Shore with the cities of Norfolk and Virginia Beach, Jimmy radioed Captain Dave and Blondie: "This is Divine. You boys catching anything?"

"Just a couple of blues," replied Blondie, while Captain Dave weighed in: "That's more than we're catching."

In other words, everything was proceeding on schedule. Soon, the channel markers brought Jimmy within sight of the massive Norfolk Navy Base, the largest military port in the world, with berths for seventy-five cruisers, destroyers, submarines, and aircraft carriers, their towering bridges and flight control decks visible for miles over the Bahamian's left shoulder.

"Divine day out here, even with no bites," Jimmy radioed, when he rounded the tip of Newport News and began his journey up the James, his fishing boat compass pointing northwest in the direction of Jamestown Island. "Caught a rockfish near the bridge, but too small to keep," Captain Dave checked in. "No fish chasing me," relayed Blondie.

"I went right into the bay and right up the river, no problems whatsoever," Jimmy says. "The scenery was absolutely gorgeous—big trees on both sides of the river, and every so often a plantation house, like the pictures I saw in my school books. It was like going back in time."

Off the starboard side, beyond the noisy shipyards of Newport News, Jimmy spotted Mulberry Island and the postmedieval-style Matthew Jones House—T-shaped, unusually enough, and built in 1727. To his left he could make out Bacon's Castle, unaware it was the oldest documented house in Virginia, having been constructed in 1665. Supporters of Nathaniel Bacon occupied the home during the Bacon Rebellion.

Farther upriver, kneeling archeologists could be seen excavating the original site of Kingsmill, both a plantation house and colonial-era tavern that was destroyed in 1843. And opposite Jamestown Island was the fourteen-hundred-acre Chippokes Plantation, acquired by governor Sir William Berkeley in 1671 and named after the Indian chief who befriended the early English settlers.

By the look of his map, it wouldn't be long before Jimmy passed the historic seaport of Claremont, home to only three hundred Virginians, several of them direct descendants of the English settlers who first camped on its shoreline in the early seventeenth century. At Claremont, the Bahamian would cut back the throttle and allow the trailing boats sufficient time to catch up with his Fisherman. Here the chart showed the winding river turning just about due north, then after a distance of ten or so miles, sharply southwest again. Where the riverbanks reach their farthest northern point and begin to bend south, one finds a thick stand of trees—for centuries named Sherwood Forest.

Jimmy was instructed to look for an ordinary post-and-plank dock, none too wide, with a white wooden bench at its deep end. If he didn't see any geese—the plastic decoy kind—crowded on the bench, then there were unforeseen problems and Jimmy was to turn the three boats back downriver and await further instructions. He eyed his waterproof watch, its dial glowing now beneath the twilight sky. He was right on schedule—one hour before sunset. With the other boats no more than thirty minutes in his wake, the contraband would all be unloaded by dusk. He looked around him at the unfamiliar scenery, which all looked the same. Given the thick foliage that surrounded his boat, the Bahamian wasn't accustomed to feeling so enclosed. Even when anchored off the distant coastline of Colombia, he had an entire sea at his back in which to retreat. On this otherwise narrow and now darkening river, there would be little, if any, room to run. He got a chill and zipped up his jacket, realizing how ready he was to close this particular chapter of a most unusual operation. He peered through binoculars, spotted six geese-a-laying on the bench, and drifted in.

TWENTY-FOUR

HE CREPT UP TO THE DOCK AND FOR SEVERAL MINUTES just sat there—Jimmy and the plastic geese, one of which had been strategically placed atop another, as if they were lovebirds trying to make goslings, or gosling decoys. Hutch's doing, no doubt. Soon, the Bahamian heard the familiar sound of sliding doors, and he glanced up to see a small army, maybe a dozen men, climbing out of four dark-colored vans—their exact color and make he couldn't determine in the dwindling twilight. But they had every appearance of U.S. government property. Jimmy immediately radioed the other boats, passing the signal to Captain Dave and Blondie that he was dockside and about to unload. In other words, "get your

butts in gear and let's wrap up this unprecedented mission."
Uncertain how the young men might react, Jimmy purposely
avoided locking eyes. Even if they didn't speak, they were
punctual.

"They had all their vans in place and out these guys came.
Every one of them was in good shape, dressed in black from
head to toe. It reminded me of a James Bond movie. They
looked like spies or perhaps even military, although that was
doubtful," says Jimmy. "For all I knew, they were baseball players. Again, I didn't want to know. They made it apparent they
were in a hurry, so I opened up the hold of my boat and we
began off-loading onto the dock and into their vans. But believe
me, this was no Chinese fire drill—these guys were timing:
boom-boom-boom-boom-boom—let's get it done, you know? That
was their attitude—no nonsense. We have a job to do; let's do
it and get out. These guys just took over."

The other two boats arrived momentarily, making for absolutely no downtime. Once the dirty dozen finished loading
their long vans, per Noah's earlier instructions—he and Hutch
were nowhere to be seen—they placed the remainder of the
hashish, which turned out to be the Chief's and Jimmy's share,
into a horse trailer that was parked near the water's edge. And
then without so much as a good-bye, the men sped off into the
night, leaving only the Tidewater dust in their wake.

"Now it was just the four of us sitting there in the dark,
but I was feeling good because our boats were empty,
although I was still hanging on to that white bag," Jimmy
notes. "I'm not one who likes to be lied to; I've always been
straight up and expect the people I work with to be straight
up. It was always that way, no question. So I decided to open

up this bag belonging to Winslow, and it had these hard bricks inside wrapped in plastic—about six inches long, four inches wide, and maybe an inch thick. They looked like rubber."

Blondie, what is this?

Not exactly sure, Divine.

Is it hashish?

It's not hashish; I know that much.

Are you sure?

Open up the hashish and look for yourself.

"So for the first time I checked out the hashish, which to me looked like Frisbees—round packages with a horse stamped on them, a horse head. Each disc was wrapped in tinfoil with cellophane over that, then another layer of paper. I've never seen anything like it before in my life. But it was definitely different than what I was carrying in Winslow's bag."

Digger, come over here. What is this?

Nothing I've ever messed with.

Captain Dave, you know what this is?

Do I look like a drug addict? Ask me if that's a halibut in your cooler, and I can tell you.

You think this is heroin, Blondie?

Wouldn't be surprised, knowing that Winslow feller. Where is he anyway?

He's up in D.C. somewhere. You know something, I'm not stupid. I'm not gonna sit here and take any more chances for this fool. I'll do time for weed, but I'm not going to get caught holding heroin. Hashish is risky enough, but they'll never charge me with bringing heroin into the United States. I'm going to dump this, and I'm going to do it now.

Are you serious?

Between us, it never came off the mother ship. Digger, did you ever see anybody hand us a white bag?

Nope, never did.

Captain Dave?

I just steer the boats. I don't even count the number of fish we catch; bad luck!

Blondie, you see any bag come off the mother?

Nope.

Besides his promise to remain all but handcuffed to the white duffel bag, the Bahamian had also agreed to stay put at the dock until a well-to-do couple in their midfifties showed up from northern Virginia—friends of the Chief who lived in the hunt country just outside Washington and who Jimmy had twice taken fishing when they were visiting Nassau. In time they would drive up in their big white four-door pickup truck, rearing stallions on the mud flaps, fulfilling their promise to the Chief that they would haul off and store his share of the illicit cargo. John and his wife, whom he called Princess, had dropped off the blue horse trailer in Sherwood Forest earlier that day and then spent the afternoon enjoying a leisurely lunch and touring colonial Williamsburg. Jimmy didn't mind waiting around for the couple, but he didn't like holding Winslow's bag. So while the rest of the crew stayed tied to the dock, Jimmy jumped into his boat and fired up the engine.

"It only took me a few minutes. I ran back out into the river, tied the duffel bag onto a spare anchor, and dropped both overboard. Unfortunately I didn't get to watch it sink because it was too dark, but I know it went straight to the bottom. And the second I let it go I said out loud, 'There are going to be some mad people and one upset dude in particular.' And then I laughed."

Jimmy despised hard drugs. He looked with nothing short of disdain on anybody who produced, trafficked, peddled, abused, or got hooked on them—with the exception of the Chief, who was now just a shell of the smiling, energetic person he'd once been. Although he didn't realize it, the Bahamian would soon get his revenge for the toll that cocaine had taken on his friend. Indeed, in due time the Western Hemisphere's biggest coke traffickers would have more reason to fear Jimmy than they would the entire law enforcement community.

≡

It was well after midnight when the crew, after stopping for a late dinner, arrived back at the Williamsburg motel. As expected, there was a message for Jimmy to call Winslow right away, regardless of the hour. And when the American answered the phone, he at least had enough manners to first congratulate the Bahamian and his hand-selected crew for a job well done. But Jimmy could hear through the receiver that the suspense was killing Winslow.

By the way, you've got my special bag, right?

No, it never came off.

Right.

I'm serious.

Don't mess with me, man. It's not funny.

I swear it never came off. It never got put on the trawler.

Cut it out, man. Level with me here.

I am leveling with you. I don't have it.

This sucks, Jimmy. Do you realize the significance of what we're talking about here?

No, I don't. You never told me anything about the bag, remember?

Jimmy, they assured me that the bag was on the sailboat and that it would come off. This was my cut of the deal, man. Don't be lying to me.

Winslow, be careful whom you call a liar.

Before the autumn sun had stirred Jimmy awake, there was a loud knock on the door. After he'd hung up the phone several hours before, he could almost see Winslow pacing nervously back and forth, trying to ascertain—while not able to question anybody—how his share of the valuable shipment had vanished into thin air. With Noah and Hutch disappearing altogether— doubtful to resurface anytime soon—they were of no help to him, and there was simply no way for Winslow to reach the captain of the schooner—who for all he knew was docked in Bermuda by now, celebrating his safe delivery with glasses of champagne. Soon, Jimmy had guessed right, Winslow wouldn't be able to stand his own company anymore, and he would jump into his rented sports car and race the 130 miles to Williamsburg. And then came the knock on the motel door.

They promised me the bag would come off. Noah confirmed it was on the schooner. So I need to find out what happened.

Well, during all the commotion it apparently got left on board the schooner. My captain did not see it. Off-loads are pretty intense, Winslow. The two crews have a job to do, and they have to do it fast, like clockwork. There's no time to remember something like a small brown suitcase, particularly when it belongs to somebody who's not there asking for it.

No, the captain of the sailboat had explicit instructions to trans-fer the bag to your trawler, Jimmy. And it wasn't brown; it was white. Do you know what was in that bag?

You still haven't told me.

It was my cut of this entire deal. It was that valuable. This is going to mess up some people.

Or not, Jimmy thought, as he wiped the sleep from his eyes and put on a pot of motel coffee. Winslow accepted a cup, but he didn't need it. His entire body was shaking while he paced back and forth across the orange shag carpet. Jimmy knew very little about heroin, but he figured the bricks stacked square in the duffel bag were the highly addictive drug in its purest form. And given Afghanistan was likely the source of the cargo of hashish, it made sense that the heroin originated from there too. After all, the central Asian country supplied the majority of the world's opium. Even the Afghan government depended on opium production to drive the country's economy, for what it was worth. Jimmy tried doing the math in his head, but he couldn't begin to fathom the value of the contents of the bag, which now likely *was* brown, resting with the catfish on the muddy bottom of the James River.

"I didn't want to be a part of it," Jimmy says. "Because if down the road they had said we smuggled in twenty thousand pounds of hashish and thirty or however many pounds of heroin, where do you think I would have been today? I'd have been under the jail, because they would have built a special jail on top of me."

Sorry, Winslow, I feel for you. And I'd like to stay and help you find this bag, but I've got three boats casting off in one hour for Florida, and I'm behind schedule as it is.

TWENTY-FIVE

THE CHIEF ANSWERED AT LEAST FIVE COLLECT CALLS from Winslow before Jimmy tied up his Fisherman in Fort Lauderdale. At which time the phone stopped ringing. Careful not to label Jimmy a liar—or a thief—the American pleaded his case every way he knew how with the Chief, imploring him to find out whatever he could from his Bahamian friend about the missing white duffel bag. But Winslow knew when all was said and done that the Chief's loyalty would remain with Jimmy. And from that point on Winslow was gone, never to be heard from again.

"No calls, no this, no that," Jimmy says. "But we still haven't made a dime—not collected a dime for the entire operation, which lasted longer than a month, when you count all the planning and organizing that had gone into it. I had captains and crew to pay, so I went ahead and took care of everybody out of my own pocket. I learned my lesson. I told the Chief good-bye, and I went home."

—
—

Jimmy was happy to be one of the Kemp Road gang again, so to speak. Or at least he was hanging out with several of his childhood friends from his infamous Nassau neighborhood, some of whom by now were on their second or third marriages. As for Jimmy, he was glad to be spending some quality time again with his daughter, who lived with her happily remarried mother on the island.

Hollywood film director Irvin Kershner soon arrived in Nassau to shoot the 1983 James Bond movie *Never Say Never Again*, starring Sean Connery, in what would be his final appearance as Agent 007, and the stunning Nicaraguan-born beauty Barbara Carrera, otherwise known to moviegoers as Fatima Blush. When the movie maker started inquiring among the locals who on the island might be capable of maneuvering a speedboat at full throttle around all sorts of floating—if not exploding—obstacles, while also towing a beautiful actress on skis, he heard a resounding chorus: "That would be Jimmy." In retrospect, Kershner should have made Jimmy the movie's martial arts instructor, given the Bahamian's expertise when it came to self-defense. Instead, the director brought in a young Steven Seagal, who actually wound up breaking Connery's wrist while trying to demonstrate a karate move.

"I was running the boat for the actress when she was ski-ing," Jimmy recalls. "Oh Lord, she looked nice. I mean, so what if she couldn't ski? Her double did most of the skiing anyway, so for me it was twice as nice to get to pull two lovely ladies around the harbor. The double would do the run-up onto the ski ramp, and in the movie the actress would wind up in James Bond's arms. They cut me out of the final picture, though. All they showed was the actress and the back of the boat. But I learned a lot about filming. It was funny to see the movie when it came out, because you saw the characters driving up the road that leads to Paradise Island, but once they arrived there they were in Coral Harbour—a completely different place."

No sooner had Jimmy finished his second brush with stardom—first with a dolphin, and now with a fictional agent of the British Secret Intelligence Services—than the Chief was calling him again, requesting another huge favor. The Chief's excuse this time was valid, however, since his intentions were to finally pay his friend for the outstanding hashish run. The Chief explained that he had lined up a buyer for the trailer of "hay," which to this day sat unhitched on the couple's several-hundred-acre horse farm near affluent Middleburg, Virginia, some fifty miles west of Washington. Jimmy had recently read an article in one of the newspapers about the horse country outside Washington, where actress Elizabeth Taylor had been living until recently announcing her divorce from her sixth husband (seven, if you count her two marriages to Richard Burton), U.S. senator John Warner. She'd said she was so bored living in the Virginia countryside—she likened the sena-tor's twenty-seven-hundred-acre Atoka Estate to a chicken coop—she'd eaten and drunk with abandon until she could no longer squeeze into her designer clothes.

I'd really like it if you and I could handle the delivery. I can't have the buyer coming to John and Princess's farm; too much could go wrong.

The entire load goes to one place?

Yes, it's a one-shot deal.

Should I really do this, Chief?

It's too personal for somebody else besides you and me, Jimmy. And I can't do it alone; you know that. Plus it's the only way you're going to recoup your money. After all we've been through—after all you've been through, I should say—we can't have something go wrong now. Too many innocent people would go down. And I'm going with you; can you believe it? It'll be our last operation. It's only fitting we ride off into the sunset together.

"The Chief was coked out of his mind," Jimmy says. "He was so messed up by this time that I wondered how he could have even set up this sale in the first place. He probably kept getting phone calls from John and Princess, saying, 'Come and haul this manure out of our barnyard.' This poor couple otherwise had nothing to do with drug trafficking, no stake in the business whatsoever. They stood to gain nothing all along. For whatever reason—I guess friendship—they agreed to tow their very own horse trailer, filled with millions of dollars' worth of hashish, from Sherwood Forest to their farm. What an incredible risk, given the consequences. But you have to know the Chief—have to be around him to understand what they were thinking. He was in the limelight, and people wanted to be there with him, wanted to do everything he was doing. He was a lot of fun to be around. Plus, he was never ashamed of the business. He did what he did for a living; he made plenty of money; and if it was okay with him, it was okay with everybody else."

⸻

His legs that unsteady, the Chief might as well have been standing on a rowboat in a gale instead of the plane he and Jimmy flew from Miami to Washington Dulles International Airport, its tarmac closer to the town of Middleburg than the nation's capital. After touching down, the pair of Bahamians rented a U-Haul truck and soon were driving west on Route 50, an old Indian path named the John Mosby Highway. In less than one hour's time they found themselves surrounded by sprawling green pastures bordered by centuries-old moss-covered stone walls that rivaled the fences in England.

"John and Princess had a beautiful farm," Jimmy says. "I remember we passed a polo club then turned off the road onto a long tree-lined dirt lane leading directly to their house."

Given all the dust hanging in the air, the couple was outside to greet the pair of drug smugglers before Jimmy could turn off the truck's engine. He was wondering what their initial reaction would be upon seeing the Chief for the first time in nearly two years. But Jimmy had hinted to the couple months before in Sherwood Forest, and even during their earlier trips to the Bahamas, that the friend they shared was, as he put it, not himself anymore. The couple had always been comfortable around Jimmy, especially enjoying the times they had spent fishing together. One thing about throwing a line into the water, Jimmy had told them: it's a great way to get to know your fellow man. Recalling his literature lessons from the Chief, he quoted Henry David Thoreau as saying, "Many men go fishing all of their lives without knowing that it is not fish they are after."

"They were very happy to see us, let me tell you," Jimmy says. "For the longest time they'd had all this hashish sitting behind their barn. I mean, can you imagine? These people are socialites—they hang out with the hoity-toity crowd. They must have asked each other a thousand times, 'What have we gotten ourselves into?' worried night after night about what the newspaper headlines would say, imagined all the *sip-sip* spreading from neighbor to neighbor. It certainly would be more titillating than some land baron's wife running off with the pool boy."

Dressed in a red plaid button-down shirt, rust-colored corduroys, and Bass penny loafers, John gladly rolled up his sleeves and helped the two traffickers transfer the packages of hashish from the blue horse trailer to the U-Haul. The diminutive Princess, dressed in yellow cords, a white blouse, and a Louis Vuitton scarf, kept a nervous watch next to the black lawn jockey who lit the way to the couple's nineteenth-century manor house. She was prepared to hightail it—in her brown riding boots—to the barn, should any unannounced visitors pull into the driveway.

Fortunately for everybody, within a half hour's time, John and Princess were standing arm in arm on their neatly manicured lawn, no doubt breathing a heavy sigh of relief while waving good-bye to the Chief and Jimmy, the two callers knowing better than to accept the couple's invitation to stay for a late lunch. Jimmy could sense that the fondness the couple once felt for the

Chief had fizzled long before their arrival in Virginia. They turned the big orange truck back onto the state road and retraced their route through Middleburg's quaint streets, where Jimmy informed his pale and sweating passenger that the Vatican had built John F. Kennedy his own church in the town so that he and his family would have a place to kneel during their weekend pony rides. Another hour and the pair of Bahamians reached Interstate 95 in Maryland, and shortly before midnight, in a driving rainstorm, pulled into an empty parking lot in an industrial section of Hartford, Connecticut.

"As directed," Jimmy says, "we left the keys in the ashtray and walked away."

As it was, a drug dealer the Chief had never personally met, likely with ties to the mob, closed the book on what by every indication was a clandestine CIA operation that had stretched from Afghanistan to Florida to Virginia and now New England.

Indeed, the question had crossed Jimmy's mind more than once while driving north that night how unlikely it was that the biggest weed smugglers in the Bahamas would end their careers in a dark, puddle-filled parking lot in the capital of Connecticut, a half hour south of Massachusetts—unfamiliar geography that would come back to haunt the pair one day.

TWENTY-SIX

SEMIRETIREMENT SUITED JIMMY. HE WAS BUILDING A cottage here and there, just like Olive used to do. He didn't keep so busy that when the urge struck he couldn't grab his fishing pole, jump into his boat, and troll the deep water off New Providence's northern coast.

It was autumn 1985, and Nassau was teeming with the season's first tourists. Paradise Island was known the world over as a destination for beach lovers and card sharks—popularity that brought with it so much development and congestion that the Bahamian hardly even recognized Kemp Road anymore. The islanders had changed too, and not for the better. Cocaine use was so prevalent among Nassauites that it had now reached epidemic proportions, and Jimmy in turn grew to hate the addictive white powder even more.

That same year crack cocaine would make its first appearance in the Bahamas, promising users a whole-body orgasm, followed, unfortunately, by a high-anxiety crash that carried with it depression, paranoia, hallucinations, and crimes of violence. Even the Black Moses—longtime Bahamian prime minister Lynden O. Pindling—was caught up in the rising sea of cocaine that flooded Nassau. Courtroom testimony that same year fingered the nation's leader for offering protection to Medellín kingpin Carlos Lehder, whose billion-dollar operation, which supplied 80 percent of the cocaine snorted by Americans, was based not in Colombia but on tiny Norman Cay between Nassau and Eleuthera.

The prime minister, according to court documents, was allegedly paid eighty-eight thousand dollars in cash on the twenty-second of every month to protect Lehder, who had purchased most of the cay and, in the words of a senior cartel member, turned it into his personal "Sodom and Gomorrah" of drugs and sex, without an honest policeman in sight. The cartel member described in court being picked up from his airplane in a convertible Land Rover filled with "naked women" welcoming him to paradise.

Lehder's cocaine-laden planes sometimes landed hourly on the island's 3,300-foot airstrip, ringed by heavily armed guards and Doberman attack dogs. Before 1985 drew to a close, Bahamian deputy prime minister Arthur Hanna stood before microphones and called on Pindling to resign—although to no avail.

Meanwhile, that same year, a jury in Miami convicted

Chief Minister Norman Saunders of the Turks and Caicos Islands—where the Chief delivered his thousands of cases of Coca-Cola—of traveling to the United States to engage in narcotics transactions. The DEA, which had long been pressuring the Bahamians to mop up Norman Cay and other cocaine-laden hotspots in the archipelago, grew tired of looking the other way. In addition, the U.S. Coast Guard stepped up its interdiction operations throughout the entire Bahamian chain. If the Bahamians, who were understandably lacking for manpower and equipment, couldn't crack down on the drug traffickers in their territorial waters, the United States would do it for them.

In the spring of 1985, the ninety-five-foot Coast Guard "grass-cutter" *Cape Current*, its smokestack painted with sixty green marijuana sprigs to indicate the ship's number of drug busts, left Coast Guard Base Miami. She was understaffed with a crew of eleven, including thirty-one-year-old reservist Alan Freedman, a Miami cruise-line manager and former Coast Guard officer required to serve two weeks of active duty a year. The *Cape Current* had aboard its bridge a new skipper, Lt. J.G. Brad R. Lee, and it was his first day in command of the U.S. cutter. He'd been transferred to Miami from Honolulu, where, as an ensign, he and his fellow officers aboard the Coast Guard cutter *Munro* spent three months in the Sea of Japan searching for the wreckage of Korean Air Lines flight 007, shot down by the Soviet Union in 1983. Now, halfway around the world, the lieutenant was finding remains of a different sort.

Electrician's mate third class Nigel Eaton—a plump, red-haired Philadelphian—was busy in the bowels of the engine room, tinkering with the cutter's two diesel-powered engines. Everybody on board had something to do as the Miami skyline disappeared and the cutter headed into the Straits of Florida.

They'd been short two seamen for several months, which meant two jobs were not getting done. Third class boatswain's mate Britt Burford, from Savannah, Georgia, was in the engine room with Eaton, and like similarly confined men the world over, they were complaining about their jobs.

"Seamen are the lowest on the totem pole," Burford griped. "They do all the dirty work."

Confident in his new command, Lee peered into the ship's radar screen at what appeared to be a large freighter maybe ten miles south of Bimini. Focusing binoculars on the vessel, he informed his helmsman that the ship was not flying a country registry flag. Quartermaster Chief Chuck Mills, the oldest guardsman on board (and who, ironically, the crew called Chief), determined that the freighter's name—*Caribbean Bee I*—was freshly painted, not quite hiding the old handle. Mills was certain it was a typical island freighter—the kind that fit the image of a mother ship—easily holding two hundred to three hundred tons of marijuana.

Radioing Miami Base, Lee requested that the El Paso Intelligence Center (EPIC) run a computer check on the freighter to see if it was on the suspect vessel list. At the same time, the lieutenant made radio contact with the captain of the suspicious ship. "Skipper, this is the United States Coast Guard. Why aren't you flying your flag?"

"Give me a minute," the skipper responded coldly. Two

minutes later a Mexican flag was raised in the stiff breeze. And as Mills had guessed, the captain told the Coast Guard lieutenant that the freighter's former name was *Salvinia*, that it had just been purchased at an auction in Nassau, and he and his crew of six men and one woman were sailing the vessel to its new owner in Mexico.

Ordering the freighter's skipper to stop his vessel, Lee requested permission to board, and given the okay, he ordered the crew of the freighter to assemble at midship, where they could be visible at all times. Should the captain of a foreign vessel not allow his ship to be boarded, the Coast Guard was forced to go through diplomatic channels, a chore it left to the U.S. State Department. That process, more often than not, could take several days, if not weeks. "But in the meantime, we follow them," Lee said at the time.

"All hands to boarding stations. All hands to boarding stations," the lieutenant's orders rang out over the ship's intercom system.

Three crew members, who would later have night duty, tumbled out of their bunks in the forward berth and were topside in less than a minute. No longer was the *Cape Current*'s crew informal, and smiles were quickly replaced by concerned expressions. For an undermanned crew, boarding another ship was a dangerous and potentially deadly operation.

On the starboard bridge, the electrician's mate, Eaton, who obviously knew as much about weapons as diesel engines, mounted a large M-60 machine gun capable of hitting a target at a thousand yards. At the same time, five crew members designated as the boarding party shed their military work clothes for bulletproof vests, handcuffs, cans of tear gas, .45

caliber pistols with extra munitions clips, and a 12-gauge shotgun—and just in case the M-60 was not sufficient, an M-16 semiautomatic rifle. Three other men lowered a rigid-hulled inflatable landing raft with a 50-horsepower outboard motor into the choppy ocean.

Should the boarding party encounter a life-threatening situation once aboard the freighter, they had orders to immediately roll over the side of the ship into the water. Eaton, if directed, would then open fire on the deck with the M-60.

"I've never had to shoot anyone," Eaton says. "Even if a suspect vessel tried to outrun us, we'd first throw lines in the water to try to tangle them. If that didn't work, we'd shoot water down their stack. If they still didn't stop, we'd shoot the big gun in front of them, then shoot into the stern, and then into the engine. If that didn't stop 'em, we'd shoot along the water line to sink them. They will stop then."

Since the Coast Guard was the federal agency primarily responsible for the interdiction of maritime drug smuggling, the crew of the *Cape Current* boarded an average of ten boats per day. They'd learned through experience that many of the drugs were smuggled into south Florida at night, hidden in the holds of boats of varying sizes; and the faster they ran, the better—for the traffickers, that is. The Coast Guard, therefore, was forced to break its own rules. The *Cape Current*, for instance, operated without navigational lights in hopes of surprising the smugglers after dark. Aluminum foil was taped over the portholes to keep the bridge and cabin lights from escaping into the darkness. The cutter also maintained radio silence.

Drug runners had their own tricks: they'd send out a false

Mayday—a distress signal—to the Coast Guard. When a cutter like the *Cape Current* responded to the location where the boat was supposed to be sinking, going, in essence, on a wild goose chase, the boats loaded with contraband were sneaking past, miles away.

Eaton expressed relief when the boarding crew radioed back to the *Cape Current* that the suspect *Caribbean Bee I* was empty. He often talked about returning to Philadelphia, perhaps working for the Coast Guard off the New Jersey shore, but he knew he was of more value here in these pirate waters. He was contributing a valuable service to his country. Not that the job didn't have its unpleasant moments. In three days' time, he would present police in Miami with a bucket of water containing the head—floating—of a young woman who, the cops later speculated, was murdered by a local drug lord out to get even with somebody. Her headless body was tossed into the ocean, as was the dismembered body of a man.

≡

As far as the U.S. government was concerned, marijuana and cocaine smuggling had grown beyond deadly—it had become all too personal. In February of that same year, Drug Enforcement Administration agent Enrique "Kiki" Camarena, a former U.S. Marine, had been kidnapped in broad daylight by drug traffickers in Guadalajara, Mexico, then tortured and beat to death. Five months later, the DEA tapped into the FBI's special agent ranks and appointed a new administrator, John "Jack" Lawn, who traveled with Attorney General Edwin Meese III to Mexico City days later and demanded answers from Mexico's government. If Uncle Sam had not declared war on drugs before, he was doing so now. Jimmy, who forever warned those he cared for about the ravaging effects of hard drugs, counted his blessings that he was earning an honest living again.

And then everything changed.

"I was sitting around one night, just chilling, when the phone rang. And the first thing I heard was, 'Will you accept the charges?' It was a collect call from the Chief, who was sitting in some federal facility in the States—I couldn't quite make out the name, but I took the call."

I might as well tell you that this call is being recorded, so if you want to hang up, go ahead, but I think you should listen to me. We've been indicted—me, you, and a few other members of the crew. They say they've got enough evidence to put me away for a long, long time, and I don't think they're lying. But here's the deal—if I tell them everything, they promise the minimum sentence they can give me, which is five years. Do you understand what I'm saying? Are you there, Jimmy?

Yeah, Chief, I'm here.

They're willing to work with me, but I've got to talk. I have to turn over property and money, obviously. It's the best deal I can hope for.

I understand what you have to do. If I was in your shoes, I would take the five years too. Don't worry about me; I'll work it out.

I'm sorry, Jimmy. I really am.

As shocked as he was to hear of the federal indictments, Jimmy wasn't surprised. What amazed him was how long it had taken the authorities to bring a case against the cowboys. He'd been out of the drug trafficking business for four years and counting—as in counting down the days to any statute of limitations if, indeed, the common law legal system covered a weed mogul such as himself.

"I had no intention of ever going back to the States, especially now with an indictment over my head," he says. "And I was wondering if they would even bother to extradite me at this point. If we'd killed a bunch of people, like some of the coke people were doing, I could see them wanting me extradited. But I knew in the back of my head that with everything going on at the time, weed people weren't as important as they once were. Cocaine was the issue.

"I heard stories later that the Chief gave the American authorities four thousand pages of testimony. Can you imagine? I don't know how he remembered everything, given how coked out of his mind he was when he got arrested. In fact, I saw his arrest as a blessing—the Americans bringing him in when they did had to have extended his life. And I was happy about that. At this point in my life, I had every reason to thank the Chief. So when he told me that he was going to roll—warned me not to come to the States because we'd been indicted—he did everything in his power to be up front with me, which was the old Chief coming out. There were no hard feelings whatsoever—although I was always upset that he sold the trawler instead of sinking it. That's how we got caught—the guy he sold it to got busted, and he told the officers, 'Hey, you don't want me. This is my first trip. This is the guy you want.' And the Chief was the guy."

Nine months passed, and still there was no knock on Jimmy's door. No orders to lie down on the floor with his hands behind his head. Which didn't mean his life was hunky-dory and care-free. The builder never knew when he left his apartment for work each morning whether he'd be coming home in the afternoon. So every time he locked two deadbolts instead of one, as if he wouldn't be returning for five or more years— granted they extended him the same generous deal negotiated for the Chief. He'd already given copies of all of his official documents to his stepbrother, Godfrey, with instructions on how to handle his estate and other personal affairs. Otherwise, he just went about his daily life and waited. Whenever a Bahamian police car steered in the direction of one of his construction sites, he would drop whatever board he was cutting or nailing, figuring they had finally come to get him. But each time the officers would simply smile and wave their hands. Everybody knew and liked Jimmy, after all. But it was not the best way to live. Finally, it was Godfrey—or else Olive intervening from her heavenly perch—who got to Jimmy.

Do you want to do right?

It all depends what is right, Bobo.

You know my friend Esau. Well, you're not supposed to know this, but he's been working a bit with the DEA. Would you like to talk to them?

Talk to the DEA?

It can't hurt, Jimmy.

I don't know. They might have forgotten all about me.

Not from what Esau has told me.

I guess it couldn't hurt. They might be interested in hearing a thing or two.

I'll set it up.

Silas Blount was head of the Nassau DEA office, which had opened in 1979, none too soon. He was tall, dark—as in black— and professional.

"Right off the top, we hit it off," Jimmy says. "Esau introduced us at his house in Blair Estates, and right from the beginning we connected—he had a good karma about him. He told me they'd been watching me for years—he was straight up about that. They'd even bugged my living room. He told me, 'You know, there's a bug in your lamp. You can check it out; it's there.' But you know what, I had already found it—it looked like a miniature speaker. I left it there, didn't mess with it, but they never heard anything come out of me. I got some X-rated tapes for them to listen to, and then I would just go into the next room. I made it so all they ever heard were couples making love. I wasn't doing anything illegal by then anyway. Plus, I hardly ever used the phone, you know? Back in the day I would jump on a plane and fly to Miami, meet face-to-face with somebody before I would ever say anything stupid over the phone. Because let's figure we did get busted—I didn't want to get another charge like using the telephone in commission of a felony.

"As for the Chief, he would always be talking on the phone. He didn't care. He'd think he was being clever, but I doubt he fooled anybody who might have been eavesdropping. He'd say, 'We just had two thousand pounds of lobster come in, and it's in the freezer at the marina.' Two thousand pounds of lobster at the marina—can you imagine?"

Jimmy and Silas met numerous times during the next several months. Every piece of information the Bahamian divulged was passed along to the DEA's Miami field office, typed up as classified intelligence, and sent to the agency's headquarters in Washington. Between the Chief and Jimmy, the identities of cocaine lords, kingpins, traffickers, and dealers were revealed or else confirmed—their methods of operation, forms of transportation, drop points, storage facilities, and contacts in the States laid out like a road map. And if the authorities wanted to look beyond a mug shot or two, Jimmy turned over to Silas his copy of the video from the Chief's retirement party.

Becoming a U.S. government informant carried its risks—especially when Jimmy saw fit to reveal that his last-ever drug run was purportedly orchestrated by CIA operatives, if not the agency itself, to stave off the Russian army and spread democracy throughout the world. Imagine the official Washington tongues wagging back and forth across the Potomac River after reading that disclosure!

It didn't come as too big a surprise, therefore, that Jimmy was soon escorted from one of his building sites to the U.S. embassy in Nassau, where a detailed debriefing lasted into the evening. By the time it was over, he had a code name.

"They code-named me 'Blue'—and they gave me a CI number," he says, referring to his confidential informant number. "And now, after all those years, I had the authorities watching me for another reason. They were protecting me—protecting me big-time. Because Nassau is small, you see? Silas soon got transferred to Miami, and when he went, I went. He always promised that he would be standing behind me."

Jimmy told the Americans everything he knew about drug trafficking, answered all of their questions and more. Now all he could do was sit back and wait for the other shoe to drop.

With the government's full knowledge, he moved to Orlando, where he became the roommate of a fellow martial-arts enthusiast who ran the neighborhood dojo. Jimmy began training again, even competing, this time politely turning down the trophies representing titles he similarly carried home as the kickboxing boy wonder of Nassau.

And then out of the blue, his telephone rang, and he was told that his arrest was imminent, and that he should be prepared, whatever that meant. And when it did come down, the federal contact added, Jimmy shouldn't take it personally. In other words, it would be done by the book.

Jimmy's next call was to Charon in Nassau, and he arranged with her for their daughter to fly to Orlando so that she and her father could visit Disney World together, something they had always talked about doing. *No better time than now*, he thought. If the DEA had only known beforehand about the Bahamian's last-minute vacation plans, they would likely have postponed the takedown, which, for the good of all interested parties, had to take place in the open, for all eyes to see—or to read about in the newspaper.

TWENTY-SEVEN

THE PLAINCLOTHES OFFICER SEATED BEHIND THE steering wheel of the black Pontiac Trans-Am, heading south on Interstate 4 out of Orlando, flipped on the emergency lights concealed behind the grille. The unmarked police cruiser could run down anything on the highway—but Jimmy, for once, wasn't running. Given the fun day he had planned with his daughter at Walt Disney World, he wasted no time pulling over onto the shoulder, keeping his fingers crossed for an expired tag or broken taillight. He turned off the engine, rolled down the window, and waited for the approaching officer's explanation—which came in the form of an M9 Beretta pistol barrel pressed against his temple.

Don't be stupid; it's all over.

Hey, I'm not stupid. You could've called me, you know. I would've come in.

Out of nowhere, a pair of SWAT teams—one local, one federal—surrounded Jimmy's car, assault rifles pointed in one direction. "It was like *clack-clack-clack-clack-clack*—guns everywhere," the Bahamian recalls. "Truthfully, I think they brought out everybody who happened to be wearing camouflage that day. It was a show of force, but I still think they were protecting me right up to the end. There was even a lady officer, who immediately consoled my daughter, which was really nice."

Had Jimmy touched base with Silas that week, mentioned that he and his teenage daughter were planning their first-ever visit to the Magic Kingdom—the two likely would have been able to spin around Space Mountain. As it was, they were transported to Miami, where Jimmy was booked and processed and arrangements were made for his girl to return home to the Bahamas.

It wasn't until his initial court appearance that he was informed his indictment had been handed down in Springfield, Massachusetts, where authorities somehow determined that some of the hashish dropped off in the Connecticut parking lot had been pressed into a pipe and smoked.

"I've never been to Massachusetts in my life," Jimmy points out. "Of all the places I've smuggled weed into and out of, I was indicted in a place I've never been to before. But even more amazing, my bail was set at twenty-five thousand dollars. I was being charged with smuggling all this hashish, and I got a twenty-five-thousand-dollar bail? Oh man."

And when that amount was posted, the Miami attorney,

who had earlier represented the crew, took his turn with Jimmy, in effect telling him there was no way he could buy a better deal than what was all but being gift-wrapped for him by the feds. He provided Jimmy with a general timetable of what he might expect during the court proceedings, which were anything but standard, since Jimmy was a confidential informant with a code name. Furthermore, Blue's case would likely be tried behind closed doors, with a chosen few in attendance. And finally, having never forgotten the way Jimmy and the Chief had draped themselves in gold the day they picked him up at the Nassau airport, Bill the attorney offered the Bahamian a few pointers on proper courtroom attire, but Jimmy might as well have been wearing earplugs.

"Bill told me to wear jeans, a T-shirt, and a pair of tennis shoes. And do you think I listened? They provided me with a court-appointed lawyer in Massachusetts. And the first day I walked into his office, I was wearing an Armani suit, twelve-hundred-dollar eel-skin loafers, a Gold Presidential Rolex, and silk shirt—unbuttoned, mind you. Right off the bat I wanted to make a statement. I proceeded to hit on his secretary—in fact, I hit on all the girls in his office. And I was in good shape too. I wasn't worried about a thing. I already had it in my mind that I would be getting five years, but I was ready. I decided that I was going to work out every day, make it time well spent, and when I got out I'd be in the best shape of my life."

Jimmy added yet another gold chain to his wardrobe when he and his lawyer met with the prosecuting attorney on the fourth floor of the federal building on Main Street in Springfield. Fortunately, he didn't flirt with the government's secretary, although had she been more attractive, he might have.

"I walked in strutting my stuff. But let me tell you, the second I shook his hand, I liked him," Jimmy recalls.

Am I to understand that you will accept the plea bargain?

Yes, I am willing to do that. But I want to be certain what exactly it is I'm being offered.

Here's the bottom line, granted the judge agrees—and he doesn't have to, of course. We'll give you five years or less.

I'm sorry?

Five years or less, whichever comes first.

"I'd thought my bail was low, and now he was telling me five years or less, whatever that meant. But I knew it was good. I could do that standing on my head walking backwards."

When the day came for Jimmy to go before the federal judge in Springfield, the courtroom was all but deserted. And if the drug smuggler was impressed with the prosecutor, he could not have been more thrilled by his draw of a judge—who, having read all the court documents, initiated the proceedings by inquiring about fishing in the Bahamas.

"The judge was a decent gentleman. He began by saying, 'Now, young man, you realize that I do not have to accept this recommendation. But you look like an honest person.'"

And with that Jimmy was sentenced to five years or less, unspecified time that it was, to be served in a federal detention center.

"I figured they were going to take me away at that point, like you see in the movies," he says. "You know, handcuff you, stick your jewelry and other personal belongings in a plastic bag with your name written on it, and then lead you away. Not so. And then the judge spoke up again."

I'm reminded that we are getting close to Christmas, and perhaps you would like to spend the holiday with your family? Of course, it would be required that they travel to Florida, because under no circumstances are you to leave the country. If this suits everybody here today, I will order that you surrender yourself the second day of January in Tallahassee. Does that suit everybody?

It does me, Your Honor. Thank you.

"And for whatever reason—don't ask me why—I clicked my heels together and saluted the judge—gave him a military salute. I've never done that before," Jimmy says. "I thanked him again; then I turned and walked out. I felt like I had just won the lotto."

The first person Jimmy looked up in Florida was Silas, who surprisingly had just announced his retirement from the DEA. He would soon be filling a senior federal parole board position in Atlanta, his hometown.

"I don't know how to describe how I felt, because he and I had been through a lot together. I told him how much I appreciated everything he did for me. Then he thanked me for everything I did for him and told me to keep my head above water," Jimmy says.

Christmas and New Year's Eve came and went, and minus his family, the recently convicted weed trafficker spent the holidays with a former Cuban-American girlfriend in Miami—actually a woman who at one time had handled some of the bank deposits for the crew. Never one to have ever experienced a hangover, Jimmy spent New Year's Day working out in a Miami gym and then made arrangements to be driven to the

Florida state capital. Three miles east of downtown Tallahassee on Highway 319, he spotted the Florida Federal Correctional Institution, a low-security detention center that housed men and women in separate facilities. Jimmy never knew a prison could look so nice.

"And they do what they have to do—scrub you down, put you in an orange jumpsuit, and then assign you a prisoner number. Mine was 14517-018."

It took the Bahamian no time to settle into a routine, and in doing so it crossed his mind to wonder whether good behavior might lead to a further reduced sentence for a prisoner in his shoes. Not that he was stupid enough to inquire. With his lenient sentence already ticking down, the dumbest thing he could do now was rock any boats. He wasn't overly impressed with the prison gym and weight room, but he discovered a small library with a magazine rack holding the latest issues of *Popular Mechanics* and *Reader's Digest*, his two favorite magazines. The following month's editions, he was told by the friendly prison librarian, could arrive in the mail as early as that afternoon, and he was advised to check back. But he would never get the chance. His bag was packed before the lunch bell sounded.

Out of the blue, Jimmy was told by a prison guard that he was being transferred to another minimum-security detention center—the Oakdale Correctional Complex in central Louisiana, some sixty miles north of Lake Charles. He'd been behind bars—if you could call them that—in Tallahassee barely two weeks, yet he didn't ask for an explanation. The prison staff seemed as confused as the inmate. He guessed it was all part of Uncle Sam's overall plan—perhaps making it safer for him should the day come when somebody asks where he served his time, and he could honestly answer not one, but two federal prisons in two different states. It certainly sounded harsh enough. So Jimmy took his pick of seats aboard the prison's white bus and got his first-ever tour of Alabama and Mississippi before entering the Bayou state, where he was issued a new toothbrush and underwear all over again.

Here was Jimmy's daily routine: eat breakfast, clean cell, pump iron in the courtyard, eat lunch, clobber boxing bag in the gym, read books/magazines, eat dinner. Given his personality, it took no time for the Bahamian to stand out in the crowd. Plus, he was not the typical lawbreaker, in this facility at least. Most of the inmates were white-collar criminals who had grown too greedy in their designer suits and neckties. One day in the cafeteria, Jimmy shocked everybody wearing a prisoner's suit by confessing that he had been busted for smuggling hashish into the United States. What with the shocked looks on their faces, you would have thought he'd admitted to being John Wayne Gacy, the killer clown.

At the start of his second week in lockup, Jimmy was assigned a job—working with the prison's paint crew, which suited him perfectly, given the number of boats he'd painted in his lifetime.

"They had a little beige golf cart that the guards would ride around in, and it needed painting. So they asked me if I could paint it," Jimmy recalls. "And I said sure enough. There were, like, four or five other guys on the paint crew with me, all used to painting walls and ceilings, so everybody was excited now to be painting something different. So I took over, grabbing some beige paint, and some cans of orange and black paint, and a roll of masking tape like I used on my boats. And we had an absolutely wonderful time painting this golf cart—shooting the breeze, telling jokes, having a good time, you know? You would not have known we were in a prison. And when we finished, the warden happened to walk by, and he hit the roof."

Who painted this?

We did, sir. We were told to paint it.

But were you told to paint orange and black flames on it?

Well, no. They didn't say how to paint it.

"The warden actually turned out to be really, really cool," Jimmy says. "Everybody who worked there got a kick out of the paint job—they took pictures and sent them around to all the other prisons to show them what we had done. But after that, the warden made me repaint it."

=
=

When the Shah of Iran was overthrown in 1979, one of the top bankers in Tehran took advantage of the chaos by walking out of the vault with millions of *rials*, when the currency was still worth something. Jafar, as Jimmy's cellmate was named, explained that he had just begun to settle down and live the American dream, when the authorities caught up with him. He'd been through one immigration hearing after another, stuck in more holding cells than he could count in English. Now here it was, well into the 1980s, and there was a none-too-urgent international tug-of-war on how to dispose of him.

"The U.S. government was supposed to give him back, if I recall, but here he'd been sitting in the States for all those years," Jimmy remembers. "But we had plenty to talk about—he was an intriguing guy, to say the least. I learned a lot from him about the world, basically that we're all really no different."

Otherwise, the artist inmates became fast friends and spent the next several weeks painting everything from prison bars to the warden's bathroom. Quickly rising to the unofficial rank of painter foreman, Jimmy was provided with a metal pushcart to transport buckets of paint, brushes and rollers, pans and drop cloths to every job site. The cart's compartments weren't custom-built, like they were on his Sport Fisherman, but it didn't take long for Jimmy's mind to start turning, those gold letters arranging in his head.

"Give a smuggler a cart and he has to put a stash in it, you know? I set it up where an inmate from India who worked in the kitchen would supply me with forbidden fruit. He'd always be sneaking me oranges, apples, and bananas, and I built myself a little stash in the bottom of the cart—a rolling fruit stand, you see? Some days I even had fried chicken to offer the detainees, midnight snacks, so to speak. So I was back to smuggling, providing extra meals for the people who needed their calorie fixes. I was having the best time you could possibly have in that jail. And then just like that, it was all over. They came and told me I was going home."

All said and done, instead of a more probable 100 years behind bars, Jimmy got a slap on the wrist. The Catholic nun's finger jabs in Nassau were more severe punishment.

Yo Jimbo, long time. Where you been?
Hubert, they got you working the airport now?
Yeah, man. It's nice and cool in here. So what's the sip-sip?
Got caught up in some stuff; you know how that goes.
Well, you're home now, Jimbo. You're home now.

TWENTY-EIGHT

THERE WAS A STRING OF FUNERALS JIMMY DONNED his suit and sunglasses to attend. The Chief got buried in Nassau. He'd died depressed, paranoid, and alone—except on his deathbed, having had a toot, a thrill, and his final breath in the space of minutes. His coke buddies had long since disappeared when he was no longer the life and blood of the party. Then again, friendships had stopped mattering to him the day he snorted out of necessity rather than pleasure. During the relatively short period of time that he was locked up in the United States, his physical withdrawal from the addictive drug was almost penalty enough for his felonious crimes on the high seas. Contrary to popular belief, cocaine addiction is extremely difficult to break. Laboratory creatures will work their bones to the point of disintegration until such time they are rewarded a taste of the drug—one experimental rodent standing on its hind legs and pressing a lever more than ten thousand times to get its fix. The creatures tend to choose cocaine over water, even when punished for choosing the powder.

The Chief was no different from the mice and rats—his craving, shaking, anxiety, agitation, vomiting, insomnia, outbursts, and fatigue not fun to witness. As quickly as he was let out of prison and told to never set foot in America again, he returned to his home in Nassau and fell victim all over again to the cocaine-induced euphoria that had blighted his mind and body. Before he opened the windows to air his place out, he mixed himself a rum and coke and cut a long line. The mucous membrane of his nose soon became so ulcerated from what he innocently referred to as snorting "candy cane" that it pained him to even breathe. It was a blessing when he didn't have to anymore.

"Heart attack, just like he wanted to go. Died in bed with a young girl," Jimmy reveals. "I got to see him just before he died. He called me one night to come over. I went by the house, and he asked me whether I had been followed. He was seeing everything—people hiding in the shadows, lizards coming out of the wall, snakes dropping down from the ceiling. I knew it wouldn't be long before his number was called."

Olive was such a force in Kirkwood's life that, like other widowers who get left behind, he was walking lost without her. He lived long enough to see Nassau sprout a skyline of glitzy hotels and casinos that stretched all the way from West Bay Street near the airport to the previously pristine Paradise Island. His wife, for all the nailing and sawing she supervised, would not have been impressed with the construction or the gamblers who followed. Now Kirkwood and Miss Olive are together again, the Church of God preachers pointed out after burying him in the cemetery near the foul line behind first base.

≡

On the day he jumped his last earthly hurdle, Jacob was still wearing his Stetson hat atop a full head of jet-black hair. He lived to be eighty-five, in doing so bolstering Billy Joel's argument that only the good die young.

"He died in 2006, and fortunately I went to see him just before he went," Jimmy says. "He'd had cancer or something like it—we never knew, exactly, because there was no autopsy. But he knew he was going, and he called me up and said, 'Come and see me, son, because I'm checking out.' And we had an amazing conversation. He had all his faculties about him. And that was when he told me about my being born with the gold letters in my head, told me about how he put me on the bow of the boat when I was real young because he knew that if I ran aground once, I wouldn't do it again."

That's when you learned to read the water, the channels, the current and tide. When I realized you had those gold letters in your head, I just let you go.

I remember, Pops. I remember.

Years later, when Jimmy was catching weed off Long Island, he liked to play dumb by purposely allowing the patrol boats to follow him into precarious waters hiding all sorts of underwater hazards. "And sure enough they would get stuck all the time—trying to figure how they were going to get out of there. And while I was floating out, waving good-bye, all they could do was sit there," he says. "If they were lucky, a high tide would free them. If not, they had to have somebody come all the way to find them and tow them out."

Jacob was buried in his black boots, right alongside Perline—"thirty feet from his front door and twenty feet from the church door," Jimmy notes. "In the Bahamas, they like to keep everybody close."

AFTERWORD

JIMMY LOOKS UP FROM HIS ARCHITECTURAL BLUE-prints, digital since Olive's day, shouting up instructions to Clint, Craig, and Calvin; Whistler and Sedrick; Eric and Genason. Jimmy's tight-knit carpentry crew, who needn't worry about sticking to nicknames, is putting the finishing touches on a replacement house that's gone up at the corner of King and Princess Streets—now awaiting a new generation of termites.

"They've all heard the *sip-sip*, as have others on the island. But nobody knows the whole story," Jimmy says. "Because Briland is so small, it's unique. Everybody knows everybody, so they think they know everything there is to know about you. But every once in a while you throw them for a loop, you know? Just the other day I went to a friend's wedding—my electrician, Raymond, got married—so I decided to wear a nice suit. I really dressed up for this occasion, and a lot of people on the island caught a glimpse of me, because you see everybody when you drive through the town to the church, then back again through the town, and up the Narrows to Palm Grove, where the reception was held.

"I could feel the eyes on me, hear everybody saying, 'Oh, look at Jimbo! He looks like the Sopranos.' And somebody else would say, 'He don't look like one Soprano; he looks like the whole TV show!' And then you see them whispering to each other, you know? They have this concept in their head, because they hear bits and pieces of what I used to do. And as soon as they see something new, like me in a suit of clothes, that adds to the mystique and they run with it—they take off. And the kids, they hear what is being said, so they will be looking at me kind of funny like.

"Actually, I'm worried about the kids nowadays. I can't comprehend them. They have everything at their fingertips, and they talk about being bored—the parents even talk about their kids being bored. That was not a word I ever knew as a child. We didn't have time to be bored. We were up before sunrise and in the field, and when the sun got too hot, you went fishing, and when you were fished out, you came home and spent time with your family before it was time to sleep— but only after you finished your chores. No, I don't understand some of these kids today.

"But you talk about a peaceful place to live. I don't have a key to my house. Once when I sold the cottage I had built for myself next door to my house, the gentleman who bought it held out his hand for the key. I said, 'You'll need to put a lock on the door if you want to have a key.'"

Jimmy still goes fishing every opportunity he gets, always accompanied by his wife, Hannah. He keeps his maroon fishing boat, *Poetic Justice*, tied up on the south end of the island between Jeff Fox's dive shop and Sully's Bar & Grill.

Otherwise, not a day goes by that he doesn't stop by the public dock—the Government Dock, as it's called—whether to pick up supplies shipped to the island aboard the bright green *Eleuthera Express* or other freighters that regularly off-load every staple, natural fiber, and raw material that one needs in order to survive on an island blessed with no bridge.

"If you want all the *sip-sip*, you go down to the Government Dock. Danny and the crew down there will fill you in on everything—give you the world according to Brilanders. Just island life, you know?"

═══

Every once in a while when he's visiting another island not terribly far from his home, Jimmy will bump into the Sarge.

"And you know, he always thanks me. Every time I see him, he thanks me for helping his family—like Ma Miller used to thank me, and all the other families. We didn't have to, but we felt better if we paid Sarge. We didn't want his help; we didn't want him to supply us with information. We just paid him to look the other way, you see?"

Blondie continues to surface from time to time. Jimmy says he's still residing on Bimini, "still doing his thing over there"—which is why he is among certain members of the crew who could not be identified by their actual nicknames. Bicycle Joe, meanwhile, went Down Under and never came back up. Jimmy trusts the Australian staked out his spread, although he has no way of knowing. Given that Bicycle hardly existed when he was a member of the crew, Jimmy doesn't hold out hope of seeing him now. But somewhere in Nassau, perhaps tossed aside in a vacant lot, or else thrown into the drink, lies the rusted remains of the Aussie's dependable bicycle.

Crazy Charlie ultimately discovered Shangri-La in the Florida Keys, choosing an upscale waterfront home with a deep-water dock on the island of Islamorada—the "Sportfishing Capital of the World." Wouldn't it be amazing if he had somehow hooked up again with his high school track stand-out! Pretty Pat sailed south, never to resurface, and Jimmy doesn't hold out much hope he ever will. A fly can only handle so much ointment, he points out.

"Ghost still comes and goes, same as always," Jimmy says, although where he appears from and where he disappears to, nobody knows to this day. As for Zeke, just months before the publication of this story, he was appointed to a term of public service in Spanish Wells. Given his important position within the community, he contacted Jimmy to make certain his anonymity was protected.

As for the irony of all ironies: a prominent member of the crew who, following his federal indictment, also cooperated with U.S. authorities—like Jimmy becoming a confidential informant, at which time he "sang like a canary," the Bahamian says—now owns and operates a delicatessen in a federal government building in Washington, D.C. Which cowboy and what federal agency, nobody can say.

As for Digger, Jimmy will only say that he is confident his dyslexic friend found honest work that does not require perfect penmanship and pronunciation.

And in the end there was Silas, as big a friend to Jimmy as anybody in the crew.

Tell everybody you know that you went down, went down hard— that you even had to spend eleven months and twenty-three days in solitary confinement because you refused to talk. Do you understand why this is important?

Yeah, I understand.

You wouldn't talk; you refused. That's what you say. And hopefully they will believe you and you will stay safe. The time will eventually come when this chapter of your life won't matter to these people anymore—they'll either be dead or retired and living in the jungle. So, Jimmy, if you don't do anything else illegal in your life, you should live to be an old man. And maybe when that time comes, you can tell people the real story.

=

From Jimmy and Hannah's beachfront house it's a leisurely walk up the sandy path to Nesbitt Street, which winds its way into Dunmore Town, where one finds small clapboard houses of every size, shape, and color (the frequent hurricanes always bring opportunities for new additions and designs). Often in the evenings, the Harbour Island Marching Band, with its spirited tuba players, will be in loud procession up Barracks Street, marching past JJ's bar, which serves up some mean chicken souse, and the world-famous Vic-Hum Club, a ramshackle of a dive owned by the affable Humphrey "Hitler"

Percentie Jr., and where the likes of Mick Jagger and Lenny Kravitz have partied well beyond the endless wake-up calls of the island's roaming colony of restless roosters, confused breed that they are.

Another block or so, and one comes to Chapel Street, which leads to the world-famous Pink Sands and Coral Sands hotels. It is there on the corner of Nesbitt and Chapel Streets that one finds the not-so-palatial but ever-so-spiritual Lighthouse Church of God. To the right of the front doorstep is a slab of white rock that Jimmy makes a point of reading every time he happens by: "This Cornerstone Laid on March 20, 1955, by W. R. Franks."

"Yes, the same Brother Franks," Jimmy says with a laugh. "Can you believe it? No matter where I go, Olive and the Church of God brothers are never far away."

ACKNOWLEDGMENTS

A JOURNALIST AT HEART, ROBERT ARTHUR HAD ALWAYS told me there was a book or two to write on Harbour Island. He knew, in other words, what he was doing when he introduced me to Jimmy Moree, who despite the extremely delicate subject matter, spoke as openly as possible about his incredible life's journey. Indeed, Jimmy is such an outstanding storyteller, his experiences are best recalled in his words, not mine. I just came along for the boat ride.

Besides Robert, this story could not have been told without the unfailing assistance of Jimmy's wife, Hannah, who provided every answer to follow-up questions as trivial as the exact color of Jacob's horse.

I am similarly grateful to my fellow newspapermen, John Solomon, Christopher Dolan, Jason Hargraves, and Victor Morton, for having looked the other way while a certain columnist juggled his daily political beat with book writing—and in the midst of an unprecedented presidential election, no less.

Behind every marginal writer is a superb editor, in this case Jamie Chavez, who kindly introduced herself as my "cheerleader, best friend, partner, and wordsmith." That she is.

For their enthusiastic support and sustenance provided throughout this project, I wish to also thank my daughter, Kerry, and our entire McCaslin and McElveen clan; as well as Joel Miller, Kristen Parrish, Heather Skelton, Jason Jones, Nettie Symonette, Catherine Armour, Jan McGinley, Pam Verick, Crit Johnson, Mildred Coit, David Hudgins, Suzanne Runyon, Billy Winburn, Vinnie Rubeo, Ann Cutbill Lenane, Dick Hammett, Cassie Vanderslice, Carolyn Hicks, Heidi Wilson, Jennifer Lee, Erin and Spud Rigney, Nolan B. O'Leary, and the smiling ladies at Queen Conch, Angela's Starfish, and Ma Ruby's.

Finally, for making the entire Harbour Island experience—and thus this book—possible, utmost gratitude is extended to C. S. Taylor Burke III.

BIBLIOGRAPHY

The Bahamas Ministry of Tourism. *The Islands of The Bahamas.* Nassau, Bahamas, 2008.

Brzezinksi, Zbigniew. "How Jimmy Carter and I Started the Mujahideen" (interview by *Le Nouvel Observateur*, France, Jan. 15–21, 1998).

Chepesiuk, Ron. *The Bullet or the Bribe: Taking Down Colombia's Cali Drug Cartel.* Greenwood Publishing Group, 2003.

Clemence, Sara. "The Ten Most Expensive Homes in the U.S., No. 7, Star Island, Miami, Florida." *Forbes*, 7 October 2005.

Downie Jr., Leonard. "Britain Celebrates, Charles Takes a Bride." *Washington Post*, 30 July 1981.

FAST Area Studies Program: Australian English Glossary from A to Zed (University of Tampere, Finland, 1996).

Frontline (PBS). "Drug Wars, The Business: Norman's Cay." WGBH Educational Foundation, Boston; 1995–2008.

Jewish Agency for Israel: Israel Timeline (Jerusalem, 1981).

Kipling, Rudyard. "The Prodigal Son" (from the novel *Kim*, 1901).

Lightbourn, Ronald G. *Reminiscing II: Photographs of Old Nassau*, published by Ronald G. Lightbourn, 2005.

McCaslin, John. "Dope Busters: Aboard the Coast Guard Cutter *Cape Current* off the Coast of Bimini, Bahamas." *Washington Times*, 1 May 1985.

———. "Meese Travels to Mexico City in Wake of DEA Agent Slaying." *The Washington Times*, 16 August 1985.

Meditz, Sandra W., Dennis M. Hanratty, "Caribbean Islands: A Country Study." U.S. Library of Congress, Washington, D.C., 1987.

National Oceanic and Atmospheric Administration: Hurricane David (1979).

Naylor, R. Thomas. *Economic Warfare: Sanctions, Embargo Busting, and Their Human Cost*. Northeastern, 2001.

Neff, Donald. "The Colombian Connection." *Time*, 29 January 1979.

Rosenthal, Andrew. "Reagan Extends Territorial Waters to 12 Miles." *New York Times*, 29 December 1988.

Starks, Michael. *Marijuana Potency*. Ronin Publishing, 1997.

U.S. Drug Enforcement Administration: *DEA History Book 1975–1980*.

U.S. Fish and Wildlife Service. "Great Dismal Swamp National Wildlife Refuge." Suffolk, VA, 2008.

U.S. National Park Service. "James River Plantations: A National Register of Historic Places." Charles City County, VA, 2008.

ABOUT THE AUTHOR

JOHN MCCASLIN IS AN AWARD-WINNING POLITICAL columnist, broadcaster, and travel writer based in Washington, D.C. His first book, *Inside the Beltway: Offbeat Stories, Scoops, and Shenanigans from Around the Nation's Capital,* was published in 2004. Reflections about his dying mother, Wanda, and her close relationship with his daughter, Kerry, make up a chapter of *Chicken Soup for the Grandma's Soul,* released in 2005.